Guiding Learning in the Secondary Schools

Guiding Learning in the Secondary Schools

John W. Renner
Robert F. Bibens
Gene D. Shepherd
University of Oklahoma

Harper & Row, Publishers
New York, Evanston, San Francisco, London

Photograph for Part I Mimi Forsyth, Monkmeyer
Photograph for Part II Burt Glinn, Magnum

GUIDING LEARNING IN THE SECONDARY SCHOOLS

Standard Book Number: 06-045382-6

Library of Congress Catalog Card Number: 70-181543

To Carol, Evelyn and Opal

Contents

Preface

No one can teach you how to teach; you must do that for yourself. Why then, you ask, do courses in professional education exist? Surely, if these courses do not have as their focus the preparation of classroom teachers, they have no function. The answer lies, we believe, in the fact that teaching yourself how to teach requires becoming involved with the factors that shape our educational system and interacting with others who are similarly involved. Among the factors that have shaped and are shaping our educational system are (1) our educational purpose, (2) the learning characteristics of those being taught, (3) the contributions of each traditional discipline to educational purpose, and (4) the teacher's role in leading learners to achieve educational purpose.

This book is built around these four factors, and in order for it to be of value to you, you must become involved with it. For example, several times in each chapter you are asked to pick up a pencil and write something. This task is an essential part of the learning process, for it forces you to pull together your thoughts and feelings about each topic. As the chapter progresses, you will find out how we feel about these topics. We do not ask you to believe that our position is always the correct one or the one that all educators should take. Our positions are based on our experiences. Your experiences may make you feel differently about certain topics, and you should hold on to your beliefs until you have sound, logical reasons for discarding them.

Many of the positions we take are not universally accepted. We subscribe, for example, to the notion that the central purpose of school is intellectual development. Not all educators believe this. So you have in your hands a book that provides you with information, gives you an opportunity to shape your own educational philosophy, and presents you with divergent points of view.

Our orientation in this book stems from our belief that you must have an educational philosophy that is uniquely yours if teaching is to be more to you than just a job. We also believe that a person's educational philosophies are shaped only when he is led to inquire into the reasons for things. We have designed this book, as nearly as possible, so as to encourage this kind of inquiry. The very nature of the printed word militates against such a framework, but if the reader takes the time and opportunity to do more than merely read, a book can help him to develop within himself an attitude of intellectual inquiry that will be useful to him both as a learner and as a teacher. The questions we ask you to ask yourself will guide you in teaching yourself to teach. Have a pleasant, profitable set of inquiries.

John W. Renner
Robert F. Bibens
Gene D. Shepherd

Educational Purpose, The Learner And The Teacher

II

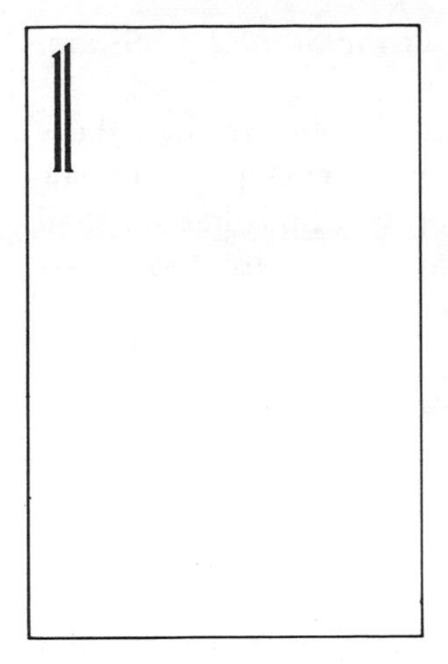

The Evolution of Educational Purpose

Schools, like all other instruments and institutions within a society, are not just given—they are established by the society. Nor are they absolutes; they can and must constantly change if they are to remain viable. Why does a society establish and maintain educational institutions? Such institutions are obviously expensive, easy to influence but difficult to change, and they often frustrate those who operate them. As John Holt maintains, "Most children in school fail."[1]

Throughout this book, as we noted in the Preface, you will be asked to write down your ideas on various topics. Doing this is important because it will influence the way you think about the material that follows; involving yourself in the learning process in this way increases its effectiveness. Now, for example:

TASK	*Before reading on, jot down the reasons you believe societies establish and maintain schools.*

Why a Society Establishes and Maintains Schools

The three points cited below form the basic concept of an evolutionary educational-purpose spiral, which may be applied not only to the historic development of education in the United States but also to the ongoing changes in our schools. These reasons why a society

[1] John Holt, *How Children Fail* (New York: Dell, 1964), p. xiii.

establishes and maintains schools are probably no better than those you formulated above, and we suggest that you develop a rationale for your reasons just as we shall for ours. You will find that we shall return again and again in the discussion that follows to these basic concepts.

To serve the present needs of the society and maintain the present social order (to maintain equilibrium)

The principle of maintaining the status quo has governed education in this country for many years, and it is still the principal focus of the majority of schools. The purposes these schools lead students to achieve will not change until society changes them. The fact that it required an investment of money by private foundations and the government to establish curricula in science and mathematics which met the needs of society is evidence that as long as the schools view their primary purpose as maintaining the status quo, the impetus for change will come from the society.

To change the existing societal structure (to promote disequilibrium)

Our society has used schools to promote societal changes since the educational system was established. For instance, when schools began to consolidate and children from one rural community began mixing with children from other communities and from urban areas, the structure of the society began to change. The 1954 Supreme Court decision concerning the desegregation of schools, by correcting an inequity in the school system, may eventually change the way of life of society itself. In this particular case the society is asking the schools to do something that must be done if we are to call ourselves a democracy but which could not (or would not) be accomplished through other social institutions. If housing in this country had not been segregated, the 1954 decision would have meant immediate racial integration of the schools. Some courts have gone so far as to say that racial balance reflecting the racial structure of the community should be established and maintained within the schools even if it means bussing children from one district to another. Although many persons consider this solution unfair, the fact remains that the schools are being asked to correct a defect that the society itself could not (or would not) correct in other ways. This is a good example of the fact that the machinery of our democratic government not only maintains a democracy but promotes it.

Autocratic forms of government, however, can also use the schools to change a society. A prime example of this was the Hitler Youth Movement of Nazi Germany. History is liberally sprinkled with other examples of how governments have used schools to change the existing social structure. *The way the youth of a society are educated determines their values and goals as adults.*

To serve the advancing needs of society

Both those who view the schools as instruments of social change and those who view them as means of upholding the status quo see the educational system as a tool of society. However, although schools do have the responsibility of carrying out the directives of society, they also have a deeper responsibility—to make society aware of the consequences of these directives. The school system must provide alternatives to the society that will increase the society's worth—*it must serve the advancing needs of society.*

The function of the school is thus to ready young people to solve problems that have not yet been defined, using techniques that have not yet been invented. Does this mean that the educational system must foretell the future? Not at all. But it does mean that *the school has the responsibility to develop citizens who are ready to accept innovation and change and who know how to learn.* If students are not prepared to continue to learn effectively after leaving school, the school then is interested only in maintaining the status quo. If the school concentrates on presenting a particular model of society so that learners will be encouraged to change society to conform to that model, it is interested chiefly in controlling social evolution. But if the school guides the learner to identify current social problems and work out alternative solutions to them, then it is interested in developing a flexible approach to future situations. *If the school's program is organized in such a way that the changes in the structure of society are brought about by the citizens themselves with no predetermined model applying, then the program itself will provide the alternatives mentioned earlier.* Schools can be organized and operated to produce persons who can solve problems as they arise, but to do this they must concentrate on teaching learners how to learn.

How an Educational System Develops These Purposes

In years to come perhaps another cycle will be added to the evolutionary educational-purpose spiral. If not, the schools of today will be operating tomorrow under point one—maintaining equilibrium. Schools do not automatically adopt one or another of the purposes described above. That choice is usually made at the nonverbal (sometimes subconscious) level. Nor will every teacher within a system subscribe to the purposes of the majority or of the system at large. A very subtle, intricate value structure exists here, and that value structure is transmitted from society to the school system to the classroom. It affects the day-by-day activities of each teacher and each learner. Both what is taught and the procedure by which it is taught will depend on the basic purposes of the educational system.

Rarely does a society seek to develop intellectual flexibility in its youth; usually it attempts to ensure the maintenance of the status quo. As the educational system evolves from a static to an open-ended view of society, there are individuals and groups who try to accelerate the process; often they are unsuccessful and, not infrequently, they are scorned or ignored.

Where is the American public school system in this evolutionary spiral? Which step is it ready to take? If you are to make a serious and worthwhile contribution, you need to answer these questions before entering the teaching profession. We believe that the most desirable system is one that encourages flexibility. If you agree, then you will wish to dedicate your efforts to moving the schools toward that point. To do this, you must first know where the schools are today and where they have been. In the remainder of this chapter we shall examine the growth of the American school system. Unless, however, you keep firmly in mind the purpose behind these pages, it will be simply a functionless narrative. If, on the other hand, you approach this history as source material from which you can gather information that will enable you to contribute to the future development of the system, it will be relevant indeed.

TASK	*Before beginning the next section, state your opinion of where the schools are in relation to the educational-purpose spiral described above or in relation to the reasons you yourself gave for maintaining schools.*

The American School System in the Seventeenth, Eighteenth, and Nineteenth Centuries

Early school patrons

The first schools in what was to become the United States were heavily influenced by the religious beliefs of those who founded and supported them. The decade following the departure in 1620 of the small group of British settlers for the shores of America was a dark one for European Protestantism. Cardinal Richelieu's troops defeated the Huguenots in France, and Catholic legions led by Generals Tilly and Wallenstein were badly mangling Protestant forces throughout the Continent. James I, for whom the King James translation of the Bible is named, was hostile toward the Puritans. When his son Charles I took the throne after his death in 1625, the antagonism toward certain Protestant groups, and the Puritans in particular, became more intense. The latter group, in response to these pressures, and perhaps motivated in part by the fact that there was a depression in southeastern England, conceived the notion of traveling to America and founding a Bible State where they could worship as they pleased. In 1630 about one thousand Puritans landed in what is now Massachusetts. An earlier group of migrants, who had left England during the reign of James I for Holland and then for America in 1620, had also been Puritans. Puritanism, therefore, was firmly entrenched in what is now the northeastern United States by the third decade of the seventeenth century.

But what is Puritanism and how is it related to the evolution of educational purpose? The religious beliefs of the Puritans were used as a basis for a theocracy, "a partnership of state and church, with the latter leading the former."[2] The church interpreted the will of God, and the law enforcement officials of the state saw that those interpretations were obeyed. Distinguishing civil law from church law in a theocracy is impossible; civil law is church law, and disobedience of civil law is a sin. The Puritans' House of God was more than a place to come together to worship; all types of civil matters were settled there—the repair and construction of roads and bridges, the salaries of government officials, and the laws of the community itself. The cardinal focus upon which the Puritan theocracy rested was the Bible, which John Calvin called God's eternal decree and the only source of authority and laws for Christian people.

The devotion to the Bible provides the first clue to the emerging educational-purpose structure. The Puritans, while viewing their relationship with God differently than many other groups, were still very much Protestants. At the heart of the Protestant tradition is the belief that reading the Bible is a Christian obligation. To fulfill his obligation, however, one must first know how to read. In fact, the instruction in what would be known today as elementary schools provided only "an ability to read and to understand the principles of religion and the capital laws of the country."[3] Since the Bible State was based on Holy Scripture, the capital laws of the country, it was assumed, could be understood only if scripture were understood. The purpose of the Puritan elementary education system, then, was very pragmatic. It was designed to maintain the Bible State; the people must read the Bible, so they must be taught to read. Think back to the three reasons given earlier for maintaining an educational system. Where does that purpose fit?

Puritan educational goals

The fact that elementary education was designed primarily to teach reading is illustrated by the manner in which this skill was taught. Often a woman who was a skilled reader would take several of the neighborhood children into her home and teach them while she went about her household tasks. This enterprise was carried out under the supervision of the ever-vigilant pastor. In addition to reading the children were occasionally taught some spelling and counting, and

[2] Adolphe E. Meyer, *An Educational History of the American People* (New York: McGraw-Hill, 1967), p. 20.

[3] V. T. Thayer, *Formative Ideas in American Education* (New York: Dodd, Mead, 1965), p. 4.

the young girls, the art of sampler making. The *school dames,* as these women became known, were compensated in various ways for running the schools, which became known as *dame schools.* Not all children were taught in the dame schools. In 1635, Boston's governing elders recommended that "Brother Philemon Pormont . . . be entreated to become schoolmaster for the teaching and nurturing of children among us."[4] However, the purpose of the schooling was the same; children needed to be taught to read in order to be able to read the Bible.

In the early years the governing members of the Puritan theocracy lived in constant dread that the clerical and secular leaders who formed the original community would die before others reared in the Puritan tradition could be readied to take their place. Although the average citizen needed only to be able to read the Bible, the production of leaders created the need for what we would today call secondary and higher education. In 1636 a college was founded. When a few years later a man named John Harvard died, leaving to the college his library of some 300 volumes and one half of his estate, 800 pounds, the grateful Puritan governors promptly named the college for him. Probably few men have purchased near-immortality as economically.

Quite naturally the young men who would attend Harvard College had to be prepared beforehand. A 1643 statute of the college clearly stated what this preparation should consist of:

When any scholar is able to understand Tully, or such like classical Latin author extempore, and make and speak true Latin in verse and prose, . . . and decline perfectly the paradigms of nouns and verbs in the Greek tongue: Let him then and not before be capable of admission into college.

A few years before the Harvard statute was written the New England fathers had started the traditional grammar schools. These schools were established to teach "humane learning and good literature,"[5] and the basic rudiments of both English and Latin grammar formed the core of the curriculum. Students attended grammar school for seven to eight years and were introduced to Greek in the last few years. The first of these schools was established in Boston in 1636.

In 1647 the citizens of Massachusetts took legislative action to ensure the production of future leaders. A law was passed stating that

[4] Meyer, *op. cit.,* p. 24.
[5] *Ibid.,* p. 26.

"when any town shall increase to the number of 100 families or householders, they shall set up a grammar school, the master thereof being able to instruct youth so far as they shall be fitted for the university. . . ." This same act also described the "one chief project of the Old Deluder Satan to keep men from a knowledge of the Scripture." The implication is quite clear: Being able to read makes scripture available to all; hence a literate people can avoid Satan. This profound purpose, then, underlay the early New England fathers' desire to build schools. The 1647 statement, in fact, became known as "the Old Deluder Satan Act."

The need to teach children to read in order that they might study the Bible and the need to supply themselves with learned leaders, particularly ministers, were the motivating forces that led to the establishment of the early grammar schools and the college. The entrance requirements for the college determined the curriculum of what is today called the secondary school. The resulting educational system was both a servant of the existing society and a function of it. The needs and desires of that society determined the purposes the schools established and, as a result, the opportunities available to students. The society determined the *direction* in which educational purpose was allowed to evolve.

The individual vs. the state in Puritan times

Before drawing any inferences about how such a procedure for determining educational purpose affected individuals, let us consider how the Bible State felt about the individual. In order to ensure that master and parents were indeed instructing their charges in (1) reading, (2) the principles of Puritanism, and (3) the basic laws of the colony, in 1642 the Massachusetts commonwealth ordered that periodic inspections of households be conducted. Such inspections were necessary because of the "great neglect of many persons in training up their children in learning and labor which may be profitable to the commonwealth." If the inspectors found that youngsters were not being instructed in the three areas mentioned above, they could be taken from their parents or legal guardians and put in a home where they would receive such an education. This, of course, gave the state absolute control over what children of elementary-school age would learn. It also established the basic principle of compulsory education. You may be tempted, as indeed we were at this point, to conclude that the schools were being used to change the existing social structure. Before you make that judgment, however, you should review the earlier discussion of that point.

To understand the 1642 act, we must know something about the basic political nature of the people writing it. Although the Puritans migrated to North America for religious (and probably also for economic) reasons, what they sought was not religious freedom for all. On the contrary, they believed that God had entrusted them with His truth and had given them the responsibility to construct and perpetuate a society exclusively in the image of that truth. Thus when the Quakers arrived on the scene, they were flogged, jailed, and often hanged—all, of course, in the name of Christ. There was considered to be no freedom of choice where religion was concerned; democracy had no place in the church. The Reverend John Cotton made this quite clear when, after long days and nights of prayer and search, he said, "Democracy I do not conceyve that ever God did ordeyne as a fit government either for church or commonwealth. If the people be governors, who shall be governed?" To support his belief, Cotton could point to no less an authority than the *Puritan Platform of Discipline,* which described the place of democracy in church and state as follows: "The Holy Ghost frequently, yea always where it mention church government, ascribeth it to elders, whereas the work and duty of the people is expressed in obeying orders."

The Puritans firmly believed in a society based on class distinctions. The decisions of the church and commonwealth, which directly touched every life, were made by a handful of ministers, magistrates, and, after the Bible State had been operating for a few years, successful businessmen. Only those at the top of the social heap were allowed to be called Mister, or gentlemen; a skilled craftsman was addressed as Goodman and his spouse as Goodwife, while unskilled laborers, servants, and anyone who worked for another were addressed by their given names. This stratified social system controlled the clothes a person wore and the place he sat in church. Obviously, the Puritans did not believe in freedom at all. Considering, however, that they, like other groups who arrived on the North American shore, came from a rigidly class-conscious society, little else could have been expected of them.

The view the early settlers had of society caused them to have an identifiable educational philosophy, which explains the educational purposes of the early schools and colleges. The individual's role was to serve the state; he was to do as the elders of the commonwealth ordered, since their decisions were made with "divine guidance." Education was "a tool to advance class interests and to nail down the prevalent social order."[6] Decisions regarding education were made for an individual, and he followed those decisions, probably because he believed this was necessary to the social order or because he did not know how to avoid doing what "the establishment" wanted done. The educational philosophy of that time was to educate a person only to the degree that would enable him to keep his place in society. The early schools were, then, at the very beginning of the evolutionary spiral described earlier.

Today education provides a way for many people to move from a lower to a higher social stratum. *Which point on the evolutionary scale does this function of education demonstrate?* In contrast, the earlier established purpose of education, was to teach everyone to read but to teach only a few to be leaders, and one of the best prerequisites to being a leader was to have the good fortune to be sired by an established leader.

The Massachusetts act did not go unnoticed by the rest of New England. Many states used it as a model; Connecticut, in fact, admired the 1642 statement so much that it adopted an identical statute. Rhode Island, however, paid no attention to this educational milestone, because there church and state were kept separate. The magistrates governing Rhode Island probably saw that to make the 1642 act workable, a theocracy would have to be established. Since they could not accept such a government, the law was meaningless to them. Rhode Island's indifference to the 1642 act raises an important point relative to educational philosophy in the colonies. Did Rhode Island ignore the compulsory-education act of 1642 because, not being a Bible State, it had no need to ensure that everyone could read the Bible or because the ability to read and education were not considered important in early-seventeenth-century America? If the latter rationale is true, Rhode Island made the same judgment regarding the individual and the state that a theocracy would make, namely, that the individual should engage only in pursuits that benefit the state and maintain the present social order.

The Americanization of the colonists

The early educational system, which the Puritans were largely responsible for establishing, began, as we have said, with the teaching of reading to enable the populace to understand the Bible and the laws. For those who wished to prepare themselves for service to the church

[6] *Ibid.*, p. 24.

or state (and who had the cash), a college education was available. The social order ordained by the Puritan fathers was neat, compact, and maintained the status quo. But the early residents of this country, and of the Bible State of Massachusetts in particular, were soon to learn that they could change their lot in life by turning from the soil to some form of commerce. Meyer explains this period in early America in this fashion: "wooed by the possibilities of a more sumptuous earthly life, more and more New Englanders began to give some earnest thought to the betterment of their material estate and condition."[7] The early New Englander found a market for his skills and his products, and he also found that the profits from their sale not only allowed him to live better but changed his social position. Perhaps he liked the sound of Mister better than Goodman or Joe. In any event, the Puritans, and all other denominations as well, discovered that the New World provided considerable opportunity for financial, and thereby social, enhancement. If these, then, are the seeds of genuine educational-purpose evolution, pin them down and make a prediction.

Institutions, however, change more slowly than individuals. In 1692 Massachusetts, which had become a royal colony in 1691, made one last attempt to enforce the act of 1642. The English presiding magistrates saw no need for the law, however, and discarded it. Throughout the early years of the eighteenth century attempts were made in Massachusetts, Connecticut, New Hampshire, and elsewhere to pass statutes that would ensure that citizens could read the word of God and the laws of the colony. But regardless of how the law was written or the penalty attached to it, those governing the colonies found loopholes that permitted them to avoid spending money to establish schools. The principal purpose for the existence of the prior educational system had been the maintenance of a Bible State. As the early religious fervor faded, there was no longer any real need for maintaining the Latin grammar schools or for rigid laws regarding reading ability. The times were changing, and the schools would have to change too.

A change in educational emphasis

In classical times, the Spartans maintained educational institutions that stressed physical development. They wanted good soldiers to protect the state and healthy mothers to increase the populace. In

[7] *Ibid.*, p. 41.

American colonial times, the Puritans maintained schools to protect the social status quo and to serve the Bible State. In both cases the educational systems were designed with a particular purpose in mind, and this purpose determined both *what* was taught and *how* it was taught. Puritan primers dealt not with children's stories as we know them but with the duties of a good citizen of the Bible State. Young children were taught such verses as

Fear God all Day,
Parents obey,
No false Thing say,
By no Sin stray,
Love Christ always,
In Secret pray,
Mind little Play,
Make no Delay,
In doing Good.

An example such as the above was meant to do more than develop the ability to read; it contained a message that reflected the purpose of the educational system itself. Consider also the following example from an early primer.

I in the Burying Place may see
Graves shorter there than I;
From Death's Arrest no Age is free,
Young Children too may die;
My God, may such an awful sight
Awakening be to me!
Oh! That by early Grace I might
For Death prepared be.

The purpose of the Puritan educational system was clearly reflected in the selection of *content* for the classroom.

TASK

Before reading on, think back to your own elementary and secondary school and college experiences. Isolate and list what you believe were the purposes these institutions were designed to achieve.

Is your understanding of the purposes behind your educational experience as clear to you as those of the Puritans would have been to a casual observer? If you cannot isolate the purposes behind the education given you, perhaps the educational system of which you are a product has not defined them clearly. More important, perhaps you, as a future teacher, should ask serious questions about whether these experiences were truly useful. An educational system without a guiding philosophy is unlikely to motivate students or to provide a philosophical yardstick by which they can measure their progress or the progress of society.

Today, most people feel they have an obligation to provide an education for their children, although they do not necessarily distinguish among the following in determining the source of the obligatory feeling. How does one decide among (1) the learning that comes from the schooling, (2) the prestige that comes to the parents because the child is attending and to the child for having attended, (3) the opportunity that education provides for upward social mobility, or (4) the purposes a child achieves in school? Regardless of the reason, people feel that the education of children is necessary.

But we have digressed from the narrative of the evolution of educational purpose in the United States. Let us return now to the colonies, where the early religious fervor was beginning to fade and the increasing concern with practical and commercial goals beginning to take root.

Two seventeenth-century men, John Locke and William Penn, were to make important contributions to American educational philosophy. Locke believed that the way men think, act, and understand is directly related to their experiences. Perhaps his greatest contribution to education was his *Essay Concerning Human Understanding*. He said:

Let us suppose the mind to be, as we say, white paper void of all characters, without any ideas; how comes it to be furnished? Whence comes it by the vast store which the busy and boundless fancy of man has painted on it with an almost endless variety? Whence has it all the materials of reason and knowledge? To this I answer in one word, from experience; in that all our knowledge is founded, and from that it ultimately derives itself.[8]

Essentially the same thing was said much later by John Dewey. Both felt that men learn through experience, not simply through accumulating information; we do not learn only by studying what has been accomplished by others. Locke was, in fact, addressing himself to the principle Jerome Bruner considered in the 1960s when he said:

[8] This excerpt appears in Book II, chapter 1, section 2. For a thorough treatment of Locke's contribution to American education, see Thayer, *op. cit.*, Ch. 3.

We teach a subject not to produce little living libraries on that subject, but rather to get a student to think mathematically for himself, to consider matters as an historian does, to take part in the process of knowledge-getting. Knowing is a process, not a product.[9]

Locke and, later, Bishop Comenius, opened the door to questions about the importance of the process of learning rather than the products of learning. This was a revolutionary idea in the evolving educational-purpose structure; emphasis on process was completely contrary to all that was being done then in the schools. Even today, there is reason to believe that the idea is not universally accepted, particularly in college classrooms. If our educational system believed that knowing is a process and not a product, *it would have arrived at point three on the evolutionary scale of educational purpose.*

TASK	*Take some time and describe in writing how an educational system that truly believed that knowing is a process, not a product, would differ from what we now have. Reread what you have written after you have finished Chapter 2.*

Earlier, the point was made that individuals who attempted to change an educational system were often ignored. Locke is one example. Only time will tell if Bruner is to be another.

When William Penn said, "cross not the genius of the child," and then added, "but match their talents well," he introduced a completely new concept into American schooling. The early primers demonstrate that those who prepared teaching materials paid little attention to the nature of the learner and, since the products of learning were what was emphasized, the pedagogues did not either. Penn believed that the child should have foremost consideration when what we today call the curriculum was selected. A few years later, Rousseau was to state eloquently the same belief. Penn made a second great contribution to education when he urged that children not be physically abused. But perhaps his most important legacy to educational purpose was his insistence that schools turn away from emphasis on memorization and concentrate instead on a few "sensible and practical truths." He also insisted that both sexes be taught to read and write,

[9] Jerome Bruner, *Toward a Theory of Instruction* (Cambridge, Mass.: Harvard University Press, 1966), p. 72. [Emphasis ours.]

an idea that was not always endorsed by earlier educational structures and one that definitely represented a movement toward changing the existing social order. Penn no doubt realized this. Although he made a great contribution to education, he did it with a somewhat ulterior motive. His interest was in preserving the government, and he knew that to survive it must have the support of the people. He saw a practical, pleasant, and profitable educational experience as a way of involving the youth in the preservation of the government—an idea that is, indeed, still worthy of consideration.

Although an exact chronology of how the educational philosophies of such men as Locke and Penn influenced the developing educational system is difficult to ascertain, the notion that the purpose of schools was to teach practical ideas certainly caught the attention of the early-eighteenth-century population. Private schools, which advertised instruction in such areas as surveying, gunnery, art and drawing, mathematics, physics, languages, and astronomy, flourished. With the exception of languages, none of these subjects had been considered suitable materials for the age group in secondary schools. The Latin grammar school had not provided such fare. One private school went so far as to offer dancing, even though the theocrats of the day condemned it as a carnal activity, particularly if both sexes participated.

These private schools were basically secondary schools; elementary education had not progressed much beyond teaching children to read and write, although the goals of the system were now more pragmatic than moral. Even though the schools at this point appeared to be pragmatic, the learner's primary function still was to acquire information, and rarely do new ways of leading students to acquire information have any lasting educational benefit. Once the new approach is no longer a novelty, the learner realizes that the educational goal is still the same; he is to learn (perhaps memorize is a better term) what the system has determined he should know. This point of view is nicely stated in the following quotation:

The method turns out to be a set of questions posed by the teacher, text, or machine which is intended to lead the student to produce the right answers—answers the teacher, text, or machine, by gum, knew all the time. This is sometimes called "programmed learning." So far, most students have been neither tricked nor intrigued by it. They recognize the old shell game when they see it, just as they recognize a lecture given on television as more of the same.[10]

[10] Neil Postman and Charles Weingartner, *Teaching as a Subversive Activity* (New York: Delacorte Press, 1969), p. 28.

Changing the procedures for transmitting information to learners does not alter what the learner must do; he must still acquire what is being transmitted. Furthermore, and perhaps more important, the educational purpose for engaging in the activity has not been altered. Perhaps this is the reason that early elementary education in this country had to wait until such men as Rousseau, Parker, Pestalozzi, and Dewey arrived on the educational scene before its purposes were really challenged.

A significant step in turning the course of American education toward more practical concerns was taken by Benjamin Franklin, a great American who is not usually thought of in connection with education. Franklin believed that the schools should teach everything that was "useful and ornamental," but recognizing that such an undertaking would require more time than was available, he was willing to settle for "those things that are likely to be most useful and most ornamental; regard being had for the several professions for which they are intended." He himself opened a tuition academy in Philadelphia in 1751. All instruction was conducted in English, and the curriculum, according to the *Pennsylvania Gazette*, consisted of "History, Geography, Chronology, Logic, and Rhetoric; also Writing, Arithmetic, Merchants Accounts, Geometry, Algebra, Surveying, Navigation, Astronomy, Drawing in Perspective, and other mathematical sciences; with natural and mechanical Philosophy, etc." The practical aspects in the curriculum of the Academy are readily apparent. Few skills were more sorely needed in mid-eighteenth-century America than surveying (most of the country was a vast uncharted wilderness in 1751), navigation (mastery of the seas was essential to survival), and merchants' accounts. The Academy curriculum was directly aimed at changing the structure of the existing society by increasing the opportunities for citizens to participate in it. Active, involved participation by concerned and interested persons is very likely to change the structure of anything. (As a case in point, consider what has happened to religion in general and Catholicism in particular since 1960.)

The Academy provided a pragmatic education that allowed the youth of the day (if he had the price of tuition) to develop salable skills, introduced coeducation, and set an example for other institutions. In today's fast-changing world, however, embracing an educational philosophy that is aimed at preparing youngsters for vocational skills may be questionable. By the time a learner develops a marketable skill, the probabilities of it no longer being needed are great. Education that provides specific job or skill training could be education for obsolescence. In the eighteenth century, however, the tempo of development was considerably different; it was probable that the skills a student developed in the Academy would be able to serve him vocationally for all of his working years.

As significant a step in the development of educational purpose as the Academy was, however, its impact was diminished by its conservatism and *adherence to point one on the evolutionary scale.* Here is how Franklin describes his selection of the board of trustees whom he himself had invited to serve: "The first step I took was to associate in the design a number of active friends. . . ." Unfortunately, although Franklin's friends may have been active, they were not particularly liberal. As Meyer explains,

Had Franklin been able to follow his own inclination, his nursery of learning would, no doubt, have laid its chief stress on the modern and practical subjects. . . . But the school's trustees, academically far more staid than the audacious Benjamin, were reluctant to follow him in such a mad caper. Consequently, when the academy tolled out its summons to its first clients, they could cross swords with Latin and Greek, as generation upon generation of learners had done before them.[11]

Thus the purposes Franklin visualized for his Academy were never fully realized. The traditionalists' view that such subjects as Latin and Greek were "good for the mind" and necessary for entrance into and success in college prevailed, and the evolutionary movement that the Academy might have fostered was partially frustrated. Furthermore, the curriculum of the Academy was based upon the old notion of *acquiring* information and skills rather than on participating in an educational process that teaches one how to learn.

Mental-discipline theory

How those in charge of an educational system view the minds of the individual learners is an important clue to the educational-purpose structure. There is no evidence to indicate that the Puritans held any kind of view of the mind, and, as was stated earlier, Locke held the view that the mind was like "white paper void of all characteristics." There is, however, another theory of the mind that has had a profound impact on the educational-purpose structure of the American school system and, in many respects, is still affecting it. This theory

[11] Meyer, *op. cit.*, p. 113.

is that of mental discipline. Even though the complete theory had not been articulated when Franklin's trustees organized the Academy curriculum, the notion that certain subjects were "good" for the students prevailed.

The mental-discipline theory begins at nearly the same point as did Locke's educational philosophy. Locke took the position that the "materials of reason and knowledge" came from experience; he also believed that the mind possessed certain faculties. More than a century after his death in 1704, the concept of the mind as a void and as possessing certain faculties were put together, and *faculty psychology* was born. The mind was viewed as a muscle that needed to be exercised in order to develop. In other words, it needed to be trained by being made to perform intellectual exercises. The more intricate the intellectual gymnastics, the more exercise the mind received, and the more highly developed the mind and the person became. Certain subjects were considered better than others for this purpose. Subjects such as Latin, Greek, Euclidean geometry, algebra, and grammar were thought to be particularly effective in developing the reasoning power of the mind. And, according to the mental-discipline theory, once this reasoning ability has been developed it will be available for use in any situation. That belief is obviously the foundation of the notion of the transfer of training. Although contemporary educators do not embrace the notion that studying certain subject matter develops the mind, they are, nevertheless, concerned with mental development. As you think back over certain of the required courses you have taken during your educational career, you can probably isolate certain influences of the mental-discipline theory.

The classical subjects thought to be needed for mental discipline were the core of the curriculum until the last few decades of the nineteenth century, when the beliefs of educators like Herbert Spencer became known. Spencer believed that science, and not the classics, should form the heart of the curriculum. He argued that the educational value of a subject was intrinsic and did not depend on the effort needed to learn it, and that science was a subject in keeping with "modern" culture, whereas the classics were hopelessly out of date. Studying the scientific achievements of Newton and Galileo required just as much mental discipline as the study of grammar, and the probability that this mental training in science could be transferred to other areas was just as great as the probability that classical training could be transferred. In other words, Spencer fought the mental-discipline disciples with their own weapons; instead of a one-sided classical curriculum, the schools were to have a one-sided scientific one. He did not question the mental-discipline theory per se. The question whether the training of the mind was a viable educational purpose and the effect of that questioning upon educational purposes was to be left to others, whose views we shall examine in Chapter 2.

The Individual vs. Society: A Continuing Conflict in Education

We have examined educational purposes of various groups in our history. In the early years of this country, schools were established because the society would benefit if citizens had certain attitudes, or could use certain skills. Clearly, then, we were at point one on the evolutionary scale, with the educational system used to serve the needs of the state. Such a system was hardly democratic, but when you consider the treatment of individuals by the state in those countries from which the settlers came, the emergence of the attitude that the individual should serve the state is not surprising. Franklin's establishment of the Academy is sometimes used as evidence that by the mid-eighteenth century the educational system was oriented more toward serving the individual. Franklin's original plans for the Academy would have represented a definite and overt movement toward point two. However, the actual curriculum was really designed to fit the individual for the existing society and hence represented a movement on the evolutionary educational-purpose spiral back to point one, where the individual serves the state.

We firmly believe that the state today does not use the educational system to prepare individuals to fit its needs, and if you quizzed practicing educators, they would probably agree. But before we become too dogmatic, let us analyze certain elements of the current curriculum.

Prior to World War II the secondary school that taught driver education was quite rare; today the majority of secondary-school students have the opportunity to learn driving skills. Furthermore, if a young driver has had a driver-education course, his parents will pay less insurance if he drives his own or the family car. Now, driving an automobile is important to most persons, and it certainly fits into the pragmatic purpose structure of the eighteenth-century academy. Does it fit the recognized educational purposes of the twentieth-century school?

Within the last two decades there has been a great increase in the demand for specific vocational education. Much of the impetus for this development has come from industries and military establish-

FIGURE 1–1
What are the advantages and disadvantages of teaching specific, marketable skills to the vocational education student?

ments that wish to employ trained individuals. These organizations, however, do not usually assume the responsibility of retraining an individual whose skill has become obsolete. Organizations like the American Legion, the Veterans of Foreign Wars, and the Daughters of the American Revolution have often been instrumental in leading legislative bodies (from state governments to local school boards) to require courses designed to develop patriotism. There is also no doubt that powerful farmers' organizations have influenced the incorporation and retention of vocational agriculture courses in schools. *All these groups clearly represent an attempt to keep schools at point one or, at best, move them to point two.*

Groups such as those mentioned above, and groups formed for the specific purpose of influencing the exclusion or inclusion of certain courses in the curriculum (the sex-education issue, for example), can exert tremendous pressure on those administering the curriculum. Such groups are not usually concerned with educational purpose nor with its evolution; they are interested only in using the schools to support their point of view. Do such groups serve a useful function in our twentieth-century schools? We suggest that you withhold answering this question until you have studied Chapter 2. Also consider the evidence presented here before making your decision as to whether the state today uses the schools to accomplish its own purposes.

We have traced the evolution of educational purpose from the early seventeenth century to the end of the nineteenth century. How do the facts discussed here fit the reasons you stated early in this chapter for maintaining schools? For most of this period the needs of the individual were not seriously considered by those responsible for the educational system. William Penn, John Locke, and John Comenius tried, but failed, to shift the focus of education toward the individual. The mental-discipline theory appeared, and certain subjects were earmarked as better for training the mind than others; again the role prescribed for the individual was one of passive acceptance. Spencer and others debunked the notion that the classics were the only subjects suitable for training the mind, and what emerged was the notion that studying hard was the important thing and that one subject was probably as good as another for this purpose. Gradually, the goals of the schools shifted. At the beginning the acquisition of certain skills and the mastery of certain subjects for their own sake was considered important. By the end of the nineteenth century, although those purposes still existed, the individual was also considered in that certain subjects were considered to be good for him because they trained his mind, and trained minds were necessary to improve the existing societal structures.

At this point in the evolution of the educational system, there were no criteria by which a teacher could easily judge the effectiveness of his teaching procedures or the materials he used. If he endorsed the mental-discipline theory, his teaching method was simple; he told the students certain facts, which they memorized and repeated to him. Teaching was simply a matter of transmitting information. Those students who received the message and could play it back, passed; the others flunked. After all, Latin was extremely important to an Iowa farm boy! The individual learner followed a predetermined curriculum or his education was at an end.

The educational-purpose structure that existed at the end of the nineteenth century had been nudged along in no particular direction by various currents. Furthermore, the impetus had come from society and *not* from the educational profession itself, which remanied a passive bystander doing society's bidding. That position was to change in the twentieth century, and we shall study that change in Chapter 2.

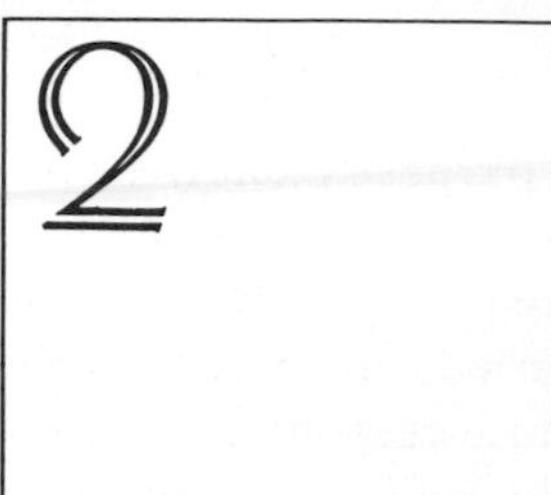

The Planning of Educational Purpose

Plato once defined a slave as one whose life is spent working to achieve the purposes of another. As you can see from reading Chapter 1, the role of the teacher in the early American schools fits this description. The lack of opportunity for initiative, no doubt, is what kept many teachers from becoming professionals and many others from becoming teachers. In this chapter we shall describe the emergence of the educational profession and its contributions to planning educational purposes.

In a 1938 publication, John Dewey described what he called traditional education (which he opposed) in this way:

The subject-matter of education consists of bodies of information and of skills that have been worked out in the past; therefore, the chief business of the school is to transmit them to the new generation.[1]

There are many, even today, who believe that the proper function of schools is the transmission of information and the training of the mind in the old sense—students should be taught to preserve what the establishment considers good in society and to change what the establishment considers bad, but not to decide for themselves what is good or bad. Dewey might have been describing the philosophy of a well-known modern conservative, who said in 1960:

We have forgotten that the proper function of the school is to transmit the culutral heritage of one generation to the next generation, and to so train the minds of the new generation as to make them capable of absorbing ancient learning and applying it to new problems.[2]

[1] John Dewey, *Experience and Education* (New York: Collier, 1963), p. 17. Originally published by Kappa Delta Pi, 1938.

[2] Barry Goldwater, *The Conscience of a Conservative* (New York: MacFadden Books, 1960), p. 86.

Have you ever stopped to consider how much time, effort, and money our educational system has poured into the transmission of information and skills since the Puritans landed on this continent? If you think back through your own educational experience, you will probably find that a great deal of your time was spent in acquiring the information and skills needed to enter college. How little such an educational purpose differs from those of the Puritans. Oh yes, students today may be told about *different* kinds of skills and information than were their forefathers, but in the majority of schools they are still only *told*. The mode and tenor of life in this country have changed drastically since the Puritans, but ask yourself how much the fundamental purposes of education have changed. Yet former United States Commissioner of Education, Sterling M. McMurrin, says this about educational purpose:

The future of American education depends in large degree upon the character of our efforts to define its aims and purposes, for without a clear conception of what the schools should achieve it is not possible to determine either the proper substance of education or its appropriate methods.[3]

The impact of McMurrin's statement is tremendous, for curricula and methods are what the teacher works with. Without those, he has two choices—he can muddle along transmitting information as his predecessors have done for centuries, or he can quit! Many do the latter.

Transmitting information is certainly the easiest way to hold class (notice we do not say teach); testing the retention of facts is likewise simple. Furthermore, an educational system that concentrates on transmitting information assumes that the information will still be viable and useful to the learner when he leaves the educational womb. Such an assumption is so inconsistent with experience as to be almost ridiculous. Consider for example, the words of a former Yale law professor and University of Chicago president, Robert Hutchins:

Almost every fact I was taught from the first grade through law school is no longer a fact. Almost every tendency that was proclaimed has failed to materialize. The facts and tendencies of today are those nobody foresaw fifty years ago. . . . I am especially embarrassed by the facts and tendencies I proclaimed myself. I can only hope that students in Yale Law school have forgotten what I taught them. The

[3] Sterling M. McMurrin, "The Curriculum and the Purposes of Education," in Robert W. Heath, ed., *New Curricula* (New York: Harper & Row, 1964), p. 262.

courts have overruled and the legislature repealed most of what I knew.[4]

Hutchins went on to say that he believed the function of schools was to provide learners with "the intellectual tools, the intellectual discipline, and the intellectual framework necessary to understand the new problems we face."[5]

McMurrin stated that the future of American education depends on its ability to determine its purposes; here we have a clue to what those purposes should be. If you think back for a moment to Chapter 1, you will see that the educational systems discussed there had many concerns, but intellectualism was not one of them. While the mental-discipline theory was influential, its focus was not on the type of intellectual tools, discipline, or framework that Hutchins describes. If the schools are truly to prepare learners for the real world, they must provide them with the intellectual experience and sophistication that will enable them to solve society's problems. What has the educational system done to define its role within this intellectual and social frame of reference?

Society and Education

For the most part, our schools have reflected those facets of our culture that are deep and abiding and they have accordingly provided the kind of education that has been expected or demanded of them. Their chief deficiencies have perhaps been their failure to more often affect the character of the culture rather than simply be a function of it.[6]

The foregoing quotation says two things: (1) that our society has the type of schools it wants and (2) that the schools (really, those operating them) have failed to exercise their inherent power of leadership. This failure is probably due to the fact that those operating the schools have been busy providing the type of education the population has demanded. If you doubt the truth of this statement, think for a minute how such subjects as home economics, driver education, and agriculture became part of the school curriculum and why you rarely find a course in, say, communism. If you carefully assess whether communism or the lack of specific vocational skills repre-

[4] Robert M. Hutchins, "Are We Educating Our Children for the Wrong Future?" *Saturday Review of Literature* (September 11, 1965), p. 66.
[5] *Ibid.*, p. 83.
[6] McMurrin, *op. cit.*, p. 266.

sents a greater danger to democracy, surely communism will win. Yet the people who support the schools, the taxpayers, expect their children to fight against and overcome an ideology of which they are totally ignorant. To take another example, consider the attitudes of many adults toward sex education. The schools are, for the most part, middle-of-the-road, noncontroversial institutions because that is what the majority of the taxpayers want them to be—they have done what has been expected or demanded of them. In some cases, the schools have become what they are because of what the society has demanded they *not* do. In other words, they are at point three on the evolutionary-purpose scale.

Milestones in Twentieth-Century Education

Dewey: the winds of change

There are several bright spots in our educational history, and those few points of light give us hope for the future. One of the truly bright lights of the past has been John Dewey, a man whose work has been called as important as, and in the same class with, that of Augustine, Aquinas, Bacon, Descartes, and Locke. Dewey was not the only one to cast doubt on the purposes of conventional education (information transmission) and its procedures. Parker, Froebel, Pestalozzi, and Rousseau did also. Dewey's efforts, however, were different, or perhaps they only seemed different. As Meyer puts it, Dewey organized "the first truly philosophically oriented school to grace this land, it has in this respect remained without a peer or even a rival."[7]

John Dewey arrived at the University of Chicago in 1894 and remained there until 1904.[8] During that decade he directed a laboratory school that was based on the premise that since both education and the development of an individual are social processes, the school should be a social institution. Education, in other words, was not a preparation for life, it *was* life. For this reason, it was the duty of the school to reproduce within the classroom the conditions typical of social life. In Dewey's school the usual academic format was replaced

[7] Adolphe E. Meyer, *An Educational History of the American People* (New York: McGraw-Hill, 1967), p. 261.

[8] Although Dewey established himself at the University of Chicago, he left that institution in 1904 to accept a position at Columbia University. He remained at Columbia until his retirement in 1930 and continued to influence American education actively until his death at age 93 in 1952.

by one based on the children's everyday activities. They learned how to read and how to handle numbers, but they did so by engaging in activities where those subjects were used and by interacting with the materials of the subject. (The phrase, *the materials of the subject,* will become very important in Chapter 5.) Science was not reading about bugs in a book; arithmetic was counting objects, not just counting; and adding meant adding something that was involved in a social process to something else on the social scene. Dewey did not believe, as did many of his contemporaries, that the child and the curriculum were born enemies; rather, he believed that if you provided learners with materials in which they had an inherent interest, they would achieve the goals of the curriculum and enjoy themselves in the process. The idea of children loving to do the things the school wanted them to do was a revelation to early-twentieth-century educators. For some, that notion is still revolutionary; they believe that if something is worth knowing, learning it should be just a little distasteful. Dewey believed that if democracy was to survive and prosper, educational institutions would have to be able to match individual learning traits or styles with the ends of society. To do that the school must recognize that people learn most efficiently and effectively when they are permitted to behave in a natural way.

Dewey has been accused of advocating complete freedom for children—of letting them do exactly as they pleased in his school. This accusation is untrue, for he did not believe that freedom without purpose was desirable. He himself said, "There can be no greater mistake, than to treat . . . freedom as an end in itself. It then tends to be destructive of the shared cooperative activities which are the normal source of order."[9] Discipline within the school has only one purpose, and that is to assist learners in developing self-control; but, "the mere removal of external control is no guarantee for the production of self-control."[10] Furthermore, "an educational philosophy which professes to be based on the idea of freedom may become as dogmatic as ever was the traditional education which it reacted against."[11] In a school devoted to developing an understanding of society and its functions, there must be freedom, provided when and as the learners develop the power to frame purposes, make wise judgments, and evaluate desires by consequences. But none of these desirable and necessary social traits will be developed if the learner is not provided freedom at the outset.

[9] Dewey, *op cit.*, p. 63.
[10] *Ibid.*, p. 64.
[11] *Ibid.*, p. 22.

In Dewey's school the teacher occupied a unique role for that period: "instead of confronting her charges from atop her podium, she was up and about, her statuelike reserve discarded, lending a hand here, suggesting there, and harkening to the lavish jabber of question and comment."[12] Dewey's ideal teacher was a participant in the learning scene, but was also responsible for providing the learners with opportunities to have the experiences necessary to integrate their natural inclinations with the social environment. He explained the role of the teacher like this:

The great maturity of experience which should belong to the adult as educator puts him in a position to evaluate each experience of the young in a way in which the one having the less mature experience cannot do. It is then the business of the educator to see in what direction an experience is heading. There is no point in his being more mature if, instead of using his greater insight to help organize the conditions of the experience of the immature, he throws away his insight.[13]

What Dewey is saying is that if the teacher does not know how to direct the learners' activities so as to provide them with the right kind of experiences, he should not be a teacher. Thus he did not believe, as some claim, that the teacher should not attempt to direct learning in any way.

Dewey shook up the educational world with his ideas. Perhaps his greatest contribution was to demonstrate that educational purpose must be planned in order for the schools to make their contribution to society; it cannot just be let to evolve. Dewey left the University of Chicago in 1904, but his impact on education is still being felt and, indeed, is just being discovered by some. In his early years, he spelled out his educational philosophy in a small book called *The School and Society*. In 1916, twelve years after he left the scene of his early triumphs, he published another volume, *Democracy and Education*. This second volume addressed itself to the place of a pragmatic philosophy of education in a democracy. Dewey stated the importance of the child-centered school when he said, "If we are willing to conceive education as the process of forming fundamental dispositions, intellectual and emotional, toward nature and fellow men, philosophy may even be defined *as the general* theory of education."[14] If we believe

[12] Meyer, *op. cit.*, p. 262.
[13] Dewey, *op cit.*, p. 38.
[14] John Dewey, *Democracy and Education* (New York: Macmillan, 1916), p. 328.

in democratic interaction as the basis of society, our school system should be guided by a democratic philosophy of education. Visits to existing schools will show you that not all Dewey's ideas have yet been put into practice.[15]

TASK	*Compare the Puritan's basic philosophy of education and Dewey's with respect to how each considers the individual.*

The work of 1918

In 1918 an event occurred that should be etched deeply into every educator's mind. This was the release by the United States Superintendent of Documents of a report written by the Commission on the Reorganization of Secondary Education. The report, *Cardinal Principles of Secondary Education,* stated that *all* education, elementary and secondary, should be aimed at achieving the following seven purposes:
1. Health
2. Command of the fundamental processes
3. Worthy home membership
4. Vocational efficiency
5. Civic participation
6. Worthy use of leisure time
7. Ethical character

These seven principles are far removed from the Puritan purpose of teaching children to read the Bible simply to perpetuate the Bible State.

The Seven Cardinal Principles are based on the concept that each individual must be able to make his own decisions; he must be able to select a vocation that suits him, take those actions that will maintain his health, and so on. He cannot do this if he does not have a reasonably good self-image. Since a self-image is acquired by interacting with others in social situations, if the Seven Cardinal Principles are to function as objectives for an educational system, the system

[15] Among those who also influenced educational purpose in this country were such directors of private schools as Colonel Francis Parker, Ellsworth Collings, Ernest Horn, and Marietta Johnson. In a description of experimental practices the contribution of the Winnetka (Illinois) Plan needs to be examined. And finally, the contributions of such men as Junius Meriam, Boyd Bode, William Kilpatrick, George Counts, and Harold Rugg would have to be examined before a complete philosophical picture of planned educational purpose would emerge.

must provide opportunities for social interaction. This is exactly the frame of reference Dewey used in building his experimental schools, first at Chicago and later at Columbia. The Seven Cardinal Principles were an endorsement of Dewey's concept of education as a social enterprise. In fact, if these principles are to be achieved, the social growth of the child must be the school's dominant concern.

The paramount psychological foundation of pre-twentieth-century education was the development of the intellect by rigorous mental exercise. As Chapter 1 explained, geometry, grammar, Latin, Greek, and many other subjects found their way into the curriculum for the purpose of improving the minds of students. Mastering subject matter *as such* was considered to develop the intellect. However, if we examine the Seven Cardinal Principles carefully, we can see that there is nothing in them which demands that any particular subject be taught. The curriculum of the average nineteenth-century school would be more likely to hinder than to help in the achievement of these principles. The Commission did, however, make one concession toward the previously all-important purpose of mental development; they included as one of the principles "the command of the fundamental processes." Had the Commission been concerned only with such processes as reading, writing, speaking, and computing, they would probably have referred not to fundamental processes, but to basic skills. (This is, of course, simply a speculation.) Since the fundamental processes were so pointedly mentioned, it is more likely that the Commission was referring to those mental processes upon which the achievement of the other six principles hinges. What are those fundamental mental processes? Unfortunately, the 1918 report does not elaborate; not until 1961 was an elaboration available, and we will return to this point later in the chapter. Obviously, though, the Commission endorsed an educational system that focused on the social development of learners, and to achieve this development, the schools needed to create and maintain a social environment within each classroom.

What, then, was the place for subject matter in the schools? There was nothing in the Commission's report to prohibit the teaching of reading, writing, science, literature, languages, or any other bodies of information. What was prohibited, if the Principles were to be achieved, was to let the acquisition of information become *the primary purpose* for teaching a subject. No doubt, students in schools where the Seven Cardinal Principles were used as objectives would develop an understanding of the specific subjects taught, but those understandings were secondary. To truly evaluate the students' progress one would have to test their progress in terms of the Seven Cardinal Principles and not in terms of their knowledge of specific facts. We leave the decision to you as to what the children were probably evaluated on.

The lack of relationship between the actual curriculum and the objectives of the Seven Cardinal Principles was probably the foremost factor in keeping the report from having a wide impact. What methods could a teacher in Potsville, U.S.A., use to develop in his students an ethical character while teaching American history, geometry, or vocational agriculture? What material in those fields was suitable for so lofty a purpose? The Seven Cardinal Principles were too far removed from what was actually to be taught to be of any use in deciding the content of a lesson or the means by which it was to be taught. They were not *functional.*

Here, then, is a frame of reference that you as a teacher can use to evaluate educational purposes. You can use them to select lesson content, teaching methods, and materials. If you can so use them, they are purposes you can lead learners to achieve; if you cannot, they are not functional for you. The need for clear purposes, usable as evaluative criteria, was pointed out in the earlier quotation from Sterling McMurrin: ". . . without a clear conception of what the schools should achieve it is not possible to determine either the proper substance of education or its methods." The Puritan purpose was a simple one, and their methods too were simple.

The Seven Cardinal Principles were not much help in changing the classroom procedures of the early twentieth century because teachers could not see how to use them. There were some few isolated spots in the curriculum, particularly of the secondary school, that seemed to reflect the impact of the report. Vocational education was much more popular after 1918 than before. Whether this was due to the Commission's report or to the general feeling of the citizenry that schools should be concerned with teaching their students marketable skills, is difficult to say. Education for citizenship also caught on in the period following World War I; courses dealing with problems in democracy, state and local government, and government were added to the usual history and geography. Organizations like the Young Citizens League began to appear in the schools. Here again, was the 1918 report a factor? We cannot tell, but the fact remains that both vocational education and social science took an a new complexion after 1918.

If the Seven Cardinal Principles of education were not functional as criteria for selecting content, materials, and teaching methods, why were we so insistent a few paragraphs ago on the importance of the 1918 date? There are two reasons. First, although these principles cannot serve as evaluative criteria for content, materials, and methods, they do indicate the several areas in which those leaving our schools should be proficient. They represent statements of policy relative to what the educational system of the United States stands for. Together, they form the basis of our democratic view of life: family, self-support, self-respect, respect for the rights of others, and responsibility for government.

The second reason why the Seven Cardinal Principles are important is basic to teaching as a profession. From the time of the first school until the early twentieth century, teachers had very little to say about what they taught. The citizenry demanded and the teachers delivered education in certain areas. Reading, ciphering, rote learning of Shakespeare, Chaucer in Old English, Latin, Greek, surveying, cake baking, and a multitude of other courses, were all taught at one time or another in one place or another. The history of the American public schools (and private schools too) is one of having what goes on in the classroom dictated by persons who are not there and, in some cases, who will never be there. That situation is not unlike having someone who is not or never has been in the oven and mixing rooms of a bake shop telling the baker how to prepare his products. Much of what went on in schools before the twentieth century (and still goes on in many places today) was controlled by persons who were not educators. The Seven Cardinal Principles, on the other hand, did represent the ideas of the teaching profession, clearly stating what the professionals believed the controlling policies of the schools should be. Here was the profession's definition of education; now dialogue could begin between the educator and the educated as to what adjustments, compromises, and developments were needed in order to move forward. But forward to what? The Seven Cardinal Principles were not, in themselves, directly functional. A more immediately relevant definition of educational purpose was needed.

A usable educational-purpose statement

In a democracy schools are for all the children of all the people. The curricula must ensure intellectual, physical, and emotional development of all students, provide them with vocational options, guide them to a wise use of leisure time, and make them aware of the responsibilities of citizenship. This, in itself, is a tremendous undertaking. Attempting to provide in addition curricula that will enable the learner, *while still in school,* to achieve purposes that satisfy his immediate and long-term needs is simply impossible. The schools do not have the facilities or financial resources for such a sweeping educational establishment, and if they did, the learner would not have the time to utilize it. Furthermore, if the schools attempted to prepare students for life by anticipating each finite need of each citizen, they would be setting themselves up as oracles. Today's educators cannot know the specific needs of tomorrow's citizens; furthermore, attempting to provide each learner with the abilities necessary to cope with every future problem assumes that learning ceases when the learner leaves school. Schools cannot and should not attempt to foretell the future, and learning does continue after formal education has been completed. If the citizen of tomorrow is to be able to cope with his society, he must be able to learn from the experiences he has every day. Only in this way can he achieve his fullest potential and greatest happiness. But to learn effectively from his day-by-day experiences, *he must have learned how to learn!* This, then, represents an objective toward which the school can lead the learner, but it does not represent the specific objectives toward which the classroom teacher must direct his teaching.

To assist us in isolating specific guidelines for use as "direction-finders" in teaching, let us remind ourselves that we live in a free society. Freedom implies individual liberty to do and think many things, a concept that is summed up in the term freedom of choice. But in order for an individual to be able to exercise freedom of choice responsibly and judiciously, he must have developed freedom of mind. Each individual in our society must develop freedom of mind for himself, and the degree to which our society will prosper will depend on his success. The schools cannot develop freedom of mind for an individual, but they can provide the conditions under which that development can occur. What is a free mind? How can we describe freedom of mind, and how can the schools contribute to its development?

If a mind is free it is able to apply certain definite rational powers to the solution of problems and the making of decisions. These *rational powers* were defined by the Educational Policies Commission (EPC) of the National Education Association in 1961 as "recalling and imagining, classifying and generalizing, comparing and evaluating, analyzing and synthesizing, and deducing and inferring,"[16] and as "the essence of the ability to think."[17] Not only, then, did the EPC give us a general purpose for education, it also identified the fundamental mental processes that constitute thinking. The 1961 report of the EPC supplied what was missing in the 1918 report; that is, it specifically defined "command of the fundamental processes" as the development of the rational powers. The schools must become intellectual institutions that develop the learner's ability to think. The EPC is not alone in this belief. Sterling McMurrin said the same thing in 1964:

In conformity to the general national disposition and temper, our schools have all too often removed knowledge and the cultivation of intellect from the center of their purposes and activities and have sometimes voluntarily, though often under intense social pressure, expended their resources and energies on pursuits that are of secondary and lesser value and are not the primary work of the schools. Wherever one looks today he sees encouraging signs in education. . . . And most important of all is that the concern for the intellectual life is moving back into the center of the school's interests and commitments. The faster the better.[18]

Notice that McMurrin emphasizes that the intellectual aspect of education must move back into the *center* of the school's concern. Exactly the same sentiments were held by the EPC, as the title of its 1961 report indicates. Both McMurrin and the EPC are making a tremendously important point; *central* to all the activities of the school must be a commitment to developing the ability to think (the rational powers). That commitment can come from no one but the teachers in any particular school; they are the ones who are in daily contact with the learners. The administration can facilitate the achievement of the goal by doing what is necessary to assist and support the instructional process. If you interpret the word central to mean basic to everything else, then the development of the rational powers is clearly something that must be accomplished before any other purpose can be achieved.

[16] Educational Policies Commission, *The Central Purpose of American Education* (Washington, D.C.: NEA, 1961), p. 5. Between 1918 and 1961 the EPC developed two other reports aimed at clarifying educational purpose: *The Purposes of Education in American Democracy* (Washington, D.C.: NEA, 1938) and *Education for All American Youth* (Washington, D.C.: NEA, 1944).

[17] *Ibid.*

[18] McMurrin, *op. cit.*, p. 267.

FIGURE 2–1
Inquiry is the teaching methodology for rational-power development.

As we discussed earlier in the chapter, the school is a social institution. But any understanding of man's social interaction depends on the ability of each person engaging in that interaction to analyze a situation, compare it with other situations, evaluate each situation, synthesize from those evaluations a future mode of behavior, and, after repeated testing of that synthesis, generalize about the current interaction. We are not saying that the school should deviate from its commitment to provide "life-now" for learners. But unless and until the school focuses on developing the rational powers as its central responsibility, it will not be able to fully achieve even its traditional purposes. *If the school concentrates on providing an environment that gives the student the opportunity to explore various disciplines through activities designed to develop his rational powers, he will develop those powers and simultaneously gain an understanding of the disciplines themselves.* The study of specific subjects does not ensure the development of the ability to think unless the teacher concentrates upon the development of that ability. Activities designed to cultivate the rational powers would have to allow the *learner* to compare, analyze, evaluate, and interpret facts and situations—all things that teachers have traditionally done *for* children. Teachers, in other words, would have to stop telling the learner things and instead help him to find them out for himself. *Only by encouraging this process of inquiry can teachers develop the rational powers of their students.* Indeed, inquiry is so important as a teaching method that most of the succeeding chapters will be concerned with it in one form or another. Learning Newton's laws of motion or Browning's sonnets does not necessarily ensure the growth of one's rational powers, but learning them can further it if the approach described above is used.

Dewey's feeling that the school must be a social institution was based, in part, on recognition of the need for intellectual inquiry. The social interaction that the implementation of his philosophy would promote would lead the learner to form certain mental habits, in particular, "effective habits of discriminating tested beliefs from mere assertions, guesses and opinions." Dewey's methods were designed "to develop a lively, sincere and open-minded preference for conclusions that are properly grounded and to ingrain into individuals' working habits methods of inquiry and reasoning appropriate to the various problems that present themselves."[19] The development of the rational powers will enable the learner to discriminate between tested beliefs and assertions, guesses, and opinions. But as Dewey made so clear, the cultivation of those abilities must be accomplished through inquiry.

Throughout this section we have focused on the need for the school to be an intellectual institution. Nowadays the word intellectual has many connotations, not all of them flattering. What is meant by intellectual? The first notion to be dispelled is that it refers only to those persons with a high measured intelligence (whatever that is). Intellectuality is *not* a concept that is applicable only to the "smart" ones among us. We use the word intellectual here to reflect the purest meaning of its root, intellect, namely, the power of knowing, or the capacity for rational thought. The power to know is not confined to only the "smart"; true, that power may be present to a greater degree in some than in others, but it is present to some degree in all of us. When we say that the school must become a truly intellectual institution, we mean that it must attempt to develop *the power of knowing* as completely as possible in each individual. Developing the ability of each student to think must be the central role of the school. The EPC referred to the development of the ability to think as the "common thread" of all educational experiences. This statement may be more meaningful if you interpret the words common thread to mean that *every* teacher, whether he teaches the first grade, junior high school social studies, or high school physics, must consider the development of the rational powers in his students as his responsibility. What does accepting that responsibility mean to a teacher? We shall explore some answers to that question in the next section.

[19] John Dewey, *How We Think* (Boston: Heath, 1910), pp. 27–28.

Using Rational-Power Development in Planning Classroom Approaches

Think about how you learn to do anything. If, for example, you want to learn to swim, you might begin by getting into the water and splashing around. If you want to learn to play the piano, you might start by exploring the organization of the keyboard. If you want to learn a foreign language, you might begin by trying out basic sentences on others. In each case you begin to learn how to do the thing you want to do by doing it. In the beginning the degree of sophistication with which you would perform each task would probably be minimal, but you would actually be using the learning while developing it. As you continue learning, your sophistication will increase. You could not, however, learn how to do any of these things by just hearing about them. To learn a foreign language you must speak it, and to truly understand the piano you must play it.

Leading a student to develop his rational powers has a great deal in common with developing any of the three abilities described above. If, for example, you want to teach someone to compare, you give him something to compare. Literary styles, tones of various instruments, painting styles, instrument readings from various electrical circuits, types of buttons, and objects with different properties (e.g., hard, soft, smooth, rough) can all be used to develop the rational power of comparison. But notice that these activities demand that the learner use the rational power of comparison while he is developing it. Just telling a student about something, or having him follow step-by-step directions, and then telling him what the answer should be is of no value in developing his rational powers. Classroom activities of this sort will not lead a learner to develop his rational powers —the central purpose of the school—and do not, therefore, contribute to the achievement of any of the school's traditional purposes. To quote the EPC, "the development of the ability to think . . . is the central purpose to which the school must be oriented if it is to accomplish either its traditional tasks or those newly accentuated by recent changes in the world."[20]

Learning activities and materials that just tell a student something are valueless as far as leading him to develop his rational powers is concerned. Does this make most of the films, filmstrips, and textbooks currently on the market useless? Can school time ever be justifiably

[20] Educational Policies Commission, *op. cit.*, p. 12.

used to show a film that is simply informative and makes no contribution to rational-power development? Certainly! Sometimes the use of purely information-centered materials can be justified because they provide the learner with facts that are nice to know or give him an enjoyable experience. Such materials can provide a change of pace in the school day or can be used to cap a unit of study that has concentrated on developing rationality. A teaching device such as a film can pull together in a few minutes information that may have taken the learner a few weeks or months to acquire by investigation. The actual investigation provides the learner with the opportunity to develop his rational powers; the film reviews and summarizes the findings. We must not, however, delude ourselves into thinking that providing factually oriented learning experiences is a substitute for investigation. The chief task of a teacher is to lead the learner to develop his rational powers, and only actual investigatory experiences can do that. There is little doubt that frequently 90 percent of the school day is spent on the development of only one rational power, recall, and only 10 percent is devoted (if any time is spent on it at all) to the development of the other rational powers. This unbalanced distribution of effort in our schools cannot and will not produce citizens with free and inquiring minds. The ability to recall is important—extremely important, in fact—but it cannot substitute for the other rational powers when decisions requiring a free mind are needed.

In short, if you are to lead learners to develop the ability to think, they must become involved in inquiring into those types of problems which demand that they use, and provide them with the opportunity to develop, their rational powers. You must select materials and activities that force them to use these powers. Every unit of study—book, motion picture, filmstrip, and all the other paraphernalia of teaching—must be judged by its potential to lead students to develop the ability to think, although you may, at times, choose classroom activities that do not contribute directly to this goal. The rational powers, therefore, represent more than a statement of educational purpose; *they are criteria by which you can select content and materials.* In Chapter 5 we shall examine the major subject areas to determine how they can be used to achieve the central goal of the school. If a learner is to learn from using all the other rational powers—comparing, evaluating, classifying—he must be allowed and encouraged to apply them to a problem and thoroughly investigate it; *inquiry is the methodology of rational-power development.* If you as the teacher are doing the classifying, comparing, generalizing, and so forth for the class, you may be inquiring but the learners are not. You can evaluate your own day-to-day classroom procedures by using the 1961 EPC report.

The primary difference between the 1918 report and the 1961 report is a very pragmatic one, and we would like you to inquire into that difference.

TASK	*List several activities in your favorite subject area that require the learner to use any or all of his rational powers. Then visualize how these activities would lead to the achievement of the Seven Cardinal Principles described earlier.*

The above task will, we believe, lead you to understand why the Seven Cardinal Principles were called policy statements and why the rational powers statement can be used, in a way that the earlier purposes cannot, to evaluate curricula.

Is intellectual development everything?

What is there about school that the student can use to increase the efficiency with which he functions? The position we have taken thus far is that accepting rational-power development as our primary purpose will allow the schools to lead students toward an increased ability to solve intellectual problems. That is, of course, a cognitive view of education.

There is another side to the development of an individual that is also extremely important. He must learn how to live in, appreciate, and conserve the world in harmony with the other human beings in it. An appreciation of differences in color, architecture, points of view, and patterns of behavior is a mark of an individual in harmony with his total environment. The individual who makes the greatest contribution to our society is one who becomes involved in situations. As part of his involvement, the constructive individual takes the responsibility for his own behavior and activities, and encourages and assists others to do likewise. The world would be very different if everyone in it were to examine all sides of an issue before making a decision, and were to exhibit faith in the powers of reason, experimentation, and discussion as procedures for settling differences. Problems would be judged in terms of the issues and the purposes to be served rather than in terms of fixed perceptions and wishful thinking. Unfortunately, as the Educational Policies Commission stated:

No society is today composed predominantly of individuals who are guided in most of their behavior by scientific modes of thought or actions. Other bases, conscious or unconscious, seem to guide most persons in most of their activity. Even where it is deepest, the penetration of the rational spirit may still be shallow in comparison with its potential.[21]

Education has a responsibility to lead the student to achieve objectives that are not nearly as tangible as his ability to analyze—objectives described by some as "emphasizing a feeling tone, an emotion, or a degree of acceptance or rejection."[22] Those objectives deal with values, emotions, satisfactions, and many other things that an individual must understand and control if he is to be a productive, valued, and happy member of society. How can the schools lead students to achieve these objectives?

Before, for example, an individual can revise his judgments and change his behavior in any area, he must have evidence that such a change is worthwhile. He can be provided that evidence by another, but, as the EPC stated, his behavior then is not being governed by scientific modes of thought. For him really to make up his own mind, he must gather his own evidence. (Gathering the evidence that governs one's behavior is particularly important in a democracy.)

How is evidence gathered? Obviously, one analyzes a situation by comparing events, classifying them to evaluate their significance, inferring future consequences, and synthesizing future patterns of behavior. In short, an individual must learn to use, and continue to use, his rational powers before he can achieve those intangible objectives that Krathwohl and his co-authors have called part of the *affective domain* (rational spirit). Rational powers, on the other hand, can be developed without developing the tolerance, value systems, and faith that constitute the affective domain; whether a student develops the latter qualities depends largely on his environment. We shall return to the relationship between environment and educational purpose in Chapter 3, where we examine the teacher's role in the classroom; in Chapter 5, where we analyze criteria for curriculum

[21] Educational Policies Commission, *Education and the Spirit of Science* (Washington, D.C.: NEA, 1966), p. 11.

[22] D. R. Krathwohl, B. S. Bloom, and B. B. Masia, *Taxonomy of Educational Objectives: Handbook II: Affective Domain* (New York: McKay, 1964), p. 7.

selection; in Chapter 7, when we study teaching procedures; and in Chapter 8, where we examine the factors that complicate the learning situation.

The future of educational purposes

In this chapter we have described a planned set of educational purposes that lead to the mental growth and development of the individual. The school is basically an intellectual institution, and these planned purposes definitely reflect that. There are, however, at least two questions that we have deliberately left open. The first stems from the premise that the teaching method which provides the maximum development of the rational powers is inquiry. What is inquiry? Historically, the role of the teacher has been to inform learners of what they did not know, a technique that does little or nothing to stimulate intellectual growth. What is the role of the teacher in a school that uses the inquiry method? Chapter 3 will concentrate on these questions.

3 The Role of the Teacher

The statement was once made that education is what remains after you have forgotten what you have "learned" from books. To a highly traditional teacher that statement is quite disturbing; for him the principal goal of education is the transmission of information—which he often confuses with knowledge. The traditionalist believes that his function in the classroom is to inform the children of what they do not know, and he tends to feel that unless learners are told (or read from a book) about something, they will not learn anything. In other words, he generally believes (1) that teaching is telling, (2) that memorization is learning, and (3) that being able to repeat factual information on an examination is evidence of understanding. When a student forgets when the Battle of Hastings was fought, what onomatopoeia is, or how to state the law of diminishing returns, the traditionalist believes that the educational purpose has been completely frustrated. When he meets a former student who has not retained the factual information he was taught, he may say that that particular student "did not study hard enough." His philosophy is that the material was there to learn; if some students did not take advantage of this opportunity, he cannot be blamed. Were he ever to meet a large sample of his students and evaluate, on an impromptu basis, their content knowledge, he might be in for a rude awakening. Biologist Albert Szent-Györgyi sums up the traditionalist viewpoint in the following quotation: "It is thought that . . . books are something the contents of which have to be crammed into our heads."[1] For traditionalists whose philosophy this is, teaching is a simple process, but those who believe that there is something more

[1] Albert Szent-Györgyi, "Teaching and Expanding Knowledge," *Science* (December 1964), pp. 1278–1279.

FIGURE 3–1
Exploration is finding out everything you can about an object, event, or situation.

to teaching would agree with Szent-Györgyi's philosophy: "Books are there to keep the knowledge in while we use our heads for something better."[2] What a challenging way to look at education!

We can now return to our initial premise, for the ability to use your head "for something better" is what is left after you have forgotten what you learned from books. But how do we learn this ability? *How can individuals be taught* to use their heads for something other than holding information?

How Learning Occurs

If you have never asked yourself this question, do so now; understanding how *you* learn is essential before you can lead others to learn. Keep in mind also the principal thesis of Chapter 2 that the central role of school experience is to develop the learner's rational powers. Basically, learning takes place through encounters with objects, events, and situations. Finding and describing the properties of an object, understanding how that object interacts with others, and perhaps changes properties as a result of the interaction, determining the cause and possible effects of an event, and examining the personal and social interactions that occur in a situation are all basic activities through which we learn. Regardless of what you are examining (an

[2] *Ibid.*

object, an event, or a situation), first you must find out all you can about it. If you are dealing with an object, you can poke, feel, squeeze, listen to, measure and observe it from every possible angle, and subject it to all types of varying conditions. If you are dealing with an event, you can ascertain when and where it took (or is to take) place; who was involved; the motivation, characteristics, and background of the participants; and something about the outcome(s).[3] If you are dealing with a situation, you can, first, identify the situation and, then, attempt to find out what caused it and what its potential is. Before you can begin to understand anything, you must *explore* it, thoroughly.

Exploration

Exploration, permitting yourself to become involved in finding out all available information about something, is the initial step in learning. Exploration can take place by having learners examine objects and observe how they interact with other objects. For example, a field trip to a legislative session is a fine exercise in exploration, because it gives the learner an opportunity to see for himself how a legislature and legislators function, if not a knowledge of the inner workings of governing bodies. Field trips are usually exploratory. Libraries and media centers where learners can read, view, and listen can also provide information.

Many educators believe that before learning can really begin a problem must be identified. Even identifying a problem however, is difficult unless you have explored the problem area beforehand. We believe that exploration must precede the statement of a problem. One cannot make statements about something to be investigated unless one has some prior information. Too often, learners are given information they should have been left to find out for themselves through exploration. By giving them the background of the problem, the teacher has deprived the learners of an opportunity to exercise their rational powers. Too many teachers believe that telling the student what background he needs will enable him to identify and solve a problem. This approach completely ignores the fact that we learn best and retain better what we learn from experience.

[3] An event is probably best thought of as a happening in the past or in the future; a situation is something that has evolved and may or may not cause an event to happen. Fish being killed by water pollution is an event, whereas the polluted aquatic environment is a situation. Events always have a dynamic quality, whereas situations may cause dynamic events or may be static.

FIGURE 3–2
Students or teachers may verbalize inventions.

Exploration is considered by some teachers as just "messing around," and sometimes it is. If, however, the teacher and the students have defined what is to be explored, the amount of messing around is likely to be minimal. (There has yet to be devised an educational scheme that will completely eliminate messing around by all students at all levels.) The exploration phase of learning allows individuals to develop their own learning styles. This, in turn, frees them to develop their rational powers and to begin to learn how to learn. Exploration is often criticized because it requires too much time. It does require time, but investments of time (like investments of money) must be judged on the basis of future dividends. If the central role of the schools is that outlined in Chapter 2, there can be no question about the dividends from exploration; it gives the learner an experimental background and a mental structure upon which to base the rest of the learning process, a point we shall investigate further in Chapter 4.

Conceptual invention

Once a learner has gained information about something through exploration, what can be done with that information to further develop his rational powers and his understanding of the object, event, or situation? Suppose that during their exploration of the United States Constitution, the students come to the conclusion that the first ten amendments deal with individual and group liberties (which they do). The students themselves might never consider calling these first ten amendments a Bill of Rights if someone did not *invent* the phrase for them. But the *concept* of a Bill of Rights is one that they will hear and work with during all their years as citizens in a democratic society. Or, consider a group of physics students who, in their exploration of magnets, have noticed (1) that iron filings sprinkled on a piece of paper held over a magnet are affected by the magnet even though they are quite far away from it, (2) that there are attractive and repulsive forces between two magnets held a few inches apart, and (3) that small pieces of iron held a few inches away from a magnet will jump toward it. In other words, the students have noticed that there is a space around a magnet that interacts with the spaces around other magnets and certain metals. Left on their own, the students would probably not think of naming that space around the magnet a magnetic field. The magnetic-field concept, like the Bill of Rights concept, must be invented for them.

Conceptual invention is an integral part of the learning process, because it provides the learner with concepts about objects (magnets), events (metal jumping toward magnets), or situations (the Bill of Rights) that they can use to discover more about that object, event, or situation. For example, understanding the magnetic-field concept and that fields interact can lead a learner to truly understand the electric motor. The concept of a Bill of Rights can lead him to think in terms of his rights and responsibilities with respect to his environment and his fellow citizens. But the learner will not achieve these conceptual understandings by simply memorizing the Bill of Rights or the laws of magnetism. He must have first explored the materials of the concept so that he is thoroughly acquainted and comfortable with them. Only then is he ready to internalize what those materials are saying to him or to develop a concept about them. Learners will occasionally invent a name for the concept, but principally conceptual invention is the task of the teacher, who invents a name for the phenomenon the learners are experiencing. Do not try to convince students that you have accidentally came up with a particular name; they have every right to know that this is an accepted name for the phenomenon. When learners are able to label something they are observing or experiencing and then use that label to represent the same thing in future situations, they have developed a concept. Helping students to integrate exploratory data into a conceptual framework is the role of the teacher.

How does conceptual invention of the Bill of Rights concept differ from the traditional method of teaching students about the Bill of

Rights? Conceptual invention represents a significant change from traditional classroom techniques, and it is important that you as a teacher understand how you are involved in this change, what the change is, and the reasons for it. Traditionally, the teacher begins a lesson by first thoroughly explaining a particular concept to his students. In a lesson on American government, for example, he might begin by saying that the Constitution of the United States of America consists of a preamble, or introduction, seven basic articles, and twenty-six amendments, added between 1791 and 1971. The first ten of these amendments constitute the Bill of Rights. Certainly it is a simple enough task then to briefly describe each article and amendment, perhaps with the aid of an outline like the following:

Basic Document
Preamble and Seven Articles

Preamble

1. *Legislative*	5. *Amendment provisions*
2. *Executive*	6. *National debts*
3. *Judicial*	7. *Ratification*
4. *States' relationships*	

26 Amendments
Amendments 1–10 (Bill of Rights)

What could be more succinct, easy to "learn" and remember, and important for every United States citizen to know? In what better way could the basic document of the nation be taught?

The answer to this question depends, of course, upon the purpose of those teaching it. If the only purpose for teaching the Constitution is to acquaint students with it, then this method is perfectly acceptable. To accomplish that goal, however, there is little need for a teacher; the students can use a textbook. Furthermore, many thousands of teenagers can listen to such a presentation on television. Programmed-learning machines, films, filmscripts, records and tapes, and any number of school-prepared materials can be as effective as a teacher, and can reach more students. Not only that, the school can test hundreds of students at one time to make sure they have "learned" the material. Do not think that this is an atypical picture. Today there are probably many school patrons, administrators, *and* teachers who believe that the transmission of information is the primary role of the school. These same people believe that educational technology can be used to sharply reduce the per pupil cost of education. The school basically, therefore, is thought of as an information dispensary. Schaefer describes the dispensary concept this way:

Embedded in this conception of the school as a dispensary is the notion that teaching, since it is thought to consist basically of distributing prepackaged information, is an essentially easy, routine, and sub-professional task. Accordingly, and this is the significant point, it seems perfectly reasonable to the public, to school boards, and even to many school men that teachers should teach all day. For the apothecary to fill prescriptions during his working hours is not considered burdensome; why, then, should the purveyor of information be unduly tired from a shorter school day?[4]

If the principal purpose of schools is to dispense knowledge, then this position is perfectly valid, and exploration and conceptual invention have no place in the schools. (Be aware that the foregoing quotation *does not* represent Schaefer's true beliefs.)

Think back, however, to Chapter 1. If the Constitution is taught in the way outlined here, the schools are still pursuing the goals of schools in that first stage of the evolutionary cycle—to serve the present needs of the society and maintain the present social order—even though the needs of today's society are quite different from the needs the schools of the Puritan era served.

Now think back to Chapter 2. The development of the rational powers of the mind was established as the central purpose of education. If you are going to lead students to develop the ability to imagine, classify, compare, synthesize, and so on, they must be allowed to *do* all these things. Thus they cannot simply be given a description of an object or an analysis of a situation or an event. In the traditional method of teaching the Constitution, its contents are neatly analyzed by the teacher. If the development of rational powers is the goal, learners must be given the opportunity to make their *own* evaluations, analyses, syntheses, and generalizations about the Constitution.

How would a teacher who is concerned both with teaching the Constitution *and* with developing rational powers go about this task? First, he must decide what he wishes the students to understand about the Constitution. He may, for example, want him to understand that the seven basic articles in the Constitution apply to

1. the operational of the federal government,
2. the maintenance of the integrity of the states, and

[4] Robert J. Schaefer, *The School as a Center of Inquiry* (New York: Harper & Row, 1967), p. 35.

3. the recognition by those framing the Constitution that it would have to be amended.

In addition, he may want them to categorize the amendments to the Constitution as

1. establishing and maintaining the rights and freedom of the individual (Amendments One through Ten, Thirteen, Fourteen, Nineteen, Twenty-Three, Twenty-Four, and Twenty-Six),
2. forbidding the government to legislate the personal and moral behavior of the citizen (Amendments Eighteen and Twenty-One), and
3. affecting the power of the President and Vice President (Amendments Twenty, Twenty-Two, and Twenty-Five).[5]

Next he must put the materials to be investigated into the hands of the students. In this case, the materials would be a copy of the Constitution itself, and books, films, filmstrips, recordings, or other media containing information on the subject. His preliminary general direction to the learners might be something like this: "Examine these materials concerned with the United States Constitution and interpret them for yourselves. Please don't be concerned with the style of the writing or, in the case of the films, with the performances of the actors. Just concern yourselves with the Constitution's content and analyze it for yourselves. You may work independently or in small groups, but let's not have more than three or four people in any one group."

Thus the exploration phase begins. The teacher, during this phase, has an important responsibility. He must work with small groups of students and with individuals. He will at times have to provide clues to get them started: "How do you interpret the first article? What responsibilities does it give you?" He may have to intervene to stop a meaningless argument: "Perhaps the Eighteenth Amendment is inclusive enough to include marijuana; assume that it is. But how does that relate to your individual interpretation of the Constitution?" He may have to redirect the thinking of some students because they are working on the basis of an erroneous assumption that could easily be avoided by more careful observation: "If you will compare the dates of the Thirteenth and Nineteenth Amendments, you will probably be able to determine whether or not the Nineteenth Amendment was primarily concerned with racial discrimination." The teacher who

[5] This is not, of course, the only way to teach the Constitution, although it is one we have found useful. Someone else may not consider these points the most pertinent, and no truly inquiry-oriented teacher would even pretend to have found the one definitive approach to any issue.

wishes to keep the learners involved will emphasize that interpreting the Constitution means deciding how it affects the student's own life. The primary responsibilities of the teacher during this data-gathering stage are to get the exploration going, to keep it going without being so dictatorial that it goes only in one direction, and to provide any additional materials that may be needed. Exploration requires time, and the time can be justified only if what is done *by the learners* leads them toward the purposes you have for teaching.

After the exploration phase has been completed, the learners must now share their information and make generalizations about the Constitution itself. Here the teacher may have an opportunity for conceptual invention, but he must remember that the concepts he invents must be the logical consequence of the findings of the young investigators. But suppose that they completely miss an important point. The teacher has two choices. He can feel that he has achieved his purpose of providing the opportunity for rational-power development, or he can suggest another investigation! "Re-examine the first ten amendments to the Constitution. What kinds of information do they contain?" From this, the concept of the Bill of Rights can be invented. The concepts that are invented and the insights that the students gain, however, must be those they feel are important and not those the teacher believes should be developed. At this point the teacher must refer to his original outline to see how many ideas were developed and whether his expectations were realistic. He may then ask himself (1) whether he should be concerned with the original points he thought should be but were not developed, (2) what kinds of activities would lead the students to reach those conclusions, and (3) whether the class has enough intrinsic motivation to investigate the matter further. Only when these questions have been asked and answered can the exploration and invention stages of the learning process be considered complete.

The discovery phase

Once the learners have developed a concept, what use can be made of these new insights? The final step in the development of the students' rational powers is to lead them to use their invention to discover more about related objects, events, and situations. For example, contemporary problems or issues involving the Constitution can be presented to the students and judgments made relative to them. Why are separate but equal school systems for the races unconstitutional? What authority in the Constitution makes taxing a tax unconstitu-

FIGURE 3–3
Discoveries occur when students begin to use inventions.

tional? What evidence exists in the Constitution that supports or denies support to the Electoral College? These questions are meant only to be representative of the kinds of investigations that can be initiated to allow the learners to discover applications of what they have learned.

Consider this example of an exploration-invention-discovery activity from physics. Students have been given wires, resistors, sources of electric current, and meters to measure current and voltage. They are instructed to design procedures for connecting the various objects in a series and to check these designs with the teacher (who makes it quite clear that he wishes to check their designs only to ensure that they will not damage any of the apparatus). After a period of exploration with the apparatus, they are then given time to record their values for the current (I), the voltage (V), and the resistance (R). Let us suppose that these are the values submitted by the students:

I	*R*	*V*
2.0	3	6.0
1.5	4	5.9
3.1	2	6.0
9.0	6	5.7
1.5	4	6.0
1.7	3	5.9
6.0	1	5.8

The teacher now asks the students how they would interpret the data. Several point out that the voltage (V) is always equal or nearly equal to the product of the current (I) and the resistance (R), with one notable exception. The learners must first decide whether to disregard this piece of information or to recheck the value. The teacher is now in a position to invent Ohm's law ($V = IR$). The students can then move on to consider all types of electric circuits, discover how Ohm's law applies to them, and use it to discover more about the circuits themselves.

In both the foregoing examples, the outcomes have been information (about the Constitution and Ohm's law) that could have been given to the students in a small fraction of the time required to gain it through the exploration-invention-discovery process. How then can this method of teaching be justified? Again, we must return to the question of purpose. If your sole purpose is the transmission of information about the Constitution or Ohm's law, you cannot justify it. If, however, your goal is the development of the learner's rational powers as well as his understanding of the lesson content, then the exploration-invention-discovery model *must* be used. *Learning goes on during the activity and is not represented by the end product.*

The Exploration-Invention-Discovery Cycle as Inquiry

The exploration-invention-discovery cycle represents the three stages of *inquiry* and the inquiry *method* is essentially incomplete if any one is missing. Often the words inquiry and discovery are equated and the inquiry method is called the discovery method. Actually, discovery is only one segment of a total inquiry, and while it can and does go on during the exploration phase, it does not reach its zenith until after conceptual invention has occurred. Looked at in another way, the inquiry method is simply the establishment of an attitude of inquiry in the classroom by the teacher during his interaction with the learners. This attitude leads the learners to achieve the objectives of the affective domain.

The value of inquiry is, as we have said, partially in the knowledge of content it produces and partially in the exposure it gives the students to the process itself. This was explained by a group of educators as follows:

Inquiry does not always result in a solution to the problem. But inquiry seldom, if ever, proves fruitless in the sense that one would have been better off had he not inquired. In fact, the really lasting educational benefit of the inquiry is the search itself, since it is during the search that the thinking ability of the investigator is being developed.[6]

Inquiry, then, is the teaching method that can lead to the development of rational powers. But quite obviously students cannot inquire into the Constitution or Ohm's law in the manner previously described and not retain a great deal of information about these academic areas. Pupils learn a great deal from an inquiry into various aspects of an academic area and, in fact, retain a great deal more factual material than they would have had traditional methods been used.

Teacher-learner roles

Putting ideas into chart form is always dangerous, because the inclination of the human organism is to follow the form as though it were a recipe. What follows reflects the way we use the inquiry-teaching philosophy. You should use these ideas as a starting point and alter them to fit your own personality. The following is predicated upon the belief that there are two *active* roles in an inquiry-centered classroom—that of the teacher and that of the learner.

Inquiry-Centered Teaching and Learning Responsibilities

Teacher	Learner
Exploration	
1. If the learners do not have a topic to investigate, the first responsibility of the teacher is *to provide such a topic.*	1. *The learners do the investigation;* they design the procedures necessary for the investigation and collects information.
2. *The teacher asks the learners for the information collected* during the investigation.	2. *The young investigators describe what has been found.*
3. *The teacher accepts the findings the learners describe,* and in so doing makes a great contribution to creating the environment necessary to lead them to achieve the objectives of the affective domain. This responsibility cannot be stressed too strongly.	3. *The learners search the information for a pattern,* usually finding it under the guidance of the teacher. Do not expect all the learners to find the same pattern; if several interpretations of the information are made, all of which are valid, the inquiry process has been especially productive.

[6] "Inquiry!" *The Oklahoma Teacher* (November 1968), p. 17.

Teacher	Learner
Invention	
4. The teacher questions the learners about the relationship of the pattern found to the topic being investigated. *Is the pattern relevant to the topic, or has some new idea been uncovered?* Obviously this question is designed to lead the learners to conceptual invention, and the teacher can, if necessary, invent the concept at this point.	4. The learners are led to generalize from their interpretation of the material collected. They are now in a position to formulate a new concept, or the teacher can invent the concept. Invention, however, must be based on the information collected by the students.
5. Questions can now be raised about *the relationship of the new concept to concepts developed during previous investigations.* The inquiry-oriented teacher will raise questions and allow the learners to discover relationships by exchanging ideas; telling learners what the relationships are (if any) is not inquiry. Questions should always be raised, even if a recognized relationship does not exist.	5. The learners are now, by using the process of inquiry, doing something that every teacher wants his students to accomplish; i.e., they are *broadening their understanding of a principle.* This broadened understanding, however, is possible because the learners have been involved in developing the information that led to the invention of the concept. They are not "broadening" their understanding simply by being told that this new concept is applicable to different situations.
Discovery	
6. *The teacher raises questions about the value, meaning, and/or validity of the concept,* keeping firmly in mind that he must accept both pro and con student arguments. For a teacher who truly believes in inquiry and who also believes that any new idea must be tested before it is accepted, this phase of inquiry teaching is the most stimulating and pedagogically worthwhile.	6. The learners now must defend not only the concept that has been developed but the procedures and arguments used to arrive at the concept. They must apply the inquiry process to the *results* of an inquiry process. As their understanding of an idea deepens through inquiry, they are learning how to learn—to inspect clinically and evaluate the results of their own thinking. The learners are now in a position to suggest other investigations that may confirm or deny the exactness of the concept. They may, of course, need the assistance of the teacher at this point.
7. The teacher may need to suggest additional investigations to test the concept's validity.	

The foregoing outline is not an attempt to "program" inquiry teaching for you. In your early use of the inquiry technique, these ideas may prove useful to you, but you must develop your own style of handling inquiry teaching. In the chart, the relationship between exploration, invention, and discovery is indicated. The inquiry method, as represented by exploration, invention, and discovery, and the relationship between the teacher and the learner, as indicated in the chart, have not yet been widely tested. As a professional teacher, you will be able to participate in this testing.

The inquiry-centered dialogue between teacher and students: an example

We have described in the preceding section how an inquiry-centered lesson might be structured. What follows is the first five minutes of an actual lesson, using the inquiry method. Here the students were continuing an inquiry they had begun into the meaning of the word *right* in three contexts.

1. *It is* right *for a man to give a woman his seat on a bus.*
2. *It is* right *for children to be vaccinated against polio.*
3. *It is* right *for citizens to vote.*

In this lesson, the students are dealing with the divergent question "What does "right" mean in statements about language, such as the statement "It is right to say "He doesn't" instead of "He don't." Notice the number of new questions that the students produce in five minutes.

Teacher: *We have spent a few sessions exploring the shifting meanings of the word "right" in the sentences (1) It is right for a man to give a woman his seat. (2) It is right for children to be vaccinated. (3) It is right for citizens to vote. Now I have written a fourth sentence on the board, which I would like you to look at: "It is right to say 'he doesn't' instead of 'he don't!' And what we'll be exploring today is what the 'right' means in that sentence. Now who will start us off? You might, if you like, compare its meaning there to its meaning in any of the other sentences.*

Marcia: *I think that in that sentence saying "he doesn't" instead of "he don't" that "right" means "accepted." This is what educated people do, or people who have been brought up well. I think that number 1 about the man giving up his seat is pretty much the same thing.*

Teacher: *Are you saying that in sentence 4 we are dealing with a question of etiquette, just as we are in sentence 1?*
Marcia: *No, it's not exactly etiquette; it's more a reflection of your training and the way you've been brought up. If you've been brought up by hillbillies, you'd probably say "he don't," but if you've been brought up by parents who went to Oxford, you'd say "he doesn't."*
Teacher: *O.K. Dan?*
Dan: *I'd like to ask one question. She said, "If you've been well educated." Who decides who is well educated?*
Marcia: *Who decides whether you are well educated? O.K. Well, let me give you a couple of examples! Would you say that someone who had had a sixth-grade education was well educated?*
Dan: *I wouldn't know.*
Marcia: *You wouldn't know?*
Dan: *It depends on the individual. A person who didn't even go to school but went around the world and just discovered things and read and everything might know more than a person who went to college all his life!*
Teacher: *We may have here then right at the beginning a problem with another word. We started out exploring the word "right" and in just three or four minutes of conversation we've come across the word "educated." I think Marcia was suggesting that people who have been to Oxford are educated and hillbillies aren't. Is that what you meant to say?*
Marca: *Well, that's rather the extremes, but yes, more or less.*
Dan: *Well, you can take a look at our President Lincoln. I don't think he had too much schooling. He had a few private lessons for a couple of years and he was a pretty well educated person. His speeches weren't bad. They were well written.*
Bob: *Most Presidents hire someone to write their speeches, Dan.*
Dan: *But he didn't. I remember seeing a film on that. He wrote on the train.*
Teacher: *On the backs of envelopes, I think. Well, let's get Judy's ideas here.*
Judy: *Well, Marcia also said that you speak correctly, but you may be well brought up if you live in slums; your parents might, you know, want to give you what they didn't have and they send you to a good school and things, but still in the house they say "don't" instead of "doesn't" and you most likely will pick up "he don't" instead of "he doesn't."*
Teacher: *Well, are you saying, Judy, that one who says "he don't" is not speaking correctly?*

Judy: *Maybe in his own home he is speaking correctly. It's his accepted way in his own home.*
Teacher: *Oh, well now let's stay with this point for a minute. If I interpret what you've said correctly, you are saying that you cannot say that one thing is correct?*
Judy: *That's right.*
Teacher: *That what may be correct here in our classroom, might not be correct some place else?*
Judy: *Yes, maybe you might say "he doesn't" in school, but when you go home, you say "he don't" because this is how your parents might understand you or someone who lives with you.*
Teacher: *Well, Bill, what do you think about this point of view?*
Bill: *Just because your parents say "he don't" and you say "he don't" in your home, that doesn't make it right. That's just what you do. We do a lot of things that aren't right.*
Teacher: *Well, this is what we are trying to find out, Bill. What do we mean by "right" or "correctly"?*
Bill: *I think in that sentence it means that in the language "he doesn't" are the words that are accepted and used to convey that idea.*
Teacher: *Well, who accepts these words, and who uses them, and who tells you not to use them?*
Bill: *The English teachers.*
Teacher: *In other words, what English teachers say you should do, becomes right or correct?*
Bill: *In the classroom, but they get their information from books and other sources.*
Teacher: *Well, you have a touching faith in English teachers and I appreciate this. Do you listen to your Social studies teacher with as much attention as you listen to your English teachers? For example, if the History teacher tells you that a Republican candidate is a better man that some Democratic candidate or vice versa, would you value his judgment as much on that as you would an English teacher's on what's right?*
Bill: *No, because he's conveying an opinion. The English teacher is telling you a rule that was set down, not by the English teacher, but by somebody else.*
Teacher: *Sue, what do you think about this?*
Sue: *Well, I disagree with him because I think you learn patterns of speech in the years that you are going to elementary school, and when you come up to the junior high and senior high schools, you learn* why *they are right. But the way you learn to talk is taught in your*

early ages. I don't think by the time you're in high school you can change your pattern of speech, because, I mean, they are like different dialects really.
Teacher: *Dialects. What do you understand the word "dialect" to mean?*
Sue: *Well, like the Southern people might say "you-all" before they start their sentences, and the people in the East won't say this.*
Teacher: *They don't say this?*
Sue: *No.*
Teacher: *Well, now, is "you-all" a correct pattern of speech or not?*
Sue: *Well, perhaps down there it might be, but I don't think it is a correct pattern of speech. I mean I don't really know.*
Teacher: *Eric, what do you think?*
Eric: *When you spoke of dialects, and you can't change a dialect, my mother came from Richmond, Virginia, and when she came up north she used to say "you-all." She doesn't say that any longer. And now when she goes back to Richmond, Virginia, they all say she has a northern accent, and she has completely changed her dialect.*
Sue: *You might be able to pick something up after a while, but I mean like he said you learn how to speak from your English teachers, but you didn't have an English teacher when you were down in—*
Bill: *I didn't say you learn how to speak. I said you learn the rules that govern how you speak. You learn to speak when you're a little kid.*
Richard: *I think there have to be some certain rules that are set down by people who think they know what the rules should be. I think in the English language the rules are written in the dictionary and English teachers have followed these rules, and these rules are necessary because, if nobody obeyed the rules, you would not understand what the next person was saying. He might be speaking English, but certainly the rules have to be followed even if you don't like them.*
Teacher: *What is your reaction to that? Richard says there must be rules because, if there were not, we could not communicate with each other very well and these rules are written down in books called "dictionaries." Jim?*
Jim: *These dictionaries—the way people are making it sound as if some small group is sitting in a dark room and they decide how they think about this rule and they decide no, we don't like this rule. We will throw it out. Well, this is not the way it is done. The lexicographers sit down and they—*
Teacher: *The what?*

FIGURE 3–4
For inquiry to flourish, the classroom environment must encourage it.

Jim: *The lexicographers.*
Teacher: *Let me just put that down. Is that how you spell it, do you know?*
Jim: *I don't know.*
Teacher: *(writes on the blackboard): I think that's it, but I think you have to know how to spell it in order to look it up in the dictionary.*
Jim: *Well, lexicographers. They sit down and they read. They read all the books put out; they read newspapers, magazine articles, speeches; they listen to speeches; they listen to television and radio; and they pick out the way the majority speak. Say they want to see whether you say "he doesn't" or "he don't." They read books, they listen to everything, and they see what the majority uses; and therefore, the dictionary dictates what the majority says.*[7]

Those watching and listening to this classroom dialogue would ask, if they did not understand modern purposes, what was learned. From the traditional content standpoint, practically nothing; but after many such experiences the students in this class will begin to learn how to learn. These students are doing what Bruner was urging teachers to allow learners to do when he said that students should take part in the process of knowledge getting.[8] Bruner justifies that stand by declaring, "Knowing is a process, not a product."[9] The teacher in this example obviously agrees with him.

[7] Reprinted from *Teaching as a Subversive Activity*, pp. 70–74, by Neil Postman and Charles Weingartner. Copyright © 1969 by Neil Postman and Charles Weingartner and used by permission of the publisher, Delacorte Press.

[8] Jerome Bruner, *Toward a Theory of Instruction* (Cambridge, Mass.: Harvard University Press, 1966), p. 72.

[9] *Ibid.*

Notice how the teacher in the foregoing example was careful to keep the discussion moving and assist in isolating problems of interpretation as they arose but did not impose his own value judgments on the students. He accepted all their contributions and did not tell any student that he was wrong. The teacher in the example is truly interested in rational-power development and realizes that it will happen only when those powers are used. This illustrates beautifully the most important ingredient that must be present before inquiry can take place—*a learning environment* conducive to freedom of expression.

Creating the right classroom environment

What is classroom environment? Environment refers to our total suroundings, not only our physical surroundings but also the mental attitudes of those around us. In the classroom, the most important aspect of the environment in which inquiry is to take place is the attitude of the teacher.

Let us review the way we wish to see learning take place. Students and teachers are to interact with one another and with the materials of the subject. That interaction may take place in the assigned classroom, or it may require the out-of-doors, the library, the gymnasium, or even the county courthouse. Regardless of where it takes place, however, interaction must occur. Furthermore, the type of activity that the particular subject requires must be permitted and encouraged to take place, and interaction does not make for a quiet classroom. Consider this enigmatic situation. No one doubts that a certain amount of student-produced sound is required in a music program. Schools often build special rooms for the music programs, rooms that permit all types of sounds to be produced without bothering others. Sound (whether it is noise or music may depend on the sensibilities of the hearer!) is recognized as a necessary by-product of teaching music. Now consider any type of school language program. Language is a form of communication, and to learn communication you must communicate with something or someone. But many persons in the schools believe that a noisy classroom is probably one in which not much learning is going on. How is it possible to learn to communicate with others by interacting with them without producing a certain level of sound? If schools desire learning to take place through interaction, which is the foundation of inquiry, those in charge must be willing to live with the byproducts of that activity.

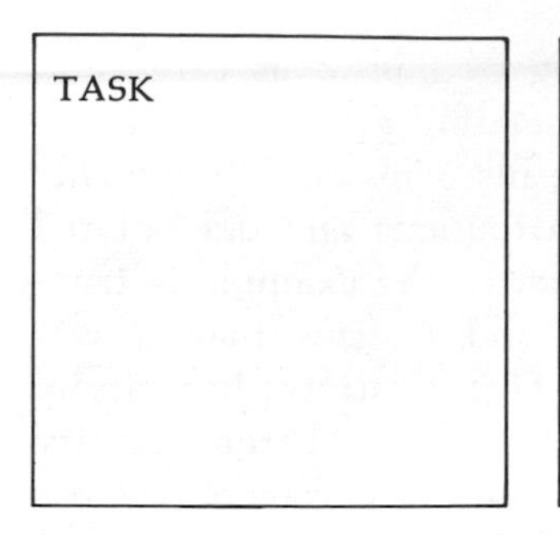

TASK

In what type of environment does interaction thrive? Ask yourself when you are the most willing to say what you think, to relate what you have observed, and to advance an honest opinion that you want others to react to honestly. Sit and contemplate for a few minutes before reading on and before jotting down your own ideas.

Our opinions about the above situation may conflict with yours. Since the medium of a textbook, however, does not permit us to incorporate your ideas in our discussion of classroom environment, you must integrate your ideas with ours. If your notes differ substantially from the following discussion, the differences should provide much food for thought.

A human being's ego usually does not permit him to advance opinions, observations, or honest hypotheses unless he feels reasonably sure they will be accepted (or at least considered) and that he will be treated with respect for holding such views or making such observations. In short, the first responsibility of the teacher in establishing an environment in which inquiry (and thereby the rational powers) can flourish is to *accept the student for what he is* and treat his ideas with respect. By setting the tone he will encourage students to do likewise and treat one another in the same way. In order, therefore, to have a classroom environment conducive to inquiry, the teacher must be an "accepter." This attitude on the part of the teacher also makes possible achieving the objectives of the affective domain. This will not, of course, happen unless the teacher feels good about and accepts himself.

TASK

Where do you get your ideas about anything? Before reading on, jot down your ideas.

The list you made above probably contains activities such as reading, observing, experimenting, and asking others. In addition, somewhere in your list you probably wrote "listening." All of us gain ideas, pleasure, and information from listening, and equally important, we like to be listened *to*. When someone listens to us voluntarily, we feel that what we have to say is important and worthwhile. Secondary school students are no different. If a teacher listens to a student, the student is encouraged to develop respect not only for the idea he is advancing but for himself for holding the idea. Furthermore, he is developing confidence in himself to generate ideas. Listening to students brings out their best abilities; and when a teacher accepts and uses their ideas, the responsibility for learning is shifted to where it truly belongs—to the learner himself. Thus a teacher must listen to his students.

Consider a class in which a student advances an idea and the teacher says, "No, that's wrong," "No, that's not what I had in mind," or "No, that's not in accordance with the facts." You have probably been in many classrooms where you heard the foregoing reactions; and unless you are very unusual, you have been the victim of such teacher responses yourself. Consider what the teacher has told the learner with those responses. First, the student has been told that there is one, and only one, answer to the question and that his responsibility is to find that one right answer. Second, the teacher has told the learner that he, the teacher, has the answer and that if the learner handles him right, he will provide it. Finally, the learner is told that his ideas are not nearly as important as those of the teacher. Since the teacher did not listen to him and use his ideas to lead the class toward a solution of the problem, the learner can, in the future, almost immediately assume that what he has to say is not important. If a teacher is interested in retarding the development of a positive self-image by the learner, there is probably no better way to do it than by not listening. When an individual is told by word or action that his ideas are not as important as the teacher's, that the teacher has absolute authority to reject his ideas at any time, and that one day he will be held accountable on an examination for the ideas of the teacher and the textbooks, he is well on the way toward developing a negative self-image. Only a strong personality can survive this type of treatment throughout his school years. If you accept the hypothesis that only those who think positively about themselves will think positively about others, the damage this kind of teaching does to future citizens is probably incalculable and may rank in importance with overpopulation and pollution. John Holt sums up the effect of such a teaching approach in these words: "It is a rare child who can come through his schooling with much left of his curiousity, his independence or his sense of his own dignity, competence and worth."[10]

[10] John Holt, "School Is Bad for Children," *Saturday Evening Post* (February 8, 1969).

If children leave school without a feeling of dignity, competence, and worth, the type of teaching that caused the lack is as great a problem as any other in our society.

Many teachers seem to have a disease known as *lysiphobia,* "the fear of loose ends." Unless they can summarize a lesson into a neat, compact package, they are not happy. In an inquiry-oriented classroom on the other hand, lessons tend to be open-ended so that the learner will think about them and formulate his own conclusions. Again, many teachers believe that they must make sure that the learners think as they do or as the authors of the textbook they are using do. In an inquiry-centered lesson, this is not the goal.

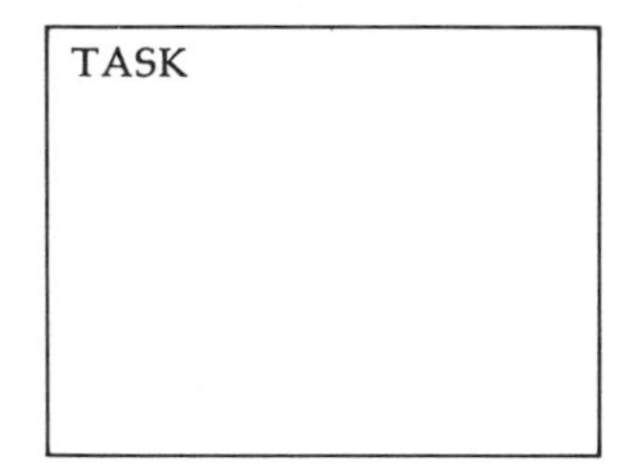

We have been looking at the factors which establish and maintain a classroom environment conducive to inquiry-centered learning. Who is responsible for ensuring that those conditions are present? What is an inquiry-centered learning environment? List your understandings.

But teachers need to do more than just listen to their students. A well-trained animal will listen. The ideas and opinions presented by learners to the teacher and their fellow classmates is information from which the solution to the problem under consideration will come, and the teacher has the responsibility to submit all the students' ideas and data to the group for consideration. Once a particular problem has been solved, it may be found that some of the ideas and data developed by the learners will not have been used. This should not have a negative effect upon the learner. Nor should it damage his self-image. This would happen only if he were made to feel foolish for obtaining erroneous information. The learner will probably see why he did not receive positive results; reviewing what he did wrong can only contribute to his negative feelings toward himself and toward learning and make him less eager to submit his ideas the next time. It is the responsibility of schools and teachers to lead children to develop the attitude that success or failure must be treated as information and not as reward or punishment.

The freedom to fail is much less evident in our schools than the freedom to succeed. Yet if the freedom to fail, to be wrong, and to make incorrect interpretations is not present, inquiry becomes impossible. One begins inquiry by asking questions, and the probability of asking a question that will produce negative results is very high. If negative results are not accepted, the learner will be less inclined to inquire in the future because he might again have negative results to report; yet, one cannot learn how to inquire except by practice. Listening to the students is important, but it is not enough. The teacher must ensure that each learner's contribution is considered.

From what has been said so far you could conclude that your job as a teacher is simply to decide what understandings you want the students to develop, secure the materials, be sure the students understand the problem and the materials, and put them to work. From the students' work will come information that can be used to explain the topic being investigated. But consider how you would feel if the person asking you to participate in some activity simply sat back and watched.

Becoming a fellow-investigator

Unless you as a teacher become a fellow-investigator, the students are likely to feel that you are just waiting for them to finish so that you can provide them with the right answer. Your involvement tells the learners that the evidence they are being asked to provide is needed before a satisfactory explanation of the problem can be found. Furthermore, unless your students are very unusual, they are accustomed to accepting a new concept not on evidence but on the authority of a textbook or a teacher. When you involve yourself in the investigation and use the evidence as a basis for conceptual invention, you are, by example, teaching the members of your class how to learn. You have used inquiry, then, to lead the learners not only to an understanding of content but also toward the development of their rational powers.

Being a fellow-investigator has other positive effects, one of which has to do with content.

TASK	*Ask yourself how the content you were taught was selected. Before you read on, write down your beliefs about content selection.*

Probably the most common basis for selecting content is tradition; geometry and biology have usually been tenth-grade subjects, and

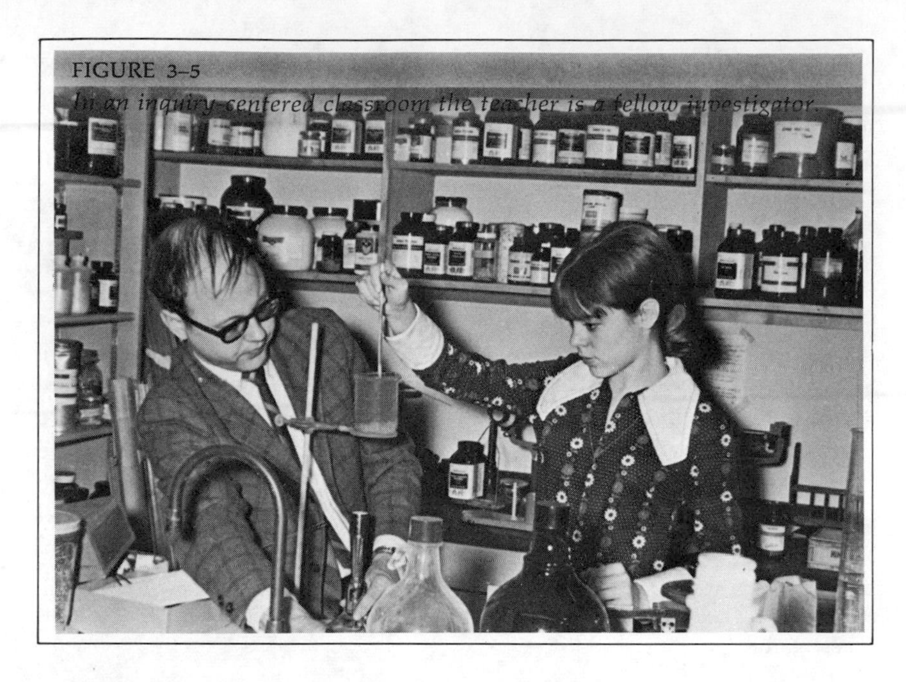
FIGURE 3–5
In an inquiry-centered classroom the teacher is a fellow investigator.

American history traditionally has been an eleventh-grade subject. Not only has the grade placement of a subject been somewhat arbitrary but the content has been selected in a completely arbitrary way. Content is usually selected because *it represents American history.* And although a lot of talking has been done about the characteristics of the secondary-school learner, historically little attention has been paid to these characteristics when the final decisions on content are made. In Chapter 4 where we discuss the learning characteristics of students in precollegiate schools, we shall also describe a procedure whereby you can make some judgments about placement of various kinds of content.

Becoming a fellow-investigator with your students will let you experience on a firsthand basis the problems that different learners have with various kinds of content. A student can tell you he is having trouble with the equation $ax^2 + 6x + c = 0$, but until you begin to work with him as a participant in the learning process, you will not be able to diagnose the difficulty. Once the diagnosis has been made, the precise assistance the learner needs can be furnished. One day, for example, an instructor was watching a chemistry class explore various chemicals in order to permit the instructor to invent the concept of chemical properties. One student was standing back and writing down data rather than conducting any of the explorations himself. The instructor took a piece of sodium, placed it in water, and tested the resulting solution with litmus paper. He then invited the reluctant student to repeat the experiment to see if he could confirm or deny the findings. When the student declined to do so, the instructor asked him why he did not want to enter into the exploration. The learner said that he was afraid because he had been told that all chemical reactions produced poisons. Once the instructor knew what the problem was, he could encourage the student to overcome his fear. Inability to read, fear of failure, personal problems, disinterest in the content and in school, improper materials, and failure to understand instructions are all learning disabilities that can be suspected by watching a group work but can be confirmed or denied only when the teacher involves himself in the actual exploration, invention, and discovery. Becoming involved with the students in their inquiry-centered investigations permits a teacher to understand their likes and dislikes, needs, and abilities in the subject area.

Thus far, we have stressed three guidelines for the teacher: (1) that the central responsibility of the school is to engage the student in activities that will develop his rational powers; (2) that learning by inquiry can provide the experiences needed for rational-power development; and (3) that inquiring into problems in an academic area leads the learner to understand that area. In other words, when a student *investigates* a problem on the Constitution, he is learning something about the structure of political science, *investigating* a particular equation leads the learner to begin to understand mathematics as a mathematician does, and *inquiring* into the nature of a work of contemporary literature teaches him something about literature itself. Thoroughly investigating any problem in an academic area gives the young investigator a better understanding of the entire area. Why, then, do schools and teachers insist that all students "cover" the same topics within a course? If the basic premises discussed above have merit, every student need not (and perhaps should not) cover every topic in a physics course, for instance, in order to learn the structure of physics. Up to now, teachers and schools have insisted on this kind of regimentation, in part because they were afraid of being accused of not providing adequate preparation in a discipline (the above discussion suggests that this argument is not valid), and in part because they did not know how to provide each student with what he needed. Providing every student with what he needs is, of course, individualizing the instruction and, as such, represents the ultimate educational opportunity for the learner. Imagine a school in which each student can investigate in each of his classes those topics that interest him, and that are suitable to his academic level. Imagine an environment in which a teacher need not be concerned if all students are not studying the same thing. Educational utopia? Perhaps, but clearly within the reach of every classroom teacher if he truly understands and uses inquiry.

Acceptance of the teaching philosophy of inquiry provides teachers with the opportunity to investigate problems with the learners and, in the process, to diagnose their strengths, weaknesses, needs, likes, and dislikes. The teacher is thus in a unique position to suggest to each learner a particular subtopic of the investigation upon which to focus. The latter investigation can easily absorb the student's time for the remainder of the period during which the general topic is studied and permit him, at the end of the investigation, to make a unique contribution to the investigation. Thus he not only develops his own understanding of the topic but, by contributing uniquely to the class's understanding, he develops his own self-image. Involving yourself as a fellow-investigator with your students opens the door to individualization of instruction.

A teacher also has other responsibilities in the classroom. He must, for example, make sure that the materials the learners need to conduct their investigations are available, a responsibility that entails some advance planning in order to alert the administration to the need to secure materials from outside sources. He must also, as we shall see below, maintain classroom discipline.

Maintaining discipline

Classroom discipline often causes a beginning teacher some anxiety, generally because he has not thought through the role and function of discipline.

TASK	*Jot down what you think the role of discipline in the classroom is and how you feel it should function.*

Neither we nor anyone else can tell you how to establish and maintain discipline within your classroom. This is an area in which you must make decisions for yourself. Regardless of the methods you choose to employ, you may want, however, to be aware of certain major principles. To begin, consider these following questions:

1. Why is social control of the students in your classroom necessary?

2. What is the ultimate objective of classroom discipline?
3. What type of discipline will permit the use of inquiry?

The answer to the first question is quite straightforward; social control in the classroom is necessary in order to allow the learners to achieve the objectives of the course. More control than that is oppressive and may give students a lasting distaste for teachers, school, and learning; less control will not give the students an adequate opportunity to achieve the course objectives and will probably be disturbing to the school in general. The line between too little and too much social control is very fine, and at times may become invisible. There are, however, some criteria for judging when to tighten and when to relax controls.

The place to begin is with the objectives of the course being studied. If the students are not working with or discussing the materials and ideas relevant to the course, they are probably not moving toward those objectives. Occasionally an issue may arise that is so much in the minds of the students that class time should be devoted to discussing it rather than to being concerned with the subject matter and rational-power development. One of the authors once taught in a secondary school where a student lost his life in a football game. On the first day of school following the tragedy the students were more concerned with the value of football to their education than they were with the formal courses being taught. Little may be accomplished in the cognitive domain, but a great deal may be accomplished in the affective domain by interrupting the customary routine.

As a rule, however, the students should consider the content of the course. If they are unwilling to do this, perhaps the course work does not interest them, or the materials are above (or below) their intellectual level, or they haven't isolated the part of the problem that interests them, or they have not had sufficient encouragement to become involved on an individual basis. In order to ascertain whether any of these factors are the cause of classroom discipline problems, consider some of the points we made earlier in the chapter about the teacher's role. Do you listen to the students? Do you accept what they have to say about an investigation? Are you investigating with them rather than setting yourself apart as a supervisor? Have you attempted to find a subtopic of interest to each learner so that he may "go it alone"? If your answers to all these questions are affirmative, perhaps you need to seek assistance from a fellow teacher or a school administrator—someone from outside the classroom who can objectively observe the interactions between you and the students and make some positive suggestions. Do not feel that just because you ask for help with discipline you are a failure. Nothing could be further from the truth and neither your fellow teachers nor your administrator will feel that you are. It requires a strong personality to ask for assistance; weak individuals often do not know they need help or are afraid they may profit from it. If your administrator feels you have failed just because you ask for help to achieve the objectives of your course and of education, it may be better for you to look for a new position where the administrator has a better understanding of his role in the school system. Always ask yourself, "How much social control must there be in my classroom in order to provide the learners with the opportunity to achieve the objectives of the course and of education?"

Do not be alarmed if you must separate a student from the class. The ultimate goal of classroom and school discipline is for the student to develop self-discipline. Self-discipline cannot be acquired if the individual is not given the opportunity to set his own boundaries of behavior and then examine those boundaries objectively in a nonthreatening situation. An inquiry-centered classroom is an ideal environment for such an examination, as long as teachers and students together inquire into why one type of behavior is more satisfactory than another to the classroom society *and* the individual students. When a student has had the opportunity to participate in such examinations and you as the teacher are certain you have done everything in your power to assist him, but he is still a disruptive influence, removing him from the class may be helpful *as a last resort*. Before doing this, however, remind yourself that you have absolutely no influence over or opportunity to rehabilitate the student you eject from the learning environment.

The type of discipline needed in an inquiry-centered classroom is that which interferes least with the inquiry going on. As a rule, as the students' involvement in the inquiry process increases, discipline problems decrease; and as the investigation becomes individualized, discipline problems virtually disappear. An interested, involved student has neither the time, the inclination, nor the opportunity to become a discipline problem. This is only natural, for inquiry is a teaching technique that invites the learners to study those aspects of an investigation which appeal to them. They are already doing what they want to do. No method can solve all discipline problems, and it would be misleading to believe that you now have "the word" on maintaining a classroom free of social control problems. We hope, however, that these last few paragraphs have provided you with some ideas about what to look for when classroom discipline problems arise.

Guiding student inquiry

Assume you have an inquiry well under way; you have involved yourself with the learners, have reached the point where everyone is making his own investigation, and have no discipline problems. At this point you may be tempted to feel that you have it made! But don't feel too sure of yourself—getting an investigation started is like starting to grow a plant; the next step is to keep it growing! Student investigations, like plants, must be nurtured. Often the only care they need is simple encouragement to keep on doing what they are already doing; a pat on the back or a "Well done" often pay large dividends. There will be times, however, when students are pursuing a completely erroneous idea or one that leads to a dead end. In such a case, you must decide whether pursuing a fruitless notion will be a good learning experience. For strong students following an idea that is potentially useless can sometimes be a valuable experience. However, if a student is just beginning to stand on his own "inquiry-centered feet," the realization that his best idea is valueless can be quite traumatic and may make him reluctant to generate new ideas. Students sometimes also reach a point in an investigation where they cannot see the direction in which they might go. Here, too, you must step in to guide the learning process.

You can, of course, provide direction for students in need of assistance. However, in doing so you deprive them of opportunities for developing self-reliance and self-respect and using their rational powers. You are making the learner dependent on you, and you will not always be around to do his thinking for him. How can you lead the student to do his own thinking about where he should go next? Generally, learners themselves will suggest alternate ways of proceeding in answer to questions from the teacher.

Not only are questions the best way to guide a student at crucial points in his investigation but they are indispensable in initiating an inquiry and in evaluating an inquiry experience. They enable the learner to focus his attention on the data most useful in generalizing about the investigation. Questions, are an essential tool of the teacher who uses inquiry techniques and is concerned with rational-power development. What kinds of questions can be used in an inquiry-centered classroom, and how are they used?

TASK	*For a few minutes, think how different kinds of questions might be categorized, then jot down your ideas.*

While the categories you used are doubtless meaningful to you, on this particular topic there are some additional ideas about questions and questioning that we believe may be useful to you.

When something is unknown to you, you ask questions. Furthermore, the understandings you subsequently develop about the unknown will very probably depend directly on the type and caliber of questions you ask and the responses you receive. Teachers can respond to a student's questions in two ways: (1) by providing him with a finite answer, or (2) by providing him with the motivation and ideas necessary to continue the inquiry himself. Giving a student a direct answer often supplies him with all the information he needs and inquiry and learning stop. On the other hand, responding to a question with another question or with an alternate suggestion about the investigation can stimulate the learner to continue thinking about the problem and thereby continue learning. Questions that focus the attention of the learner on a specific factor in the investigation or give him direct information are *convergent.* A convergent question tends to cause the student to look inward toward what has been done and not outward toward what might be done; in other words, it tends to terminate an investigation. Such questions encourage the learner to concentrate on retaining facts rather than using his head for something better, such as evaluating a suggestion from the teacher, analyzing what needs to be done to implement a thought triggered by a question from the teacher, or synthesizing data from an investigation and drawing inferences and generalizations therefrom.

Convergent questions can be used to advantage in inquiry-centered teaching *if* the teacher uses them to focus attention on a particular portion of an investigation with which the learner is having difficulty. If the learner is led to analyze his error through a series of convergent questions, he can correct it and move on to fitting that piece of information into the larger picture. A question that is direct and factual can often be used to jolt back to productivity a student who has mentally left the group for a moment, or as a means of social control. Once the student is thinking in a convergent manner, however, the teacher has the responsibility for asking questions that will stimulate the student to think in a wider scope. This type of question is a *divergent* question.

Divergent questions invite the learner to think in a multiplicity of directions and to consider a number of possible explanations for the data collected. T. C. Chamberlain stated the ultimate use of divergent questions when he explained that an investigator should advance several hypotheses regarding the solution to a problem and not "fasten his affections unduly upon any one."[11] This type of question is particularly important at the secondary-school level where the students are just *beginning* to think abstractly, for it invites them to participate in one of the greatest abstractions—What would happen if . . . ? A teacher stimulates this type of thinking by asking the learner for an interpretation of the data he has gathered, the inquiry procedure being used, or the computation or observation he has made. The best type of divergent question is, What do you believe the data you have tell you? or Why did you select (or design) this particular procedure to collect information? A typical convergent question often asked by teachers is, Does the information you have found support the idea we have been studying? Convergent questions tell the learner that what is really important is not what he thinks or what his information tells him, but that the proper thing to believe is what he has been told. Divergent questions tell the learner that it is what *he* has to say that is important.

If your purpose in the classroom is the transmission of information about a particular discipline, divergent questions are of little value because they tend to lead the learner away from what is and toward what might be. The principal purpose of asking divergent questions is to find out the direction of the learner's thinking and what he is thinking. But before you ask a divergent question, be sure you want to know what the student is thinking; not all teachers do. As Robert Karplus has pointed out,

Teachers usually ask a question . . . to get an answer already formulated in their own minds or to make a point of their own choosing. Teachers rarely ask a question because they are really curious to know what pupils think or believe or have observed. The pupils, of course, adapt quickly to this situation. After a few years in school, answering questions is for them more a mind-reading proposition than a matter of reasoning about the substance of a . . . problem.[12]

When answering questions becomes a matter of figuring out what response the teacher wants, inquiry generally stops and guessing begins.

[11] T. C. Chamberlain, "The Method of Multiple Working Hypotheses," *Science*, (May 1965), pp. 754–761, first published in *Science* (February 1890).

[12] Robert Karplus, *Theoretical Background of the Science Curriculum Improvement Study* (Berkeley, Calif.: Univ. of California, Science Curriculum Improvement Study, 1965), p. 41.

Just as no one can tell you exactly how to establish and maintain discipline in your classroom, no one can tell you precisely how to ask questions. At one point in our research, we asked a group of fifty experienced, inquiry-centered teachers to contribute their ideas on asking questions. We have summarized their responses on the following pages but have left to the reader application of their ideas to convergent or divergent questions. Each teacher was asked these six questions:

1. Why do you ask questions?
   (Responses)
   a. To start the learner thinking.
   b. To see if the learner is thinking in the direction of the problem.
   c. To put the learner on a definite track if necessary.
   d. To invite learner participation.
   e. To see what the learners know about a particular problem before beginning an investigation.
   f. To create interest.
   g. To allow learners to develop confidence.
2. What do you expect from a question?
   (Responses)
   a. An honest reply.
   b. A response that leaves both the teacher and the student free to ask another question (questions that invite a Yes or No answer are of limited value).
   c. An opportunity for the student to ask himself a question.
3. What do you want a question to do to the learning situation?
   (Responses) The question should . . .
   a. free a student to ask questions.
   b. personally involve the learner.
   c. lead the learner or suggest to him.
   d. stimulate interaction among the learners.
   e. lead to further investigations.
4. What kind of question should be asked?
   (Responses)
   a. An important one.
   b. One to which the learner believes the answer is important.
   c. One that stimulates inquiry.
   d. A question devoted to one idea that is small enough to comprehend.
   e. A question that can be built on.
   f. A question that is not misleading.
   g. One that requires more than Yes or No.

   h. Use "why" questions sparingly, since they can be indefinite; instead of asking why something happened or is true, ask the student what evidence he can give that something happened or is true.
5. When do you ask a question?
   (Responses)
   a. When you want the learner to move on.
   b. When a learner's mind is wandering.
   c. To get learners back on the track or away from a dead end.
   d. To solicit problems and develop areas for investigation.
   e. To check the group's understanding.
   f. To stimulate group discussion.
   g. To improve a learner's self-image.
   h. To focus attention on the inquiry at its beginning.
   i. To see if a learner is ready to undertake an individual inquiry.
   j. To provide the teacher with the opportunity for conceptual invention.
   k. To initiate exploration.
   l. To begin discovery experiences.
   m. To lead the learner toward another concept.
   n. To find what the learner is doing and thinking.
6. How do you ask questions?
   (Responses)
   a. Ask for the attention of the class.
   b. Ask with enthusiasm and genuine interest but easily and informally.
   c. Ask the question and then select a respondent.
   d. Encourage the students first to listen carefully to the question and then to volunteer answers.
   e. Don't rush the student to respond.
   f. Generally use volunteers to answer.

You know, of course, that all answers must be accepted. These six general, teacher-made categories provide you with the information to develop your own questioning techniques. We present them to you not as rules but as data on which to build your own solutions.

A Reflection

This has been an intricate and complex chapter, for the role of the teacher in leading students to achieve educational purposes is intricate and complex. Essentially, however, we have tried to make the following ten basic points.

1. What is the traditional view of teaching and how effective is it?
2. What are the roles of exploration, invention, and discovery in inquiry?
3. What is the role of the teacher in a traditional or in an inquiry-centered classroom?
4. How should the teacher and learner interact in the inquiry-centered classroom?
5. How can a classroom environment conducive to inquiry be established and maintained?
6. How does inquiry teaching facilitate individualized instruction?
7. What is the place of discipline in the classroom?
8. What responsibility does a teacher have once individual investigations are under way?
9. What types of questions do teachers ask, and what is their purpose?
10. How do experienced teachers use questions?

This brief review is intended as a summary, but not as a conclusion. Perhaps it will serve to help you find your way through the complex, intricate, and important task of classroom teaching.

Throughout this chapter we have referred repeatedly to the type of content the learner can or cannot handle. Do students at various ages have learning characteristics that make learning certain types of content impossible? According to Jerome Bruner, "any subject can be taught effectively in some intellectually honest form to any child at any stage of development."[13] Does Bruner mean this statement literally? Does the human organism pass through various phases of intellectual development that should be considered before content is selected for a particular age group? If so, how can those intellectual levels be identified? The questions and others like them form the framework for Chapter 4.

[13] Jerome Bruner, *The Process of Education* (New York: Vintage Books, 1960), p. 33.

The Impact of the Learner's Characteristics on Educational Purpose

The American public spends a tremendous amount of time, energy, and money on education in order to bring its children to intellectual, emotional, and physical maturity as fully and efficiently as possible. In Chapter 2 we examined the objectives of the affective domain, which are primarily aimed at emotional development, and saw how achieving these objectives depends on development of the rational powers. In Chapter 3 we explored the three phases of inquiry—exploration, invention, and discovery—and found them to be the methodology for the development of the rational powers. The question now arises as to what content, materials, and activities will promote intellectual development in the learner. In order to answer that question, we must examine even more closely how learning occurs and the patterns that the human organism follows in growing intellectually.

TASK	*Before exploring with us the intricate fabric of learning, take a few minutes to write down what you think the learning process consists of. At the end of the chapter, review your notes to see whether any of your ideas have changed.*

How Learning Occurs

Interaction and structure

Traditionally, intellectual development has been thought of as the sum of all of a person's discrete learning experiences. Jean Piaget, however, tells us that "development is the essential process and each element of learning occurs as a function of total development, rather than being an element which explains development."[1] In other words (although improving Piaget's statement is difficult), what a person learns depends on his intellectual development—that is, what he has learned does not account for his development, but rather vice versa.

Assuming, then, that the material to be learned is clearly suitable for learners in a particular stage of development (how this is achieved we shall discuss later), how actually do they learn it? Piaget's basic hypothesis is that we know something if we can act upon it or interact with it. We do not know an object, an event, or a situation simply because we have looked at it and made a mental copy of it. Suppose, for example, that you wished to teach Newton's first law of motion, which says that moving objects will continue moving in a straight line and objects at rest will remain at rest, unless they are acted upon by some outside force. A learner can make a mental copy of this law in a few moments and make perfect scores on any examination he is given, but when he meets with instances of this law or its results, he will not be able to apply it because he has no *mental structure* he can use to categorize and assign meaning to the information he receives. If, however, he has had a learning experience during which he acted upon and interacted with moving and resting objects, he will begin to build mental structures about them, and when he next encounters a situation that involves moving bodies, he will be able to process the information.[2] Whether the concept of inertia is invented by the teacher or the learners find it for themselves is probably not too important because the mental structures necessary to process information about moving and resting bodies have already been built. Once, however, the conceptual invention of inertia is introduced, the structure becomes more defined and discovery can go forward.

One of the most useful concepts in our world is that of "property." A property is hard, soft, sticky, rough, sweet, sour, and so on, and we speak of the properties of objects, materials, sounds, events, situations, and all manner of things. One approach is to give learners materials that have various properties and have them make mental copies of these properties. This procedure may produce students who can answer questions about the property of a particular object, but

[1] Jean Piaget, "Development and Learning," *Journal of Research in Science Teaching*, 2, No. 3 (1964), pp. 176–186.

[2] Piaget's theory is that knowledge *of* the world is developed by acting upon objects *in* the world. Each action builds a schema of the object and the sum of the schema (the schemata) plus their interrelationships represent an individual's mental structure.

when the object whose properties are to be copied is changed, no mental structure exists that can be used with familiar objects. Now suppose that instead of having the learner mentally copy the properties of various things, we ask him, beginning in the first grade, to work with those properties—to act upon liquids by mixing them, to interact with the language by producing stories, and to act upon sandpaper by feeling it. All the while this interaction is going on, the learner is finding out not so much the properties of specific objects (that would be copying reality) but something about the property concept itself. That is, he is developing mental structures that will enable him to process similar data in the future. This is what Bruner meant when he said, "Knowing is a process, not a product."[3] True learning proceeds by the interaction of the learner with an object, an event, or a situation, and the construction of mental structures to assimilate the results of these interactions. The materials and ideas that are selected for the learner to interact with must obviously be suited to his level of intellectual development or a proper mental structure cannot be developed. You cannot, for example, expect a first grader to interact with calculus and construct mental structures from that interaction.

Cognition

Piaget's learning model is *cognitive,* as opposed to a stimulus–response model. Many people have contributed to the field of developmental learning, but the greatest contributions have no doubt come from Piaget and his longtime associate, Bärbel Inhelder. Piaget explains the necessity for establishing his learning model as follows:

Classically, learning is based on the stimulus–response schema. I think the stimulus–response schema, while I won't say it is false, is in any case entirely incapable of explaining cognitive learning. Why? Because when you think of a stimulus–response schema, you think usually that first of all there is a stimulus and then a response is set off by this stimulus. . . . I am convinced that the response was there first. . . . A stimulus is a stimulus only to the extent that it is significant and it becomes significant only to the extent that there is a structure which permits its assimilation, a structure which can integrate this stimulus but which at the same time sets off the response. . . . The stimulus is really a stimulus only when it is assimilated into a structure and it is this structure which sets off the response. Consequently,

[3] Jerome Bruner, *Toward a Theory of Instruction* (Cambridge, Mass.: Harvard University Press, 1966), p. 72.

it is not an exaggeration to say that the response is there first. . . . Once there is a structure the stimulus will set off a response, but only by the intermediary of this structure.[4]

Stimulus–response, then, is a viable learning model only because of the existence of cognitive structures, which arise from the learner's action on and interaction with materials, ideas, objects, and other materials found in the learning environment. When a learner interacts with his environment, he is *inquiring.* But only if the teacher believes in it as the strategy for a classroom will it be used in the schools.

Inquiry has already been designated as the methodology of rational-power development, and now it emerges as the methodology of cognitive development.

Equilibrium

What has been said so far about the development of mental structures leaves unanswered a crucial question. How does a learner deepen his understandings of anything through the cognitive-structure model of learning? Such understandings are developed because the human organism desires always to be in a state of mental and physical harmony, or *equilibrium,* with the environment. If an individual is mentally or physically uncomfortable with his situation, he tends to act to reestablish equilibrium. For example, suppose that a teacher is leading children to develop the concept of property and the need arises for the concept of a pentagon. If this concept is not part of the learners' cognitive structures, this event (the need for the concept) will produce a state of disequilibrium. In order to reestablish a state of equilibrium, the teacher must invent the concept of a pentagon. Once the conceptual invention has been made, the learners are again in equilibrium with their environment; they can employ the concept and make further discoveries that will sharpen other structures—for instance, those having to do with geometric shapes.

The introduction of new concepts may also disturb the learners' equilibrium by affecting their perception of other concepts and the environment in general. Hence, they must again act to reestablish equilibrium and the learning cycle continues. Phillips explains equilibrium states in this way:

Structures continually move toward a state of equilibrium, and when a state of relative equilibrium has been attained, the structure is

[4] Piaget, *op. cit.*

sharper, more clearly delineated, than it had been previously. But that very sharpness points up inconsistencies and gaps in the structure that had never been salient before. Each equilibrium state therefore carries with it the seeds of its own destruction. . . .[5]

The teacher's responsibility is to provide activities that lead the learners to reach a state of disequilibrium and from which they can gain information whose interpretation will restore equilibrium. But in reaching this new state of equilibrium, the learner has developed a cognitive structure that is sharper and richer than that which existed in the disequilibrated state. When he views objects, events, and situations from this new structure, he is likely to see gaps, inconsistencies, and contradictions that again create disequilibrium. Thus, as Phillips said, each new equilibrium contains a potential for self-destruction.

In Chapter 3 we presented a plan for inquiry-centered teaching. In essence, that plan establishes and subsequently destroys equilibrium. In fact, equilibrium is the thread that weaves together the teaching design so that the learner becomes completely involved in the learning process and his understandings grow deeper and deeper. However, in order to acquire this deeper understanding the learner must develop his intellect. He must move, *by himself,* to a new equilibrium.

Intellectual development must come from within. It is because of this fact that the traditionalists fail. Telling a student that his ideas are wrong does no good because he must find this out himself if it is to have any real impact. He must be confronted with new and contradictory evidence that will disturb his equilibrium. Through successive disequilibriums the learner's cognitive structures are changed. This constant change of structure leads to intellectual development and explains why a response seems to be delivered to a stimulus. In reality (as Piaget said), the response is present in the organism before the stimulus; thus the stimulus *does not generate* the response—instead it is a result of the cognitive structures built up through prior learning experiences. Thus the stimulus-response view of learning is incomplete and inadequate without the concept of cognitive structures.

Equilibration, the constant progression through disequilibration to new equilibrium states, according to Phillips, is an "overarching principle."[6] It is the one concept that ties together the cognitive view of learning and furnishes the basic rationale for inquiry-centered teaching. As a teacher the establishment and destruction of equilibrium

[5] John L. Phillips, Jr., *The Origins of Intellect: Piaget's Theory* (San Francisco, Freeman, 1969), p. 10.
[6] *Ibid.*

must be constantly in the foreground, for this is the path to intellectual development. Establishment and destruction of equilibrium are compatible with the goal of rational-power development.

TASK	*Take a few minutes now to describe for yourself that compatibility. If you do not feel that these two purposes of teaching are compatible, explain your feelings.*

Teachers must always be on the alert for opportunities to establish, destroy, and reestablish equilibrium in *individual* learners. Time-consuming as this may be, it represents the only way to true intellectual development.

Factors Affecting the Changing of Cognitive Structure

Intellectual development results, as we have seen, from changing the learner's cognitive structures through equilibration and disequilibration; thus the equilibrium concept is one of the important factors in cognitive development, but not the only factor or even independent of other factors. We shall discuss below some of the other factors, such as the *maturation* process, that also influence intellectual development.

Language

TASK	Before reading this section, *try an experiment: What do you hear when you read the following sentence? The government should outlaw automobiles because they are the major contributors to air pollution, which is injurious to our health. Write down your answer, then read the statement to three other persons and record their responses.*

We have tried this experiment and have found that different people hear different things. Some people fasten their attention on government, some argue that an electric automobile, for instance, would not contribute to pollution, some say that many factors in the environment are injurious to our health, and still others insist that there are many objects and functions in our society which do more damage to our air than cars. In other words, the same words call to mind different things for different people.

We—all of us—attach meaning to anything from our particular linguistic frame of reference; we are truly trapped by our language, and when one begins to think about changing a person's cognitive structure, this is a tremendously important notion. Earlier we saw how mental structures are changed by disturbing the learner's equilibrium. We can disturb a person's equilibrium only by communicating with him; if his language development is severely retarded, he will be difficult to communicate with and hence difficult to disequilibrate. Consequently, changing the cognitive structures of learners with language deficiencies is more difficult than changing those of learners who have no such deficiency. Language develops through social interaction with other human beings; a factor that Piaget has called "social transmission."[7] A learner cannot be disequilibrated if he is not in a position to receive information, that is, if his language development is not sufficient to perceive what is being said. Sometimes it is said that every teacher should be a teacher of language. Many teachers interpret this phrase to mean that they should teach grammar. A far wiser interpretation would be that they should teach students to receive information about and descriptive of their environment. Then, indeed, they would be doing much more than teaching language; they would be preparing the learner for the disequilibration-equilibration process and hence for intellectual development. By teaching a learner language he can use in describing his environment, we mean, of course, teaching him through conceptual invention at a point when his exploratory experiences have prepared him for it.

A person's experience, as Piaget states, is the fourth factor that influences cognitive-structure development. There are, according to Piaget, two types of experience—*physical* and *logico-mathematical*.[8] Physical experience derives from interactions with objects in the environment and with the environment itself. This type of experience is essential to the very young learner. Through such interaction he begins to develop mental structures about objects, environment, and their interactions. Physical experience is also needed by many adolescents

[7] Piaget, *op. cit.*, p. 180.

[8] Jean Piaget, "Foreword," in Millie Almy, *Young Children's Thinking* (New York: Columbia University, Teachers College Press, 1966), pp. v–vi.

because their intellectual development has not reached the point where experience involving logic is meaningful. Even an adult who encounters something new and unusual will attempt to secure information through physical interaction with it. Physical experience, especially when it is obtained directly from the objects themselves, would appear to be most conducive to the formation of basic cognitive structures.

At some point in a child's education he begins to learn such things as that when he counts four groups of three objects, he gets the same total as he does from counting three groups of four objects. He has learned that doing something to the objects (rearranging them) does not change their total number. Although he is manipulating objects, he is learning from his own actions and not from the objects themselves. Piaget calls such experiences *logico-mathematical,* that is, they come from the operations and not the objects.

[*When the learner*] *learns that the sum is independent of counting he is discovering the properties of the actions of ordering and uniting. He is learning something from the actions themselves, rather than from the objects independent of these actions.*[9]

In the example above the learner performed a physical *action,* i.e., rearranging the objects. To quote Piaget once again: "A child learns very little . . . when experiments [investigations] are performed for him . . . he must do them himself rather than sit and watch them done."[10] Learning from logico-mathematical experiences takes place when actions are internalized, that is, when they become part of the learner's cognitive structure and he is able to make decisions based on internalized actions and not on physical manipulations. Such internalized actions are called *operations* and are the foundations of logico-mathematical experience. These experiences require that the learner coordinate his actions very carefully in order to avoid contradictions. He must exercise a good deal of *self-regulation,* or contradictions will continually dominate his reasoning patterns. Self-regulation is the learner's internal mechanism for achieving equilibrium. As he checks his logic and seeks out possible contradictions, he sharpens his cognitive structures and moves in and out of equilibrium. This, however, will occur only when the learner can internalize his actions and reverse his reasoning in order to get from any point in his reasoning

[9] *Ibid.,* p. vi.
[10] *Ibid.,* p. v.

back to the beginning. Young children cannot reverse their thinking and hence cannot have logico-mathematical experiences.

TASK	*What do the factors described above have to do with classroom teaching? Before reading on, jot down your answer.*

We have described how the learner's equilibrium is destroyed and reestablished by his interactions with objects and the environment. If a student is provided with experiences commensurate with his language and maturity level, he will eventually reach the point where he can sharpen his own cognitive structures by learning from operations instead of having to rely continually on the information he gets directly from objects. In order to reach this point, the learner must be allowed a maximum of opportunity to investigate and interact with the materials of the discipline being studied. This applies not only to the way in which children get information from objects but also to logico-mathematical experience. Piaget sums up his feelings on the subject as follows:

In the area of logico-mathematical structures, children have real understanding only of that which they invent themselves, and each time that we try to teach them something too quickly, we keep them from reinventing it themselves.[11]

In other words, Piaget's theory of how experience aids intellectual development demands that teachers use exploration, invention, and discovery—inquiry—in all classrooms, for all subject matter, and at all grade levels.

Levels of development

At several points in this chapter we have said that most logico-mathematical experiences are beyond the level of children in the early grades and that content suited to the learners' level of development must be selected. In the sections that follow, we discuss the intellectual level of children from kindergarten through the twelfth grade. *Do not try to read only that part which is applicable to the particular level at which you intend to teach.* The intellectual-levels concept is a continuum, and to really understand any part of it you must have some knowledge of the whole.

[11] *Ibid.*, p. vi.

The Piagetian Model of Development

The physical development of the human organism begins at conception. Although cognitive development probably begins some time before birth, there is no evidence to support this conclusion. There are, however, data tracing the intellectual growth of children from birth. The most complete picture has been supplied by Jean Piaget. According to Piaget, a human being has the ability to pass through *four* distinct phases of intellectual development. In each of these stages the mental functions have certain characteristics, or properties; *as an individual moves from one stage to another,* these properties change. Eventually intellectual function undergoes a gradual but complete metamorphosis; what was before impossible can now be accomplished.

This picture of intellectual development is based on data Piaget obtained from working directly with individual children over a period of many years. His methods of data collection are unique and are largely clinical:

He observes the child's surroundings and his behavior, formulates a hypothesis concerning the structure that underlies and includes them both, and then tests that hypothesis by altering the surroundings slightly—by rearranging the materials, by posing the problem in a different way, or even by overtly suggesting to the subject a response different from the one predicted by the theory.[12]

Perhaps, for our purposes, Piaget's procedure could be described as giving the child a task to perform that involves materials and reasoning, letting him perform the task, and then asking him what he did and why he did it. Piaget's model of intellectual development is important for teachers because it comes from *direct* association with learners of all ages. As a teacher you will work directly with your students, and any model you use to select and employ content and materials should be directly relevant to them.

The sensory-motor stage

The first stage of intellectual development in Piaget's model is the *sensory-motor* phase, which begins at birth and continues until the child is approximately 2½ years old. During this phase the child learns that objects are permanent, that is, just because an object dis-

[12] Phillips, *op. cit.*, p. 4.

appears from sight does not mean it no longer exists. The characteristic of object permanence explains, for example, why a 1-year-old child will cry when his parents leave him. This separation anxiety does not occur earlier because until the child develops the concept of permanence, what is out of sight is out of mind.

During the sensory-motor period, the child begins to develop language skills.[13] Basically, he learns how to attach sounds to the objects, symbols, and experiences he has had. But the invention of an appropriate sound for something depends, as does later learning, on the child having an exploration experience with that something. During the sensory-motor period the first signs that intellect is developed, and does not just occur, begin to emerge. Now, certainly, the way a sensory-motor child goes about inquiring is quite different from the way an adult inquires, but the extent of this early learning has much to do with his later development.[14] Thus culturally deprived children, who receive little help from their environment in developing the beginnings of a language system, may need more than the conventional reading readiness programs *before* they can begin to participate in activities. Although you may never work with sensory-motor children, you should be aware that this is the stage in which intellectual development begins and that unless the child accomplishes certain goals in this stage, later learning must wait. Perhaps we as teachers need to spend more time determining when the learner is ready to begin doing and less time being concerned about the specific content being covered.

The preoperational stage

Before the second stage of intellectual development in Piaget's model—the *preoperational* stage—is investigated, we need to make two important points. First, there is only one stage in Piaget's model whose start can be pinpointed—the sensory-motor stage begins at birth and ends at about 2½ years of age. A child will *begin to enter* the preoperational stage at about 2½, and will begin to leave it at about age 7. In other words, the precise age at which a learner will begin to move from one stage in the model to another cannot be stated, for the child himself determines his progress. Piaget has described the relationship of the stages in his model and age in this way: "Although the order of succession is constant, the chronological ages of [children

[13] *Ibid.*, pp. 13–49. In these pages Phillips presents a thorough picture of the sensory-motor child.

[14] *Ibid.*, p. 17.

in] these stages varies a great deal."[15] A child does not move *completely* from one stage to another at a single point in time. He may be in the sensory-motor phase in regard to some traits and preoperational in regard to others. As his development progresses, he moves deeper and deeper into a particular stage in some respects, while he is only entering it in others.

TASK	*A few moments ago we used the term* trait. *How would you define a trait, and what do you think are the traits referred to here?*

Earlier in this chapter we discussed the difference between *actions* and *operations.* An action is generally physical, whereas an operation is always intellectual. When a child is able to reverse his thinking during an action and get back to the starting point, he has performed an operation. For example, suppose you were given a mathematical formula that you did not completely understand, say $x = (-b + \sqrt{b^2 - 4ac})/2a$. Now, suppose that in order to pass the course you had to use this and other formulas to solve problems. No doubt you memorized the formula and several examples; then, when presented with a problem, you searched for clues as to which formula to apply. In other words, you acted upon each problem with a number of formulas until you found a match. While there is a silght hint of an operation in matching the formulas and problems, this kind of procedure is primarily an action. Operations must be completely reversible and internalized by the learner. The term *preoperational* is wonderfully descriptive of what children at this age are like. They cannot mentally operate with ideas that require them to take information into their cognitive structures or do even simple mental experiments. They are *perception bound;*[16] that is, they see, they decide, and they report—in short, they *think,* but they cannot *think about* their own thinking.

A complete description of all intellectual characteristics of the preoperational child is far beyond the scope of this book.[17] However, in

[15] Piaget, "Development and Learning," p. 178.

[16] We would like to take credit for inventing this phrase, but we cannot. We first heard it used by Dr. Celia Stendler Lavatelli in the film *Piaget's Theory: Conservation,* produced by John Davidson Films, Inc., San Francisco.

[17] If you wish to investigate further the characteristics of preoperational children, you are urged to consult the book written by John L. Phillips, Jr.,[5] referred to throughout this chapter, or Piaget's *The Psychology of Intelligence.*

order to use Piaget's model to select and use content and instructional methodology, you should understand the five basic characteristics of this stage:[18]

1. Egocentrism
2. Irreversibility
3. Centering
4. The inability to perceive states in a transformation
5. Transductive reasoning.

Egocentrism in the young child is one of the most prominent preoperational traits; the child sees the world from only one point of view—his own. The world, as far as he is concerned, revolves around him, and he is completely unaware that he is a prisoner of his own frame of reference. In other words, the child cannot see another's point of view or take that point of view and coordinate it with his own. His opinions are based on his perceptions, and he feels no need to either justify or look for contradictions in them. A preoperational learner has developed a certain language pattern, which he uses to communicate, and he does not have the ability (or see the need) to adapt his language to the needs of his listener. Considering his single, ecocentric frame of reference, the language patterns of a preoperational learner are entirely predictable. In his perception-bound view of the world he learns only by interacting with his environment. Experiences must be provided for him—he cannot gain understanding by being told about something or by being given its abstraction; he thinks only about what he perceives. This egocentrism continues throughout the preoperational stage, which ends when the child is between 6½ and 7½ years of age. Teachers of this age group must be continually aware of the need to provide experiences that permit the child to have a maximum of physical experiences and a minimum (if any) of logicomathematical experiences, and this raises serious questions about the viability of some firmly entrenched activities found in the early years of schooling. Reading, for example, involves basically a set of abstract sounds represented by a series of abstract symbols. There is, after all, no intrinsic reason why a series of lines hooked in a certain way should be called *A*, *B*, or *C*. The alphabet is an abstraction, a defined series, and to really understand it the child must be able to take the point of view of those who defined it. This may be asking too much of a child in the preoperational stage whose egocentrism is strong. Do reading difficulties, which can plague a person his entire life, begin

[18] As you study Piaget's model, keep in mind the equilibration concept discussed earlier. Remember that it is called the overarching concept of intellectual development.

when (as an egocentric, preoperational learner) he is placed in a situation where those in charge demand that he internalize abstractions that he cannot comprehend? Comprehension of an abstraction demands that the learner take it into his cognitive structure and operate with it. According to the empirical data upon which the Piagetian model is based, a preoperational learner is not able to perform intellectual operations. Perhaps much of the time spent teaching reading in the first grade could be better spent allowing the children to interact physically with objects (some of which might be letters) or socially with one another and with the teacher to expand their language skills. Furth (note his use of the phrase "must be exposed") expresses his feelings about providing reading experiences for young children in this way:

Reading and writing should have no more emphasis or focus in a child's early school years than toilet training has in an infant's first years. . . . Seriously, while the written word is the means par excellence for expanding a mature intelligence, the early pressure on reading must be exposed not merely as contributing little or nothing to intellectual development, but in many cases, as seriously interfering with it.[19]

Reading, however, is not the only subject that needs to be critically reexamined from the preoperational child's egocentric point of view. Since the egocentric child is perception bound, his understandings of the social world must be developed from experience. Thus a social studies program for early elementary grades that concentrates on such topics as "Children of Other Lands" is of questionable value.

The second trait of the preoperational child that should be considered in choosing the curriculum for the early grades is *irreversibility.* In order for a human organism to begin to perform intellectual operations, he must be able to reverse his thinking. The irreversibility of thought in young children is beautifully illustrated by this dialogue with an 8-year-old boy:

"Have you got a brother?"
"Yes."
"And your brother, has he got a brother?"
"No."
"Are you sure?"
"Yes."
"And has your sister got a brother?"

[19] Hans G. Furth, *Piaget for Teachers* (Englewood Cliffs, N.J.: Prentice-Hall, 1970), pp. viii–ix.

"No."
"You have a sister?"
"Yes."
"And she has a brother?"
"Yes."
"How many?"
"No, she hasn't got any."
"Is your brother also your sister's brother?"
"No."
"And has your brother got a sister?"
"No. . . ."[20]

The dialogue with the child continues until he finally recognizes that he is his brother's brother. The following dialogue with a 4-year-old girl also demonstrates the irreversibility concept nicely:

"Have you got a sister?"
"Yes."
"And has she got a sister?"
"No, she hasn't got a sister. I am my sister,"[21]

Reversibility is the ability to return a thought to its starting point. For example:

$8 + 6 = 14$, and $14 - 6 = 8$

Here we started with 8 and ended with 8. However, preoperational children cannot reverse their thinking. Consider what this means in terms of mathematics programs for the early primary grades. The reason many people today shy away from mathematics might very well be that they were introduced to it at too early an age, before they had developed mental reversibility.

Testing a child for irreversibility is not difficult and can be informative. One method is to give the child two equal quantities of modeling clay or plasticene (we have found that using different colors facilitates communication). Form the pieces of clay into two balls and explain to the child that you want to start the experiment with one ball exactly the same size as the other. Allow your subject to work with the two balls until he believes they are just the same size. Now deform one of the balls; a good way to do this is to roll one of the balls into a long, cylindrical shape. Next ask the child (a 5-year-old child will probably be best to work with) if there is more clay in the ball, more in the roll, or if there is the same amount in each. (Be sure to give him all three choices, and ask him why he believes as he does.)

[20] Jean Piaget, *Judgment and Reasoning in the Child* (Paterson, N.J.: Littlefield, Adams, 1964), p. 86.

[21] *Ibid.*, p. 85.

TASK	*Record the child's answer and his reasoning.*

A child who has not developed the thinking trait of reversibility will tell you that there are different amounts of clay in the cylinder and the ball—our experience has been that most preoperational children will select the cylinder as containing more clay.

If the subject is preoperational, he will not be able to make the reversal in his thinking from the cylinder shape that exists now to the clay sphere that existed previously. He cannot do the analysis and synthesis needed to mentally reconstruct the sphere, although he knows that it existed. (If you ask him to restore the roll of clay to its original shape, he will produce a sphere and tell you that now there is the same amount of clay in each.) At this age a child thinks, but he is so irreversible he cannot think about his thinking.

Why does a child usually focus on the cylinder rather than on the ball? This is explained by another characteristic of the preoperational stage—*centering*. When the one clay ball was deformed, the child probably fixed his attention on the detail of length, and his rigid, perception-bound thinking structure prevented him from seeing anything else about the transformed object. Educational experiences provided for young children should avoid using materials or prescribing activities that encourage the centering trait. If, for example, colors are used, they should all be attractive and appealing. Centering is a characteristic of preoperational children, and teachers should not be surprised when a child focuses his attention on one aspect of an object, event, or situation to the exclusion of all others. Insisting that a child decenter and consider other aspects of an object is useless, and if the teacher is too insistent, the child may simply say that he sees some other property just to get the teacher to leave him alone. Whether it is a child's inability to reverse his thinking that causes him to center or whether it is the centering trait that causes irreversibility is not known, but since the two traits are not mutually exclusive which comes first is not really relevant.

The extreme perception boundness of a preoperational child is also illustrated by another characteristic trait known as *states and transformation*. Figure 4-1 represents a wooden rod that is held upright (position 1) and then released (positions 2, 3, and 4). The rod eventually comes to rest in position 5. Obviously, the rod was in a state of rest when it was held in position 1 and is again in a state of rest in

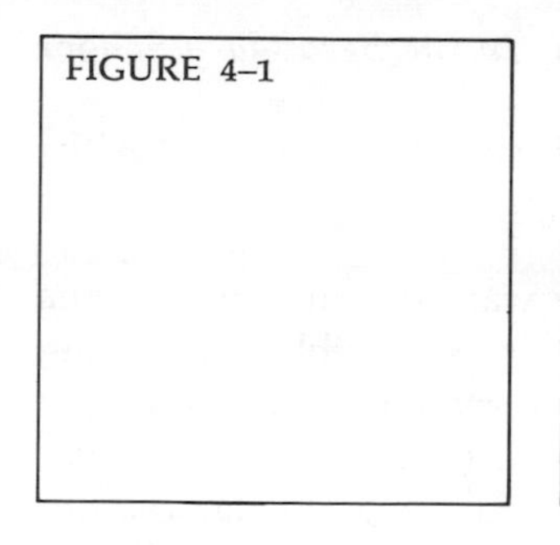
FIGURE 4–1

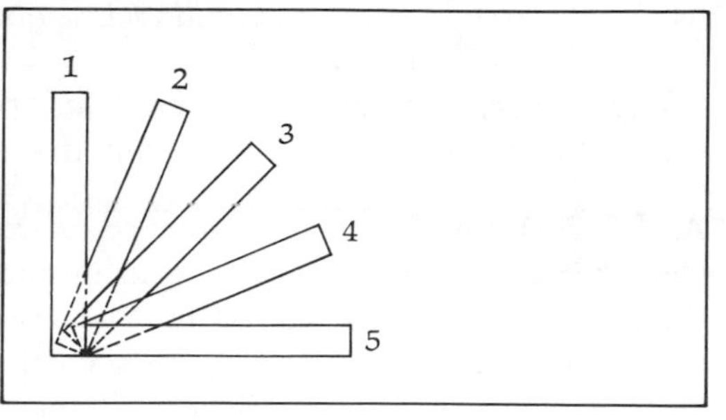

position 5. In the interim, it passed through a series of other states, represented by positions 2, 3, and 4. This series of states resulted in a *transformation* in the stick's position from the vertical to the horizontal.

If a preoperational child is shown this experiment and is told that he will be asked to draw a diagram of it, he will not draw what is shown in Figure 4–1, nor will he indicate in any way what successive states the stick went through in being transformed from position 1 to position 5. Our experience has been that the preoperational child will draw *only* positions 1 and 5; he sees only the beginning and final states and does not see the transformation. The preoperational child's inability to comprehend the transformation of one thing into another (which also shows irreversibility and centering) is particularly important when young children are being taught a process, e.g., in a plant growing experiment. There is little use in trying to get them to see the importance of the several states in the transformation from seed to leaf, for they cannot. They will perceive the first and final stages and nothing else. The process that allows the final state to be a function of the intermediate states cannot be seen by preoperational children. Similarly, giving young children music lessons that require learning a technique involving several mental transformations to get to a final state, or expecting them to grasp mathematical processes such as addition, or forcing them to learn the ground rules of spelling seems doubtful.

In his book *Play, Dreams and Imitation in Childhood* (translated by C. Guttegno and F. M. Hodgson),[22] Piaget relates an incident that occurred when his daughter Jacqueline was two years old:

Jacqueline wanted a doll-dress that was upstairs: she said "Dress," and when her mother refused to get it, "Daddy get dress." As I also refused, she wanted to go herself "To mommy's room." After several repetitions of this she was told that it was too cold there. There was

[22] (New York: Norton, 1951), pp. 230–231; original French edition published in 1945.

a long silence, and then: "Not too cold." (I asked) "Where?" "In the room." "Why isn't it too cold?" "Get dress."

As far as Jacqueline was concerned there was no difference in the logic that a warm room makes securing the dress possible and getting the dress makes the room warm. She was reasoning from particular to particular and not from general to particular (deduction) or particular to general (induction). Piaget calls particular to particular reasoning, *transduction*. It begins to appear in the child with the beginning of language and lasts until he is about 4 years of age. As a teacher, do not be surprised if you encounter transduction in kindergarten and first-grade children. If you do, be patient; it usually disappears with the increased experiences provided by the school environment.

Identifying whether a child can see the relationship between states and transformations is a simple task; identifying the other preoperational traits—egocentrism, irreversibility, centering, and transduction —is somewhat harder. There are, however, procedures for identifying preoperational thinking. We have already described one technique, the clay balls experiment, for identifying irreversibility. This experiment illustrated the inability of a preoperational child to mentally hold on to the image of an object and see that distorting the object does not change the amount of material it contains. Mentally holding the original image of an object is called *conservation,* and preoperational children do not conserve. They make decisions about the distortion of the object on the basis of what they perceive. This rigid perception boundness, however, is due to their irreversible thinking, their not seeing a transformation among several states, their tendency to center, their extreme egocentrism, and their tendency toward transductive reasoning. Isolating a child who does not conserve allows you to describe his stage of intellectual development in terms of the five preoperational traits already discussed. Conservation is an *overt* manifestation of whether a child is a preoperational thinker. As we said earlier, this stage of development begins at about 2½ years of age. In describing the beginning of a child's ability to conserve, Piaget also provides information about the end of the preoperational period:

. . . there always comes a time (between 6½ years and 7 years 8 months) when the child's attitude changes: he no longer needs to reflect, he decides, he even looks surprised when the question is asked, he is certain *of the conservation.*[23]

[23] Jean Piaget, *The Psychology of Intelligence* (Paterson, N.J.: Littlefield, Adams, 1963), p. 140.

The beginning of the ability to conserve and the beginning of the child's entry into the third stage of the Piagetian model—concrete operational—occurs, then, in the late first or second grade. In designing about 70 percent of a first-grade curriculum, the teacher should consider that the children are preoperational.

The experiment with the clay balls tested the child's ability to conserve *solid amount*. Several other experiments are also very useful in identifying preoperational thought. These experiments, which involve the conservation of number, liquid amount, area, length, and weight are described below. As you read the description, keep in mind the definition of conservation: A child who conserves can hold a concept about an object in his cognitive structure while a second object like the first is distorted, and he can see that the distorted object is still like the non-distorted object in many specific ways.

Experiment I: Conservation of Number.[24] Have the child line up six black checkers in one row and six red checkers in another row, as shown in Figure 4–2.

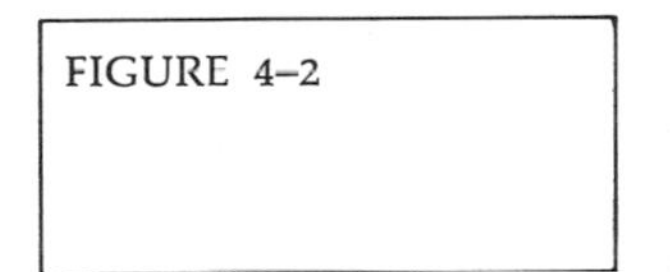
FIGURE 4–2

Ask the child if he agrees that there are the same number of red checkers as there are black checkers. After he agrees, stack the red checkers one on top of the other, and leave the black checkers as they were; the checkers will now appear as in Figure 4–3.

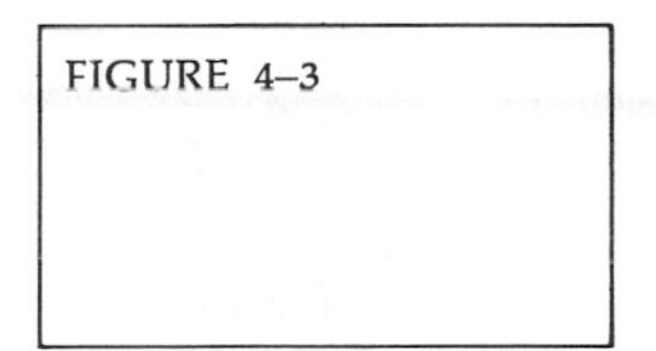
FIGURE 4–3

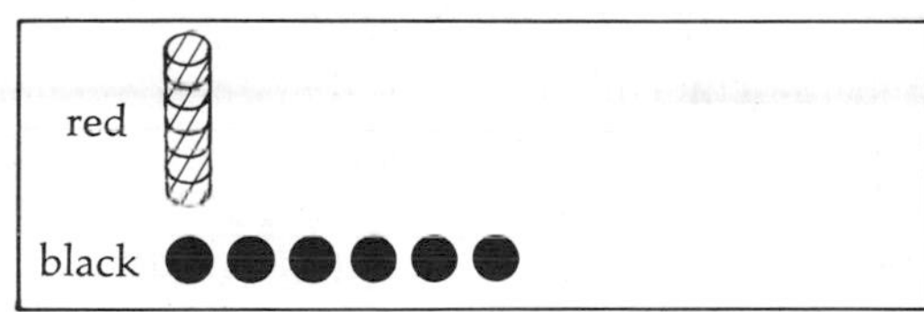

After the checkers have been rearranged, ask the child if there are more black checkers, or if the number of black and red checkers is equal. If he reports that the numbers are equal, he conserves number.

[24] The utilization of these tasks is illustrated in the film *Piaget's Theories: Conservation*, produced and distributed by John Davidson Films, Inc., San Francisco. The directions for these tasks have been tested by several hundred elementary school teachers, whose suggestions and contributions we appreciate. We are especially indebted to Dorsee Bennet Cohenour and Sandra Thompson Quigley, who, after extensive work with children, assisted in rewriting the directions for each test.

FIGURE 4–4
A child often counts the checkers when completing the conservation-of-number task.

Experiment II: Conservation of Liquid. Pour the same amount of water into two containers of equal size as in Figure 4–5. (For convenience, you may wish to color the water in one container red.)

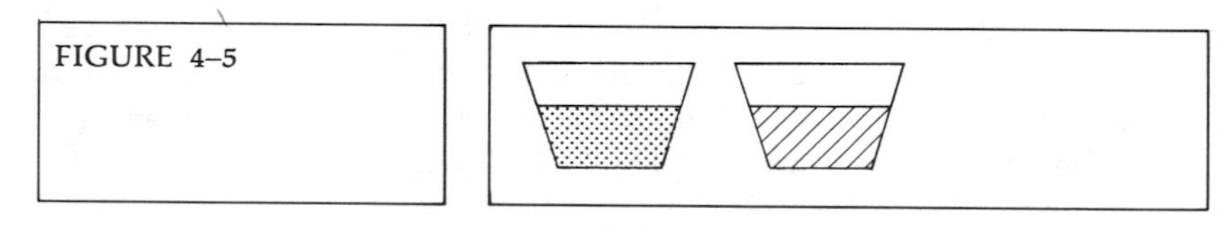

FIGURE 4–5

Ask the child if he agrees that the containers are the same size and that they contain the same amount of liquid; let him adjust the levels if he wishes. After he agrees that the amounts are equal, have him pour the clear liquid into a taller, thinner container (see Figure 4–6), and ask him if there is more colored water, more clear water, or if the amounts are equal.

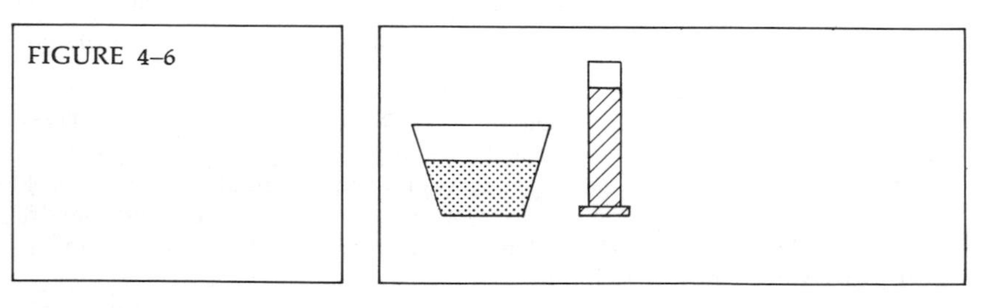

FIGURE 4–6

If he says that the amounts are equal, he conserves liquid; if he believes that there is more water in one of the containers, he demonstrats a lack of liquid-conservation ability.

Experiment III: Conservation of Solids. We have already described this task in our earlier discussion of irreversibility. Prepare two clay balls of equal size, as in Figure 4-7. (For convenience, you may wish to use two colors of clay, say, blue and red.)

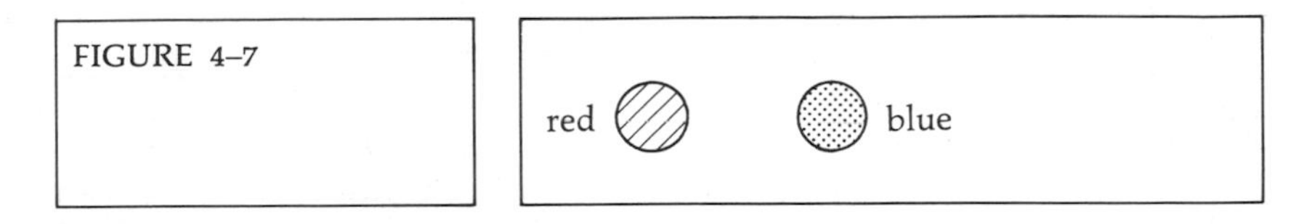

FIGURE 4–7

Ask the child if he agrees that there is the same amount of clay in each ball; let him make any adjustments he wishes in the balls in order to convince himself they are indeed of equal size. Next, deform one piece of clay by rolling it into a snakelike or cylindrical form as in Figure 4–8.

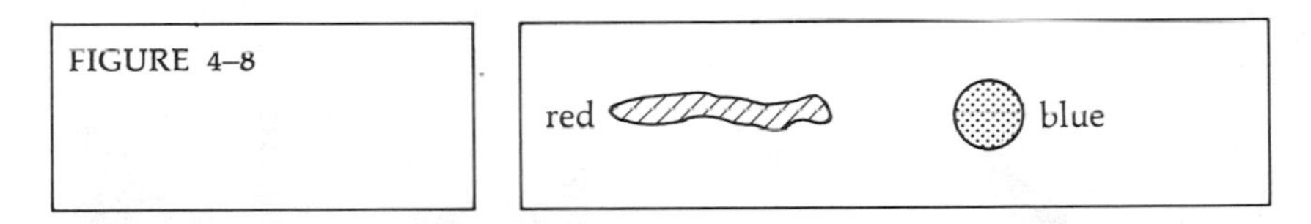

FIGURE 4–8

Ask the learner if there is more clay in the ball, in the snake, or if there is the same amount in each. If he recognizes that the amount of the solid remains constant, he has developed the ability to conserve solid amount.

Experiment IV: Conservation of Area. Show the child two fields of grass (green construction paper) of *equal size;* be sure he is satisfied that the fields are the same size before going on. Explain that each field is owned by a farmer; Mr. Green owns one, and Mr. Jones owns the other. Mr. Green and Mr. Jones each builds a barn on his own field. Place a barn made of red construction paper or a toy barn on each field and explain that the barns are exactly the same size (see Figure 4–9).

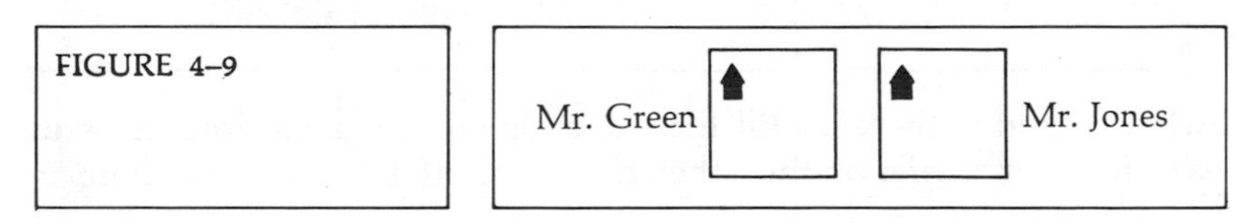

FIGURE 4–9

Ask the child if there is still the same amount of uncovered grass on each field, or if one or the other has more. Record his answer. Then tell him that Mr. Green and Mr. Jones each builds another barn. Mr. Green builds his second barn right next to his first barn, but Mr. Jones leaves a space between his two barns (see Figure 4–10).

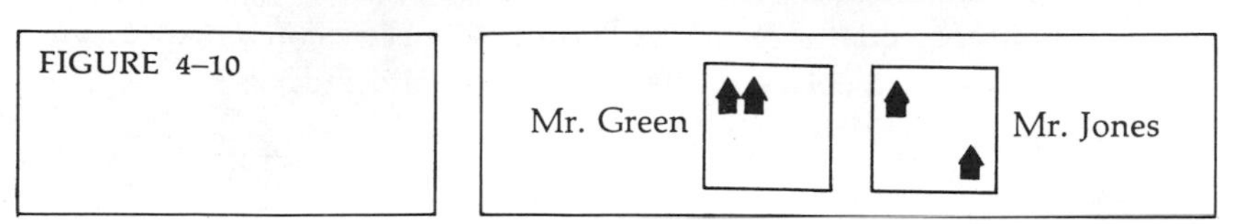

FIGURE 4–10

Again ask the child if there is still the same amount of uncovered grass on each field. After he answers, explain to him that Mr. Green and Mr. Jones each builds a third barn. Mr. Green builds the third barn right next to the second barn, and Mr. Jones again leaves a space between his barns (see Figure 4–11).

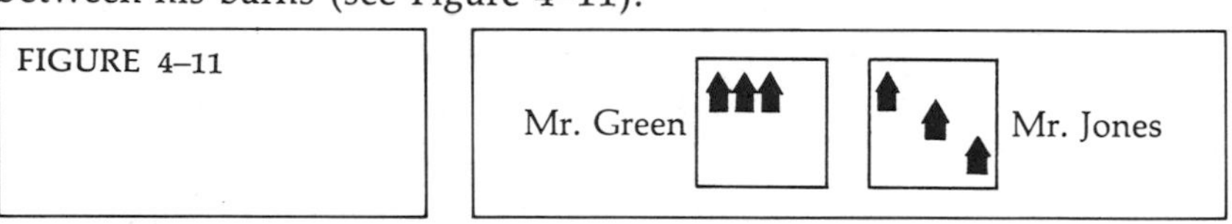

FIGURE 4–11

FIGURE 4–12
Children frequently need to arrange and rearrange the "barns" during the conservation-of-area task.

Ask the child if there is still the same amount of uncovered grass in each field, or if one or the other has more. If he says that there is still the same amount in each field, he can conserve area. Be sure the child is not just counting the barns and conserving number.

Experiment V: Conservation of Length. This task requires a wooden dowel 12 inches long and four dowels 3 inches long. (The exact lengths are not important, but the combined lengths of the four smaller dowels must equal the length of the longer dowel.) Two identical toy cars are also helpful. Place the long dowel and the short pieces parallel, as in Figure 4–13.

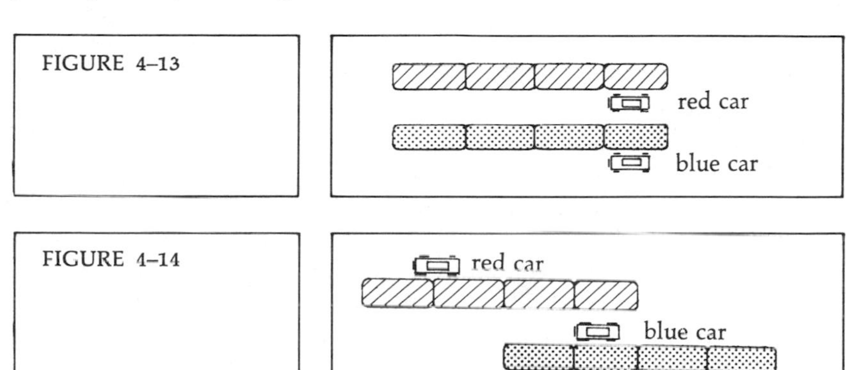

FIGURE 4–13

FIGURE 4–14

FIGURE 4–15
Starting the conservation-of-length task with the "roads" equal in length is important.

Be sure the child agrees that the line made up of short pieces is exactly the length of the long piece; let him make adjustments if necessary. Then tell him that the dowels represent roads and that there is going to be a race. Place *identical* toy cars (say a red one and a blue one) at the same ends of the roads, as in Figure 4–13, and then ask the child whether, if the cars travel at the same speed, the red one or the blue one will reach the end of the road first. Or whether they will reach the ends of the roads at the same time? The child will generally agree that the cars will reach the ends of the roads at the same time; if he does not, discuss it with him until he sees that they do. If he does not ultimately agree that the cars reach the ends of the roads at the same time, abandon the task. Next move two pieces of the four-piece road as shown in Figure 4–14, and repeat your question about the race. If a child now states that the cars will reach the end of the road at the same time, he conserves length.

Experiment VI: Conservation of Weight. Give the child two balls, one red and one green, containing equal amounts of clay. Add and subtract from each of the balls until the child agrees that the balls weigh exactly the same. Then take the two balls of clay from the child and flatten one of them into a pancake or distort it in some other way. Do not let the child lift the two clay objects after you have done this. Next ask the learner if there is more green clay, more red clay, or whether the amounts are still the same. If he fails to recognize that the amounts of red and green clay are still equal, the child does not conserve weight.

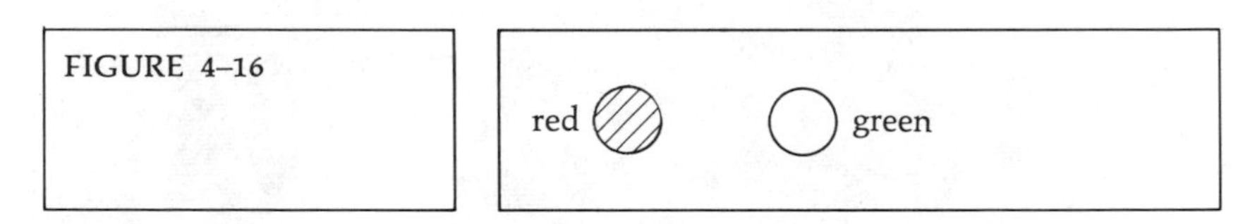

FIGURE 4–16

If these tasks seem very simple to you, it is because you are not preoperational. To really be able to appreciate and understand the significance of preoperational thought, you should try these experiments with children of different ages. A 5-year-old, a 7-year-old, and a 9-year-old will probably give you a wide enough age range to see the movement away from preoperational thought and toward the concrete operational stage. Be sure to ask each child the reasons for his answers and give him the opportunity to explain his reasoning to you.

If you combine your results with those of your fellow students, you will see that age alone does not determine when a child leaves the preoperational stage. Also, the fact that a child conserves on one task does not necessarily mean that he will on the others. As yet, there is no adequate data to indicate the task on which the child will demonstrate conservation first, second, and so on. Our experience suggests that a child learns number first and then liquid. Other than that there seems to be no definite pattern.

What is the relationship between the five traits of preoperational thought described earlier, conservation, and the curriculum? In order for you to see the relationship between the traits and conservation, you must analyze each conservation task for instances when centering, irreversibility in thinking, transductive reasoning, egocentrism, or the inability to perceive intermediate states in a transformation will cause the child to fail. In order to conserve the child must overcome these tendencies. As Phillips explains,

> *. . . the Preoperational child tends to be dominated by his perceptions, to center on a single attribute of a display and to "reason" transductively. In order to conserve, he must shake off that domination. He must decenter, and he must realize that an object can change in one respect without changing in other respects.*[25]

The curriculum, therefore, must provide opportunities for preoperational children to work within their limitations, while still providing them with experiences that will ultimately lead them to lose their perception boundness. The following lesson plan for first-grade science is a good example of how to work with children at this level.

Advance Preparation
Select groups of objects to provide as wide a variety as seems reasonable. Buttons, beans, rocks, shells, wires, wood blocks, metal pieces, bottle caps, birthday candles, and pipe cleaners are available in the kit [which accompanies the program]. You can also add rubber bands, crayons, paper clips, chalk, and 3" × 5" cards to the array. Use all or just some of these objects during the first session. Place each kind of object on a separate tray, and display these in front of the room. Put a tray, plastic dish, and magnifier on each child's desk.

Teaching Suggestions
Beginning the activity. *Ask the children what objects are on their desks. Discuss the properties of the dishes and magnifiers as well as their similarities and differences. Allow the children some time to explore with the magnifier before you give them any instructions. . . .*

[25] Phillips, *op. cit.*, p. 115.

Describing properties. *Ask each child to select one object from his collection. Volunteers may show their objects to the group, describing the properties they observe.*

Pick up one object from your collection, and ask each pupil to choose a similar one from his collection. Call on a child to tell you about the properties of his object. . . . Repeat this procedure with several pupils. Choose other objects from your collection in order to discuss as extensively as possible a list of properties.

Defining sorting. *If necessary, introduce a definition of sorting by citing a simple example such as, "The class is made up of children. We can sort the children into boys and girls." Or you can sort crayons by colors, as a classroom demonstration. Now invite each child to sort the objects on his tray. Many chlidren will sort according to the properties already mentioned; others will use different criteria. When the children have sorted all the objects, suggest that each child display his tray to a neighbor. Each child then tries to guess how his neighbor sorted. Encourage the children to discuss their guesses and the reasons for them. After a few minutes, suggest that they tell each other how they sorted. Informal conversation and description among children is most important to their continuing development of language skills. You also have an excellent opportunity at this time to provide individual help to those children who need it. After this informal discussion, some children can describe their sorting methods for the class, or you can proceed to the sorting-by-specific properties activity.*

Sorting by property. *Name a property (color or shape, for example), and ask each pupil to group some or all of his objects into piles on his desk while thinking of this property. Let individual children describe how the objects in their piles differ from one another. If they cannot sort or describe the objects at this time, do not become concerned since they will have many more opportunities for similar experiences.*

The day-to-day science work in the classroom can consist of any activity that helps children become aware of objects and their properties. The number of sessions spent on this activity depends upon the needs, interests, and abilities of your particular pupils.[26]

Earlier in this chapter we said that experience is an important factor in intellectual development and identified two kinds of experience, physical and logico-mathematical. In the curriculum example just given, the experience at first inspection seems to be largely physical;

[26] Science Curriculum Improvement Study, *Material Objects* (Chicago: Rand McNally, 1970), pp. 29–30.

perhaps it is. There is, however, a real element of basic logic that the child encounters in such learning experience.

TASK	*Look carefully at the curriculum example above. What opportunities does it provide for the children to break away from the five preoperational traits listed earlier?*

Do experiences like those in the example produce results that are significant enough to warrant including them in the curriculum? Stafford and Renner[27] used these materials with two groups of sixty first-grade children. The two groups were selected from schools with the same socioeconomic background, the same general type of educational program, and the same general caliber of teachers. The children's ability to conserve was first measured in September, 1968, at which time more children in group A could conserve number and area (on the latter task, group A surpassed group B by a very wide margin). Group B had more children who conserved weight and length, while the same number of children in each group conserved solids and liquids. Group A was then given a conventional first-year program; group B was given the same program, *except* the Material Objects unit was used. Group A had a science program that required the children to look at pictures in a book and talk about what was in the book but gave them no direct experience with the objects. The conservation ability of both groups was measured again in January, 1969. At that time, group B markedly surpassed group A in all conservations except area, and the margin between groups B and A on that task, which was very wide at the beginning of the experiment, was now very small. But perhaps the most significant result of the experiment was that group B outgained group A in *developing the ability to conserve* on every task, despite the fact that in September, 1968, group B had a mean IQ of 103.2 on the Otis-Lennon scale and group A had a mean IQ of 106.2. Since the only difference in the educational experience for the two groups was the Material Objects unit described above, the researchers concluded that a program emphasizing physical interactions and introducing children to logico-mathematical experiences leads them to develop the ability to conserve.

[27] Don G. Stafford and John W. Renner, "SCIS Helps the First Grade to Use Logic in Problem Solving," *School Science and Mathematics*, (February, 1971), pp. 159–164.

In terms of achievement in school subjects, what good does it do a child to develop the ability to conserve? If you analyze the type of thinking needed in subjects like mathematics, social science, and reading, and the type of reasoning needed to conserve, you can see the connection. The extent to which a child demonstrates this ability tells the teacher how logically tight he can make his teaching. Almy has this to say about the relationship between the child's ability to conserve and his progress in beginning reading:

The findings in our studies of a rather substantial correlation between performance in conservation tasks and progress in beginning reading suggest that, to some extent, similar abilities are involved. A program designed to nurture logical thinking should contribute positively to readiness for reading.[28]

If children can be trained to succeed on conservation tasks, will they be better readers? Maxine Jeter and John W. Renner[29] found that they could train kindergarten children to conserve colored liquids. But when salt or sand (which pour like a liquid and take the exact shape of the container, as a liquid does) was substituted for the liquid, the subjects did not conserve. That suggests that the children memorized the answers to the test for conserving liquids rather than internalizing the process; they had not yet converted actions into operations. Do children memorize when they are asked to use reasoning that is beyond them? Training to develop conservation has attracted a great deal of attention in recent years.[30] At this point the results seem to show that a child cannot be trained to conserve and have the development of that ability mean educationally what it means if the child develops it naturally or through educational materials that provide physical and logico-mathematical experiences.

The conservation concept is a potent tool in the hands of a teacher who knows how to use it. Because he can identify preoperational thinkers and those who have gone beyond this stage, he can select the type of curriculum for his students that matches their level of intellectual development. There is no point in asking a preoperational thinker to become involved in an educational activity that requires him to reverse his thinking; he just cannot do it. He can, however, observe, perceive, and report his perceptions. He needs educational experiences that will enable him to use his perceptions. Experiences

[28] Almy, *op. cit.*, pp. 139–140.

[29] Unpublished research at the University of Oklahoma, 1969.

[30] See Irving E. Sigel and Frank H. Hooper, eds., *Logical Thinking in Children* (New York: Holt, Rinehart and Winston, 1968), Chap. 5, "Training Research."

that would disequilibrate a learner in later stages of development will not affect a preoperational child; a preoperational child does not internalize his perceptions and do mental experiments to test their equilibration properties. Activities like those cited in the sample lesson tend to give the learner physical and simple logico-mathematical experiences that lead to a change of mental structures and thus to disequilibrium. Understanding the characteristics of preoperational thought enables the teacher to recognize the types of activities that will be valuable to his students.

The concrete-operational stage

We have stressed the preoperational period in this chapter because it makes understanding the next stage, in which the child is capable of concrete operations, much easier. The simplest way to describe a concrete-operational child is to say that he can do things a preoperational thinker cannot, that is, he decenters, equilibrates, does mental reversals, begins to reason inductively and deductively rather than transductively, and sees the relationship between states in a transformation. His egocentric structures begin to thaw out, and he can see objects as other people do. He also conserves. Just as the ability to conserve does not develop in all areas at one time, however, a child does not move from the preoperational to the concrete-operational stage all at once. The process is a gradual one.

The concrete-operation thinker can truly do the mental operations that Piaget says represent the beginning of logical thinking. He can take data derived from the investigation of objects, manipulate them, do mental experiments with them, and make statements about the results of these manipulations. *He can think about his own thinking.* Piaget describes concrete operations in this way: "In a third stage the first operations appear, but I call these concrete operations because *they operate on objects and not yet on verbally expressed hypotheses* [italics ours]."[31] The ability of concrete-operational learners to make mental reversals and do other types of thinking that preoperational children cannot do will be wasted unless they are given actual objects to work with. Concrete thinkers operate on objects and not on verbally expressed hypotheses.

This stage of intellectual development begins somewhere between 6½ years and 7 years 8 months and continues, according to Piaget,

[31] Piaget, "Development and Learning," p. 177.

until the child is 11 to 12 years of age. Friot and Renner's findings[32] suggest that this stage may last even longer than Piaget suspected. Of 258 eighth and ninth graders studied, 253 exhibited concrete-operational thinking. The average age of the students in this sample was approximately 14 years 6 months. McKinnon and Renner[33] provided data which suggest that the upper age limit on concrete operations is much higher for some people than for others. In a sample of 143 entering college freshmen, 72 were found to be concrete-operational. Based on these studies, it seems safe to say most junior high school students are in the concrete-operational stage. The probability is also high that a good percentage of senior high school students think on a concrete-operational level. The implications of these findings for the curricula in both the upper elementary grades and the junior and senior high schools are quite clear. Obviously, the bulk of the curricula must consist of direct experiential kinds of learning, learning that allows the students to interact with the objects of the various disciplines. Pre- and concrete-operational thinkers must interact with the objects of the discipline before learning can take place. The interaction is inquiry, and inquiry leads to the development of the rational powers. (We shall discuss categorization of disciplines and their objects at length in Chapter 5.)

TASK	*Why is understanding the preoperational stage important to a secondary-school teacher?*

The formal-operational stage

The preoperational thinker often indulges in the wildest kind of fantasy. If the real world does not suit him, he just imagines it to be different, the kind of world he does want. The concrete-operational thinker is concerned with the actual data he extracts from objects, with organizing those data and mentally experimenting with them. He does not take departures from reality as the preoperational thinker

[32] Faith Elizabeth Friot, *The Relationship Between an Inquiry Teaching Approach and Intellectual Development*, unpublished doctoral dissertation, University of Oklahoma, 1970.

[33] Joe W. McKinnon, *The Influence of a College Inquiry-Centered Course in Science on Student Entry into the Formal Operational Stage*, unpublished doctoral dissertation, University of Oklahoma, 1970.

does; he accommodates his thinking to events in the real world. He can categorize, compare, seriate, and perform all sorts of mental operations that lead to rational-power development as long as he is given experience with real objects. We now reach the last level of intellectual development in Piaget's model, the *formal-operational* stage, which can begin at about 11 or 12 years of age.[34] Piaget himself has pointed out that there is little consistency in the entering age level. "Although the order of succession is constant, the chronological ages of [children entering] these stages varies a great deal."[35] Formal-operational thinkers have imagination, but their imaginings are firmly rooted in the information they receive from the world around them. Phillips explains the formal-operational thinker as "capable of departures from reality, but those departures are lawful; he is concerned with reality but reality is only a subset within a much larger set of possibilities."[36] A preoperational thinker cannot think about his own thinking, a concrete-operational thinker can think about his thinking as long as objects are present for him to manipulate, and *a formal-operational thinker can think about the consequences and implications of his own thinking.* He can think in the abstract; he does not need to have objects to manipulate. He can take data and treat the pattern they form as only one of many possible patterns. To the formal, abstract thinker, *the possible is as real as the here and now.* He not only performs mental operations with real data but performs operations on the operations used in mental experimentation. Only when learners achieve the formal-operational level of thought can they deal with abstract ideas, and our information suggests that this does not occur, at the earliest, until sometime during senior high school. This has important implications for the curricula in the highest grades. Consider, for example, the task of diagramming sentences; when done properly, it is clearly an operation on an operation. Thus assigning this task to children of junior high school age, as is usually done, is pointless. Or consider the concept of acceleration. Acceleration is the rate (in feet per second) that velocity (in feet per second) changes; it is a rate of change of a rate of change. It is usually taught in the twelfth grade, probably the earliest level at which such an operation can be comprehended.

The concrete-operational thinker can obtain information, classify it, seriate it, and so on, but according to Piaget, formal operations "consist essentially of 'implications' (in the narrow sense of the word)

[34] Piaget, *The Psychology of Intelligence,* p. 148.
[35] Piaget, "Development and Learning," p. 178.
[36] Phillips, *op. cit.,* p. 101.

and 'contradictions' established between propositions which themselves express classification, seriations, etc."[37] Bruner describes formal thinking as the same types of logical operations that "are the stock in trade of the logician, the scientist, or the abstract thinker."[38] In short, the learner who has passed into the formal-operational stage can reason from ideas; he does not need objects.

What are the implications of the Piagetian model, particularly the formal-operational level, for the curricula? In relation to today's schools some interesting, disappointing, frightening, and enlightening factors become apparent. The intellectual-levels model of Piaget tells us that to be useful, any experience that children below the formal-operational level have, must be an experience with objects they can seriate, classify, analyze, compare with other objects, evaluate, and, in general, *act upon*. Those experiences are necessary if the learner is to progress through the various stages of the Piagetian model. If the schools were to truly embrace this model and use it to select curricula that would lead children to achieve the formal-operational stage, the school day would be organized very differently. First of all, there would be much less emphasis on textbooks. Today, the principal concern of many college and secondary school teachers is selecting the right textbook. While textbooks are important, they are only one of many sources of data on the objects of the various disciplines, and their importance depends very much on the age level of the learner. School activities that stress only the memorization of material in textbooks do not provide the kinds of experiences that will allow children to move through the various stages of intellectual development. Inquiry-oriented activities, like those described in Chapter 3, *do* give learners this kind of experience. In other words, *inquiry is not only the methodology for rational-power development, it is also the methodology which gives students experiences with the objects of a discipline that will lead them through the levels of development described in the Piagetian model.* Earlier in this chapter we quoted Piaget as saying that every time we try to teach a child something too soon, we keep him from reinventing it himself. A learner invents an explanation only when he is in disequilibrium; regaining his equilibrium sharpens his ability to look at what is being considered. In addition, the continual process of equilibrating and disequilibrating moves the child upward through the several stages of intellectual development. *Inquiry, then, is the methodology of intellectual development because*

[37] Piaget, *The Psychology of Intelligence*, p. 149.

[38] Jerome Bruner, *The Process of Education* (New York: Random House, 1960), p. 37.

it provides opportunities for the learner to disequilibrate and equilibrate himself. It is the methodology of equilibration.

If the curricula selected for the schools do not provide experiences suited to the learners' level of intellectual development, none of the foregoing will happen. In Chapter 2 we saw that the students' rational powers were one criterion for selecting curricula. Here, then, is a second criterion: *The curiculum (content and materials) used must be compatible with the developmental level of the learner.* Only then will he progress through the several stages of development and reach the formal-operational stage. In order to become concrete-operational, the child does not need to work with concrete-operational content while he is preoperational; in fact, he cannot do so. If a child were left to his own devices, i.e. not sent to school, he would probably provide himself with the proper experiences to become concrete-operational. However, unless a learner has ample and proper concrete-operational experience, he will not become formal-operational; he will not be able to make decisions that require a high degree of abstract thinking. The number of concrete-operational college students found in McKinnon and Renner's study suggests that many of today's schools are not providing experiences at the concrete-operational level that will enable the learners to become formal-operational. In many schools little actual learning occurs because teachers provide only formal-operational experiences for concrete-operational learners. Would "pushing content down" result in providing formal-operational experiences for concrete-operational learners?

Are developmental levels related to school discipline? In many schools the noise that results when children are engaged in inquiry is considered a discipline problem. Many teachers and school administrators believe that a quiet classroom is a productive classroom and that there should be little or no talking among students. Yet social transmission through conversation is crucial to intellectual development. Discipline is being maintained not when there is no conversation among students but when the conversation is directed at the topic under consideration.

TASK	*Record your own generalizations about the quiet classroom.*

Disciplinary problems are most likely to occur when a child is asked to learn material that is over his head. If the task assigned is too difficult for him he may refuse to attempt it at all or become frustrated and give up after a few tries. No student is more likely to become a discipline problem than an idle one, and there is no surer way to turn a student off than to give him tasks he cannot do. *Cannot* is not at all the same thing as *does not want to,* and teachers should be alert to the difference. A preoperational thinker cannot do work designed for a concrete-operational thinker, and the latter cannot do work that requires formal thinking. You have probably heard teachers describe certain material as too difficult for certain classes; what they probably meant was that the work being offered was suited to one operational level and that the learners were at another. Giving learners activities that are suited to their level of intellectual development can have the effect of immediately engaging their attention and thus wiping out many potential discipline problems.

Identifying the formal-operational thinker is a more complex matter than picking out those in the concrete-operational stage. Less work has been done in this area than at the preoperational–concrete-operational boundary. At present, Robert Karplus in California and Jan Smedslund of Norway are among those engaged in inventing ways of identifying formal thinkers. There are, however, several simple tasks that will give you information about a learner's ability to think formally.

As a learner enters the formal-operational stage, he begins to conserve volume. You can test this ability with two cylindrical containers, each about one-half full but containing equal amounts of liquid, and two small weights of equal volume but different weights that can be lowered by a string or wire into the cylinders. (See Figure 4–17.)

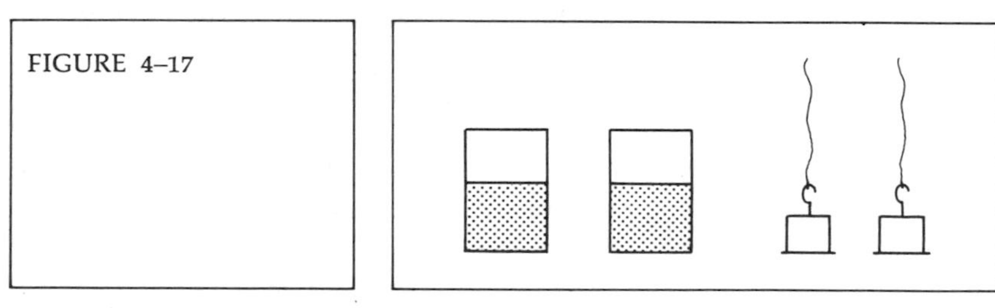

FIGURE 4–17

Have the student adjust the level of the water in the two containers until *he* feels they are identical; be sure he understands that the weights are identical in volume but different in weight. Next, ask him what will happen to the water level in the cylinder if one of the weights is submerged in one of the containers. When he tells you that the level will rise, ask him if the heavier weight or the lighter weight will raise the water level more or if they will each raise it the same amount. A thoroughly concrete-operational thinker will say that the heavier weight will raise the water level more, and a student who has begun to enter the formal-operational stage will report that each weight will raise the water level the same amount. Next, have the student lower the lighter weight into one cylinder. Then give him a rubber band. After having him first mark the spot he believes the water will rise to in the second cylinder with the rubber band, have him lower the heavier weight into the container. If he positioned the rubber band incorrectly, ask him what he thinks caused the levels to come out equal.

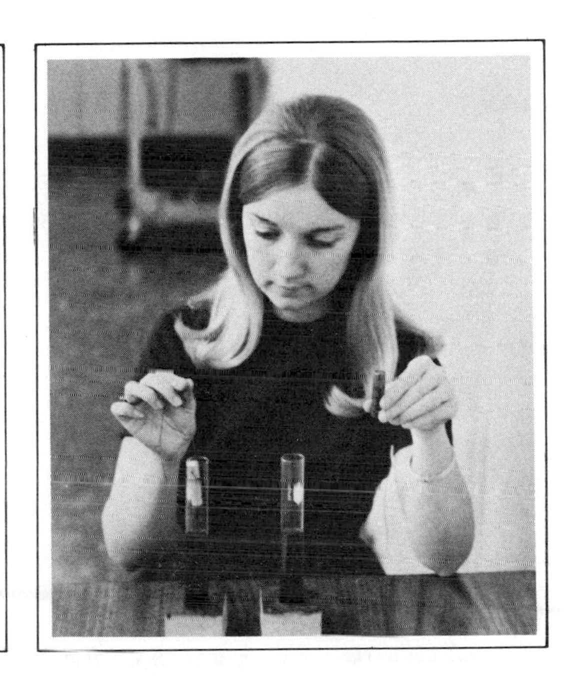

FIGURE 4–18
Student manipulation of the materials is essential when completing the conservation-of-volume task.

There are other tasks you can use to identify a learner who has moved into the formal-operational stage. The first is called the *reciprocal-implication* task. It is based on the principle that when a solid, moving object (like a marble) strikes a straight, solid barrier (like a wall) at an angle and is reflected, the object will be reflected from the wall at the same angle (r) at which it struck the wall (i). The experimental set-up is shown in Figure 4–19. The task given the student is to strike the stationary object with the moving object, but the moving object must strike the wall first. After the student has performed this task, ask him to analyze the problem and formulate a rule that will ensure his hitting the target every time. The work of Piaget and Inhelder[39] indicates that a student will not be able to tell you that the angle (*i*) at which the incoming object strikes the wall (the angle of incidence) equals the angle (*r*) it makes when leaving the wall (the angle of reflection) until he is well into the formal-operational stage.

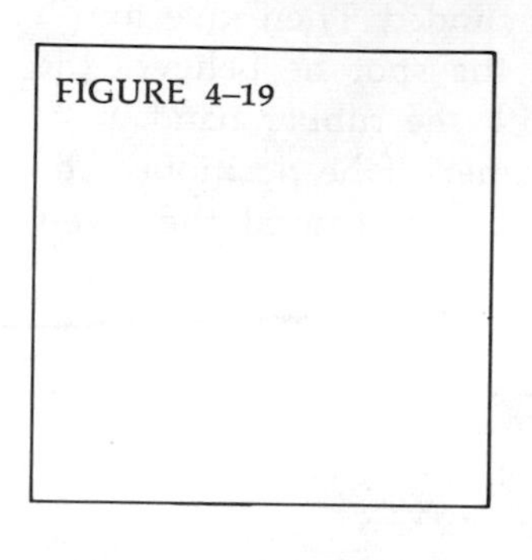
FIGURE 4–19

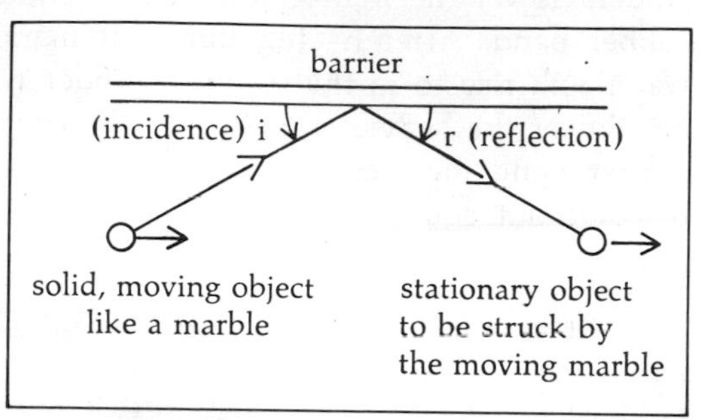

Piaget and Inhelder also tried this task, using specially constructed apparatus that they described as "kind of a billiard game,"[40] with preoperational and concrete-operational children. They reported that preoperational thinkers did not see the path of the moving object as straight-line segments but described the object's entire path as a curve. At this stage of development the child takes into consideration the "starting point and the goal, but not the rebound points."[41] Concrete-operational thinkers do see the path of the moving object as two straight lines:

[They] succeed in isolating all the elements needed to discover the law of the equality of the angles of incidence and reflection, yet they can neither construct the law a fortiori *nor formulate it verbally. They proceed with simple concrete operations of serial ordering and correspondences between the inclinations of two trajectory segments (before and after rebound), but they do not look for the reasons for the relationships they have discovered.*[42]

Not until the thinking of students becomes formal will they see how the two angles are reciprocally implicated. To do this they must organize the data, do mental experiments with them, and develop a hypothesis and put it in shape for testing—a truly formal-operational task.

[39] Bärbel Inhelder and Jean Piaget, *The Growth of Logical Thinking* (New York: Basic Books, 1958), pp. 3–19.
[40] *Ibid.*, p. 3.
[41] *Ibid.*, p. 4.
[42] *Ibid.*, p. 8.

A third test for formal-operational thinking, which uses only readily accessible materials, is one that requires the learner to do something, watch the results, isolate the factors (or variables) that can be changed, and *exclude* those that do not influence the results. This task is called the *operation of exclusion*. The apparatus used is a series of weights of different sizes that can be suspended from a solid support by different lengths of string and allowed to swing back and forth—in other words, a pendulum. (See Figure 4–20.) The stu-

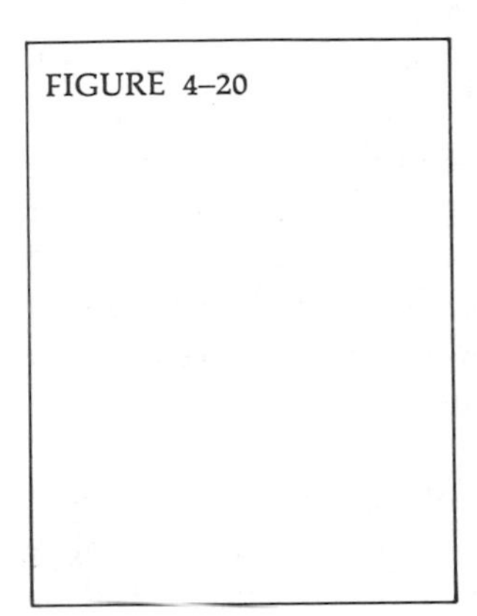

FIGURE 4–20

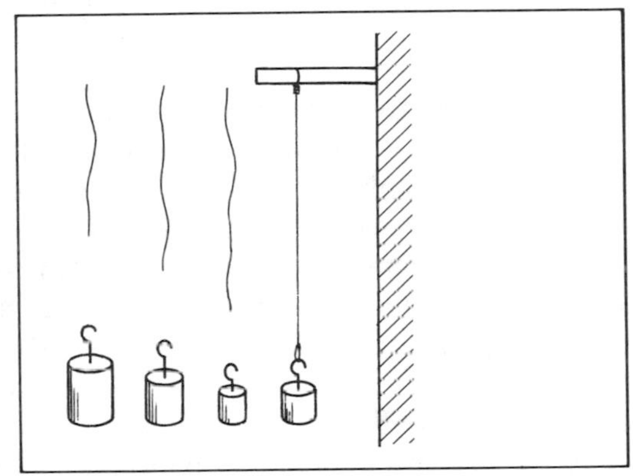

dent is shown all the materials and asked to make a pendulum. After he has it operating, he is asked what controls how fast the pendulum swings. He is told that he can use any of the weights and string lengths to assist him in solving the problem. As the student inspects the apparatus, he will see that he has a range of variables to play

FIGURE 4–21
In the exclusion task the student must separate the irrelevant factors and discard them from his thinking.

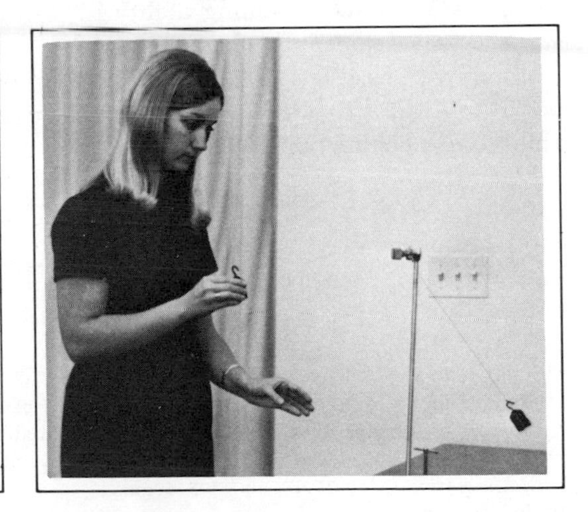

with. These include the length of the string, the size of the weight, the height from which the weight is released (amplitude), and the force of the push he gives the weight.

The variable that controls the rate with which the pendulum completes its swing is the length of the string; none of the others has any effect. The student must formulate a hypothesis that will lead him to exclude all factors from his thinking except the length of the pendulum's cord.

A preoperational thinker, according to Piaget and Inhelder,[43] will attribute all variations in the motion of the pendulum to the strength of the push. The concrete-operational thinker will find the inverse relationship between the length of the string and the oscillation of the pendulum, that is, he will realize that the longer the string the slower its motion, and the shorter the string the more rapid its motion.[44] He will not, however, attribute the motion of the pendulum to length only, but will give rather casual roles to the size of the weight and the amplitude. Only a formal-operational thinker isolates the length as the significant factor.

All experiments described thus far for isolating formal-operational thinking require that the teacher work with the students individually. Such procedures, although they are valuable, require a great deal of time. If a teacher is using the students' performance on these tasks as a guide in deciding the curricula, he probably does not have the time to administer one or two tasks to each student in all his classes. Recently, Elizabeth and Robert Karplus[45] designed and tested a pencil-and-paper procedure that can be used to gain some insight into patterns of logical thinking. Called "The Islands Puzzle," it is designed to "assess abstract reasoning ability."[46] Since the formal-operational stage of development is characterized by the ability to think in the realm of the possible as well as in the realm of reality, this paper-and-pencil tool can provide you with a quick overview of your students' ability with abstractions. A description of the puzzle follows:

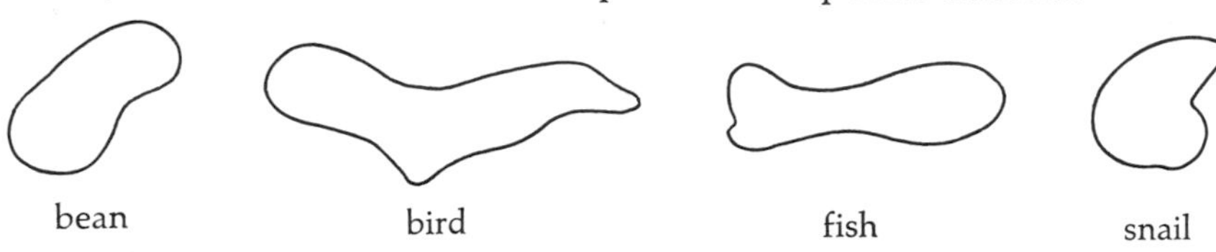

[43] *Ibid.*, p. 69.

[44] Because of the relationship between the length of the string and the length of the weight, strings shorter than 18 inches probably should not be used.

[45] "Intellectual Development Beyond Elementary School," *School Science and Mathematics* (May 1970), pp. 398–406.

[46] *Ibid.*, p. 398.

Introduction: *The puzzle is about four islands in the ocean. People have been traveling among these islands by boat for many years, but recently an airline started in business. Listen carefully to the clues I give you about possible plane trips. The trips may be direct or they may include stops on one of the islands. When I say a trip is possible, it can be made in both directions between the islands.*

This is a map with the four islands, called Bean Island, Bird Island, Fish Island, and Snail Island. You may make notes or marks on your map to help you remember the clues. Raise your hand if you have questions about the clues.

First clue: *People can go by plane between Bean and Fish Islands.*

Second clue: *People cannot go by plane between Bird and Snail Islands. Use these two clues to answer question 1.*

Question 1: *Can people go by plane between Bird and Snail Islands?*

Yes____ No____ Can't tell from the two clues.____

Explain your answer.

Third clue: *People can go by plane between Bean and Bird Islands. Use all three clues to answer questions 2 and 3. Don't change your answer to question 1.*

Question 2: *Can people go by plane between Fish and Bird Islands?*

Yes____ No____ Can't tell from the three clues.____

Explain your answer.

Question 3: *Can people go by plane between Fish and Snail Islands?*

Yes____ No____ Can't tell from the three clues.____

Explain your answer.[47]

Karplus and Peterson have designed a puzzle dealing with the ratio concept, which they describe as "an essential component of what Piaget has termed formal operational thought":[48]

Oral Introduction: *This problem is about Mr. Short, who is just like the man on your papers, and Mr. Tall (E. [the experimenter] displays the two figures on the two sides of the display chart). I will measure how high the figures are with my chain of big paper clips—we'll call them "biggies" (E. displays his chain of eight jumbo clips) and write down the results (E. writes "Mr. Short": and Mr. Tall": on the board). First we'll do Mr. Short—how high is he? (E. hangs paper clip chain from a pin at the top of Mr. Short's head. Class members count and chorus "four." E. writes "4 biggies" on the board.) Have*

47 *Ibid.*

48 Robert Karplus and Rita W. Peterson, "Intellectual Development Beyond Elementary School II: Ratio, A Survey," *School Science and Mathematics* (December 1970), pp. 813–820. Reproduced by permission of the editor of *School Science and Mathematics.*

all of you seen it? . . . Now we'll turn to Mr. Tall. (E. turns over chart to show Mr. Tall.) How high is he from the head to the ground? (E. hangs paper clip chain from a pin at the top of Mr. Tall's head. Class members count and chorus "six." E. writes "6 biggies" on the board.) Have all of you seen it? (E. puts down the chart, and it is not used again. The jumbo paper clips are also put away.)

Now you do three things. First you measure Mr. Short on your papers, using your small paper clips—call them "smallies." Then you predict the height of Mr. Tall in smallies, and finally you explain how you made your prediction. Explain as best you can what made you predict the number of smallies you chose.

Question and Answer Page:

How tall is this figure, measured with small paper clips?
Predict the height of the large figure, as measured with paper clips.
Explain how you figured out your prediction.[49]

Both the puzzles described require the learner to work with possibilities, which is a true mark of formal operations. Suppose, for example, that the statement "People cannot go by plane between Bird and Snail Islands" leads a student to conclude that traveling between those islands by plane is never possible, regardless of the plane routes designed, and that that assumption governs all his decisions. The student is dealing with a possibility. If he changes his assumption on the basis of new data fed to him, and makes known how his assumptions have changed, he is dealing with another possibility. The learner's explanations are a clue to his formal-operational ability. At the present time data are not available to forecast the

[49] *Ibid.*

explanations that known preoperational and concrete-operational learners would use. Although Piaget did not design these tasks, we feel you will find them useful in determining the degree of formal-operational ability that exists in a class.

What has been said above about identifying the formal-operational learner is only a beginning. There are other tasks that can be used, but they require materials that are less readily available. There are also many points in the interpretation of data from formal-operational tasks that should be considered in deciding exactly where on the formal-operational spectrum a student is.[50] However, the tasks presented here, because they can be administered quickly and the results can be interpreted easily, are a convenient guide for the classroom teacher in selecting content and teaching and learning materials.

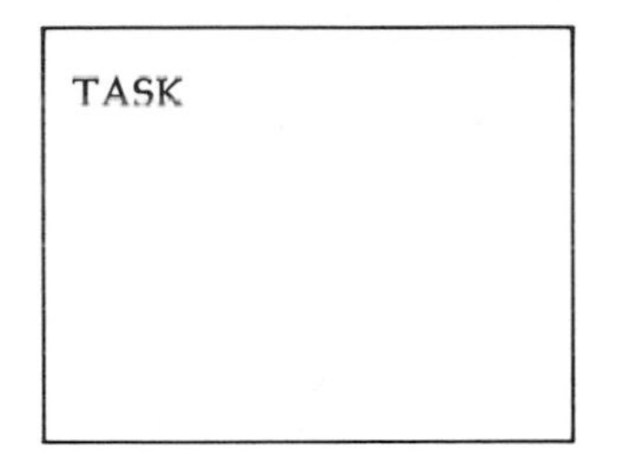

In Chapter 3 we described a model of the roles of the teacher and learner in an inquiry-centered classroom. Which of those roles can be fulfilled by learners in each of the four stages of intellectual development described in Chapter 4?

We now have two criteria—rational-powers and development and Piaget's intellectual-development model—with which to judge content suitable for inclusion in the school curricula, and you should not hesitate to apply these criteria clinically and with absolute honesty to the disciplines that will be discussed next.

[50] For a more detailed account of the formal-operational stage, see the first six chapters of Piaget and Inhelder's *The Growth of Logical Thinking*, described earlier.

Achieving Educational Purpose

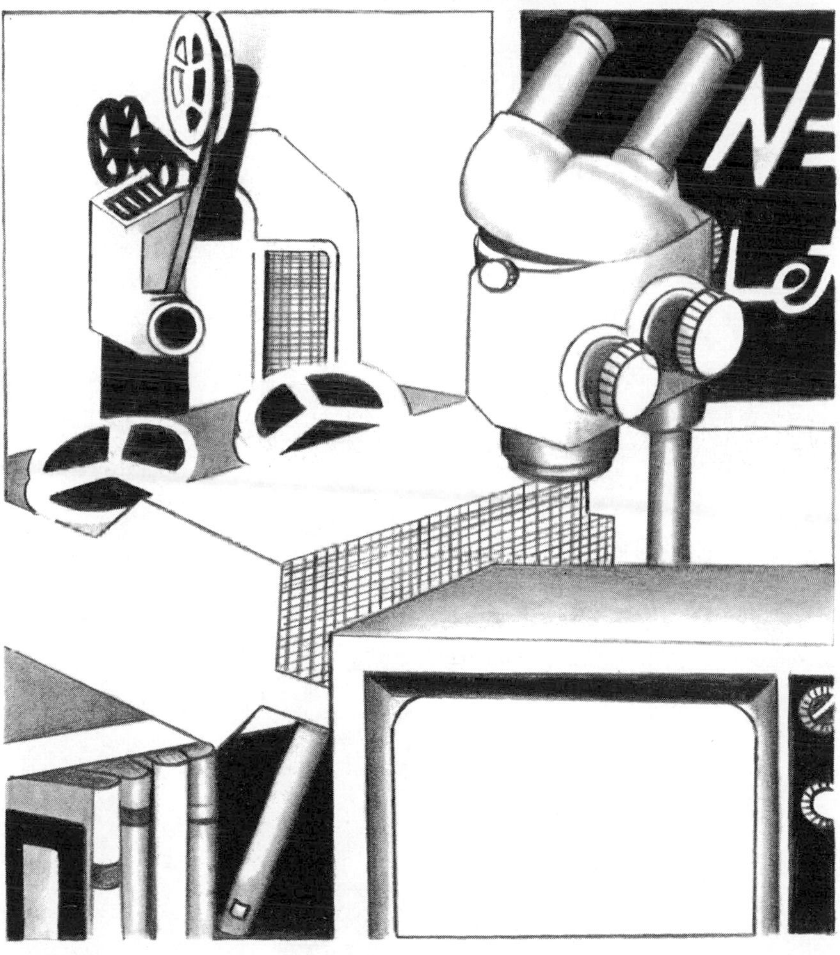

5 Using Content

An elementary school child, asked what he studies in school, may say reading, science, art, mathematics, or spelling. A secondary school student, asked the same question, may say English, government, history, French, biology, or geometry, and college students may answer architecture, political science, business administration, or music. Educational institutions at all levels use some type of content to lead learners to achieve their established purposes; in fact, content is the principal vehicle used. The most suitable type of content for a school is, of course, that which allows and encourages learners to develop their rational powers. There are, however, factors other than established educational purpose which influence the content that schools select to teach. One of those factors—the intellectual-development levels of the learner—was discussed in Chapter 4. What types of content can and should be used with pre-, concrete-, and formal-operational learners? The second factor that must be considered in content selection is the various disciplines. Mathematics, chemistry, language arts, government, and other organized bodies of knowledge are recognized as part of the cultural and intellectual heritage of man, and society expects the schools to be concerned with these disciplines. These expectations place both restrictions and responsibilities upon educators and prompt several questions:

1. What can the several disciplines contribute to the development of the learner's rational powers?
2. What facts, principles, generalizations, and other products within each discipline can and should be used to lead learners to develop their rational powers and, simultaneously, to develop an understanding of the structure of the discipline?
3. What products of a particular discipline can be used with a given age group which that age group will view as relevant and important?

Critics of modern education would answer these questions by saying that each teacher should present each child to as much content as possible and that the next teacher should pick up where the last one finished. This statement is based on *the assumption that exposure to the content of a discipline will cause the learner to develop his ability to think* and will automatically convince him of its importance. The educated person, say these critics, is one who through his years of schooling has accumulated a good deal of knowledge about many things. Phenix evaluates this view of education as follows:

The old conception of the school as a place for accumulating knowledge to be used over a lifetime is no longer appropriate, for much of the knowledge that will be needed in the future is not yet discovered at the time the student is in school, and much of what he may acquire there will soon be obsolete.[1]

If schools concentrate on teaching content that already is or soon will be obsolete, the entire educational process becomes an exercise in futility. In each discipline materials must be selected that are affected only minimally by creeping obsolescence and hence will not be irrelevant when the student matures. One way of doing this, according to Phenix, is by "teaching methods of inquiry."[2] The methods of inquiry in any discipline cannot be employed without making comparisons, analyses, evaluations, syntheses, generalizations, and, in general, employing the rational powers. Inquiry is the methodology needed for rational-power development; inquiring within the various disciplines can give the learner experience with the facts, principles, generalizations, attitudes, problems, communication patterns, software, and even jokes of each discipline.

Before starting his students on an inquiry within a discipline, the teacher must decide what types of experiences they should be given. Bruner states his position this way: "At the very first breath, the young learner should . . . be given the chance to solve problems, to conjecture, to quarrel, as these are done at the heart of the discipline."[3] Mathematics should be proper mathematics, science should be recognizable as science by a scientist, and every other discipline studied in the schools should provide experiences having the same structure found at the heart of the discipline. *What, then, are the basic characteristics of the major disciplines that can be used as guide-*

[1] Phillip Phenix, *Realms of Meaning* (New York: McGraw-Hill, 1964), p. 334.

[2] *Ibid.*, p. 335.

[3] Jerome S. Bruner, *Toward a Theory of Instruction* (Cambridge, Mass.: Harvard University Press, 1966), p. 155.

lines to prepare curricula to lead a learner to develop an understanding of the methods of inquiry of those disciplines and their basic structures? The discussions that follow are based on a broad definition of each discipline. Instead of, for example, discussing English and foreign languages, we shall discuss language; instead of biology or physics, we shall discuss science.

Language

Of all the needs a human being has, one of the deepest is the need to be understood and accepted by others. In order, to understand, be understood by, and be accepted by others, however, an individual must be able to communicate with them. The drive to communicate is probably the greatest motivation the human organism has for learning a language. Obviously, then, languages should be taught in such a way that learning them fulfills this basic human need, a need that the learner feels *now* and not one that his teachers believe he will feel at some future time.

The objective of language itself is communication, but the goal of studying a language is understanding its meaning. The study of ordinary speech patterns will allow communication, but without studying the morphemes (elemental meaning units called words) and syntax one cannot understand language. How are the morphemes and the syntax of a language established? Languages are established for three basic reasons:

1. to communicate meanings within and about a real world,
2. to share life within a social world, and
3. to express individual needs and emotions.

The world we communicate about is a real one. It exists; it has been given to us and has not been simply invented. Symbols and other methods of communicating must be invented by the members of a community to express the realities of the world. When, for example, the word *thunder* is used in an English-speaking country, it describes an event in the real world. In a non-English–speaking country, the morpheme would be different, but the phenomenon would be the same. Particular words are an invention of man; some person or group of persons at some time agrees to call a particular atmospheric disturbance "thunder." Exactly when that agreement was reached is unknown, but in all probability it was reached in an evolutionary way. While an event may be natural and not the product of man's imagination, the way it is described is man made; and the sounds of that description vary from language to language.

The social world contains fewer absolutes than the real world of natural phenomena. The mores of social groups and professions may differ vastly from country to country. To be able to communicate within a social environment requires a thorough understanding of that environment. What is being communicated about in a social situation is an invention of man, just as the language used to communicate about it is man made. Furthermore, language often has a particular meaning only in the context of the moment. For example, a fifth-grade child was heard to use the word "smunched." The adult talking with him also used the word in their conversation, and each understood the other perfectly. A second adult later inquired what "smunched" meant and how it related to the conversation. Musicians' slang is another example of how language can mean something to a particular social group but have little or no meaning in a different setting. *The social use of language can be thought of as describing an invented situation with an invented system.* Our individual needs and emotions are not based entirely on an invented situation, as is a social setting, but we still use an invented system to make those needs and emotions known to others.

As the foregoing examples show, basically language is a man-made construction which acquires meaning only through use. The principal method of acquiring knowledge of a language, then, must be through studying its use in the everyday life of the community. Furthermore, an individual will acquire skill in using the language only if he participates in its use in the community. After extensive observation of and participation in the language the learner is ready to begin to develop an understanding about the meaning of the language. To facilitate comprehension analyses can be made of patterns of language usage. Such analyses will reveal the most frequently repeated patterns, and those patterns can be used as a guide for the learner.

In making these analyses of language patterns, technical terms are often introduced to describe certain basic characteristics of the language. The traditional manner of approaching the study of English grammar was to force it into a Latin-grammar mold. Thus, we emerged with classes of words such as nouns, verbs, prepositions, adjectives, adverbs, and conjunctions. That mold cast a word in a certain role that could be changed only by altering the word's basic function or daring to use it unconventionally. But casting a word in a definite role neglects this basic fact about language: "In many cases the meaning of the word can be better understood by reference to the context in which it is used than by consulting a dictionary."[4] To say "He and I share an office" has the same general meaning as "He and I office together," but the word office takes on a meaning in each case that reflects its context. The structure of a language consists not only of the various morphemes the culture has invented but the syntax for using those morphemes. Furthermore, the structure of language varies from culture to culture and from one social group to another. One cannot, therefore, "learn a new language properly by redeploying the sounds of another language. Each language must be studied on its own terms as an integral, self-contained structure."[5]

Teaching language as a structure that is *not* dependent on some external governing force like Latin grammar requires that the learner be led first to analyze his own language. That this analysis will require the repeated use of the rational powers is immediately obvious. Secondly, the participant in language analysis must undertake this study at a level commensurate with his level of intellectual development. Using the goal of rational-power development and the students' intellectual level as criteria, a teacher can construct an approach to learning that will truly aid intellectual maturation.

But what about nouns, adverbs, and other facets of traditional language teaching? When teachers force language into the traditional Latin-grammar mold and then teach it that way, they really believe their mission is "to protect the English Language from decay."[6] Traditional English teachers are not alone in their adherence to the Latin mold. A large percentage of the population believes that grammar should be learned in the traditional way. If you probe for reasons behind such beliefs, you will usually be told, "That's the way I studied it," "The culture accepts it," or "It's a tried-and-true method." There is little need to point out that none of these statements constitutes a good reason for retaining the present approach to language instruction. Those who hold such attitudes forget that language is a man-made medium and that what has been constructed by man can be reconstructed by him. Furthermore, teaching a language through a rigidly controlled grammatical system overlooks the fact that the primary objective of a language is communication within a social system; when the communication needs of the social system change, the language structure must change also. Thus, words such as *thou, thy, thence,* and *methinks* are no longer commonly used.

[4] Phenix, *op. cit.*, p. 68.

[5] *Ibid.*, p. 65.

[6] Maya Pines, "Readin' and Writin': Imperfect Past, Indefinite Future," *Think* (March–April 1969), pp. 21–25.

Teaching a language demands that, first, its communication patterns be studied, and then that the data derived from those patterns be used to analyze the structure of language itself. Within the past few years the teaching of language has begun to shift to this pattern. Dialogues between people are analyzed, and the *placement and context* of words in those dialogues are used to analyze the language. Persons such as Charles Fries, Paul Roberts, Noam Chomsky, and Neil Postman, and groups such as the Euclid (Cleveland) Junior Demonstration Center and the University of Nebraska English Education Project have made great progress in providing evaluative frameworks to determine whether a particular linguistic idea should be placed in the curriculum. These criteria, coupled with the concepts of developmental levels and rational powers provide a framework that allows language teachers to make meaningful decisions about the language curriculum.

Literature

All the higher mental processes involve more than the simple awareness of the facts; they depend also on the ability to conceive what might be as well as what is, to construct mental images in new and original ways. Experiences in literature and the arts may well make a larger contribution to these abilities than studies usually assumed to develop abstract thinking.[7]

This quotation clearly shows the relationship of the study of literature to the development of rational powers. Literature, if it does anything at all for an individual, leads him to construct mental images. Phrases such as "a cold, grey, rainy day," "white, fluffy, rolling clouds," "the dank, musty, sour aroma of a back alley," "spilled beer, crumpled napkins, and ashtrays filled to overflowing," and "golden ringlets encircling her angelic face" produce in all of us certain mental images. The exact images depend on what experiences the hearer has had with the phrase. In other words, recall, comparisons, analyses, evaluations, classifications, syntheses, and finally generalizations must occur before mental images can be produced; or, as Piaget has stated, intellectual development depends on (among other things) the social experience of the learner. *If literature were used for no other reason than the development of mental imagery, its place in the curriculum would be assured.* There is, however, another cardinal reason for the

[7] Educational Policies Commission, *The Central Purpose of American Education* (Washington, D.C.: National Education Association, 1961), p. 18.

presence of literature in the curriculum; imagination is a rational power: "A central concept in the art of literature (as, indeed, in every art) is imagination."[8]

Before exploring the importance of literature as a stimulator of imagination, we should point out that imagination does not necessarily imply using words to produce mental images. When language is used to produce mental images, the writer is relying upon the past experiences of the learner to help him. Even a concrete-operational learner can develop mental images if experience with objects is used as a basis for the images, and such experiences contribute to rational-power development. The need of concrete-operational learners to have concrete experiences before mental operations can be performed explains why in children's stories animals take on human characteristics, flowers talk, and little engines say "I can." Literature is of great value in developing the rational powers, but the material selected must be at the operational level of the learner.

Literature does, however, stimulate the imagination, leading a person to "create new forms of experience"[9] that have no connection with everyday reality. The imagination leads beyond what is, toward what is possible. What adult has not mentally rewritten a novel to accommodate a favorite character?

Piaget describes the formal-operational person as one who "thinks beyond the present and forms theories about everything, delighting especially in consideration of that which is not."[10] This is very close to the description given above of literature as creating new forms of experience. Using literature to achieve the development of imagination is essentially a task that should be left to the later elementary grades *at the earliest.* Fairy tales sometimes frighten young children because they cannot begin to operate on the formal-operational level and hence cannot distinguish the possible from the real.

In judging a piece of literature as to its suitability for rational-power development, a distinction must be made between mental images and imagination. Both can occur as a result of language, but neither outcome is necessarily assured. Before a piece of literature can stimulate a reader to use his imagination or produce mental images, it must be interpreted *and the reader himself must make the interpretation.* Children should learn to make their own interpretation of literature, for the simple reason that when they encounter

[8] Phenix, *op. cit.,* p. 177.

[9] *Ibid.*

[10] Jean Piaget, *The Psychology of Intelligence* (Paterson, N.J.: Littlefield, Adams, 1963), p. 148.

literature, or even ordinary prose, after leaving school, no one will be available to hand down interpretations. Is there a place in the study of literature for the interpretations of "authorities"? Whether the answer is negative or positive depends on the objective you hope to lead learners to achieve through the study of literature.

How is the literature used in schools selected? Most material is chosen because it is prescribed by the schools, recommended by experts, preferred by the individual teacher, or simply available. These criteria have some validity, but a teacher should be careful in using material recommended by experts. Often an expert's opinion is valid, but not for the type of student with whom you are working. The same objection can be raised for literature prescribed by the school. Since not all learners are alike, the material suitable for some students may not be suitable for others. As a professional, the teacher should have the freedom to select those materials that best meet the academic needs of his class.

Two other criteria that are sometimes used in selecting material to be used in the schools are *relevance* and *representativeness.* Any teacher of literature (or for that matter, of any subject) must select "from the rich resources of authentic knowledge that comparatively small portion that will best serve his students."[11] Literature cannot be used to develop the rational powers or stimulate the imagination if the person reading it does not regard it as relevant. What constitutes relevant literature? You, as a teacher, are the only one who can answer that question, for what is relevant in an urban area may be absolutely irrelevant in a rural area. As a professional, the teacher must assess the environment of the school and the community, the abilities and interests of the learners, and the educational goals being pursued before making a judgment. He can and should seek advice and guidance in making that decision, but no one can shoulder the consequences of the decision in the classroom except the teacher; no one but the teacher, therefore, should make the final decision about relevant content.

The criterion of representativeness, especially as it applies to educational purposes, has wide implications not only for literature but for the other disciplines as well. There are certain ideas that represent better than others the character of a discipline. If, for example, fairy tales are to be used in the study of literature, *Cinderella* is certainly representative. The study of English literature would certainly be incomplete without an introduction to Shakespeare. Throughout litera-

[11] Phenix, *op. cit.*, p. 322.

ture there are certain forms that represent the discipline. To exclude the study of some forms, such as poetry, from the curriculum is to present students with a distorted view of the field of literature. The same is true in other fields. To neglect sculpture would be to give a distorted view of the field of art; to neglect popular music would be to give a distorted view of the field of music as a whole. Literature has great potential as a vehicle for achieving educational purpose. The operational level of the learner and the manner in which the content is employed and selected, however, are all factors that affect the usefulness of literature at any educational level.

Music and Art

E. H. Gombrich once said that there is no such thing as art; there are only artists.[12] Unlike science, in which broad generalizations are possible, art, and probably all forms of esthetic expression, are highly individualistic. Since esthetic expression is individualistic, so is esthetic understanding. It results only from direct perception. An explanation by someone else of the *New World Symphony* or the *Mona Lisa* cannot convey to an observer what Dvořák or Leonardo are saying. The need for direct perception in music and art immediately establishes the basic requirement for teaching those areas; that requirement is *involvement.*

In art involvement means direct interaction with the materials of the field. In the visual arts these materials may be paint, clay, water color, or any other medium the artist uses. Manipulating the materials with which an artist works gives the learner an opportunity to develop an understanding of the problems, the potential, and the limitations of those materials. Regardless of the field, a newcomer does not begin to develop even a basic understanding of it until he understands its materials. In art that understanding is perhaps more basic than in some other fields because the materials tell the story.

A parallel statement can be made about music. While physical manipulation of the materials of music is not always possible, aural interaction is. Aural interaction constitutes the involvement a learner must have with the subject matter of music.

In teaching music or the visual arts, the learner must be actively involved. Duckworth paints a picture of the kind of involvement that is necessary:

[12] E. H. Gombrich, *The Story of Art* (New York: Phaidon Publishers, 1958), pp. 5, 446.

The child must live with music, not trivia, before he can be expected to form concepts. Only through many concrete experiences of "playing with" music that he hears, improvises, and reads, will a child have a basis for his abstract thinking and be able to transfer his learning.[13]

Duckworth is an enthusiastic advocate of the principle of active involvement, which in the performance side of art and music is easy to see. A student who plays the clarinet in the school band, creates clay figures, or does a watercolor is learning a skill. But the vast majority of students enrolled in music and art classes will never become performers or earn their living by their artistry. There will be many learners, however, who will participate in some forms of music and art as an avocation and this fact puts a particular responsibility on teachers in those fields. Phenix explains that responsibility in regard to music in this way:

A person's musical understanding is unnecessarily impoverished if he limits himself to certain traditional, conventional, and habitual musical patterns as being the only ones he considers authentic or admirable.[14]

Clearly, then, to serve the avocational needs of today's youth and not leave them musically impoverished, the music curriculum of the school must, at some level, include all types of musical experiences. If, in fact, various types of musical experience are not included at various levels, the curriculum stands an excellent chance of being considered irrelevant by the learner. Elementary school children are such eager participators that they rarely make judgments about the appropriateness of a musical experience; they simply perceive and participate. The teacher, therefore, has a tremendous responsibility to select music that is appropriate to their intellectual level. Left entirely to their own devices, junior high school students would probably exist upon a diet of popular music alone. Students in this age group, therefore, must be encouraged to experience greater variety in order to avoid the irrelevance syndrome. The evidence suggests that this age group is not yet ready to operate on the complex level of imagination required to interpret classical music. Most popular music does not require the use of intricate mental imagery or imagination; it deals with the here and now. Then too, the attraction of

[13] Guy Duckworth, "What Are We Teaching—Concepts or Details?" *Clavier* (June 1964), pp. 45–50.
[14] Phenix, *op. cit.*, p. 150.

the junior high school student to popular music is closely associated with strong peer group ties, which are explained perhaps by the fact that this age group is in transition from the late concrete- to the early formal-operational stage and overt, concrete experiences are still a necessity. While senior high school students are also interested in popular music, they are beginning to think abstractly enough to appreciate music that challenges the intellect. Hence, they might view a steady diet of popular music as partially irrelevant. Since music, as taught in the schools, is not designed to produce performers, it has little place in the educational system if its relevance is not considered.

Some persons take the position that children at all levels should be taught music and art because they are part of our cultural heritage. No doubt they are, but so are dressmaking, baking, and automobile mechanics. These subjects are not included in the curriculum because they are irrelevant to all or a significant portion of today's precollegiate students. Just because a subject has always been taught is not necessarily a good reason for teaching it in today's schools.

What then are the criteria that teachers can use to select the curricula for courses in music and art? Two—relevance and appropriateness to a given developmental level—have already been discussed. But there are two additional criteria that can prove useful in leading learners to achieve the purpose of education. The study of music and art must have potential to develop the learners' rational powers. This will be accomplished, however, only if the learner is allowed to interpret for himself the sounds of the music and the various forms of visual art. Learning how someone else hears a sound or views a painting is important only if these interpretations are treated as data. Simply accepting, or imitating, the views of experts will not help the learner to develop ideas of his own; he is simply accommodating his ideas to some predetermined frame of reference. On the other hand, playing with ideas allows the learner to assimilate them.[15] There is far more intellectual growth in assimilation than there is in accommodation; accommodation does not *demand* the use of comparison, evaluation, analysis, imagery, and many of the other rational powers, but assimilation does. Leading learners to interpret works of art and music is a tremendously important responsibility of the teacher. Earlier in this chapter we discussed the use of literature to encourage the use and development of mental imagery and imagination. Art

[15] John L. Phillips, Jr., *The Origins of Intellect: Piaget's Theory* (San Francisco: Freeman, 1969), p. 9.

and music have just as much potential for developing these intellectual characteristics as literature. The teacher, however, must always be willing to allow and encourage individual interpretations of material to be made in order to foster this development.

The subject matter selected for art and music at the various grade levels must accurately represent the discipline; it must be good art or good music, and the content selected must be representative and appropriate to the particular level being taught. Art and music are indeed part of the cultural heritage of the world, but in order for them to make a maximum contribution to education, they must be employed from an educational-purpose frame of reference.

Social Science

The word *social* can be defined as relating to the interactions of an individual and a group. Since these interactions can be subjected to analysis, synthesis, and generalization, inquiring into them is properly called *social science.* The interactions which an individual has with groups are generally political, economic, religious, educational, or "just for fun." The interactions an individual has with himself as a result of other types of social interaction are psychological. Psychology is not rooted in the social sciences alone; its causes and effects overlap the biological sciences. History has as its focal point the chronological study of social interactions, but the study of chronology, events, and people does not constitute a proper treatment of history. To be complete, a historical study must examine the causes of certain social interactions. Sociology is concerned with the objective interpretation of social interactions to determine their causes, isolate their effects, and predict future interactions. Political science is the study of interactions within and among groups organized specifically for the governance of others. Economics concentrates on the impact of social interactions, on the ability of a culture to financially sustain and improve itself. Of all the social sciences, anthropology is probably the most comprehensive, including as it does the study of all aspects of man's socially constructed world—language, religion, mores, laws, tools, and manners.

In discussing the discipline of social science as an area of inquiry for the schools, there are several points that must be considered. The social sciences are concerned with the man-made world rather than with the physical and biological worlds that are the concern of the natural sciences. However, the social interactions that occur in the man-made world can have a profound effect on the physical and biological worlds. Air and water pollution, for example, are problems for whose ultimate solution we look to the natural sciences, yet they are the direct result of social interactions in the man-made world.

Since the social sciences are concerned with the results of human interactions, they can be truly understood only through participation in such interactions, both in the classroom and outside. To study the functions of government from a textbook without observing those functions firsthand or interacting with those performing the functions is to deny to the learners experience with human interaction, which is the foundation of social science. Furthermore, to develop the learner's rational powers, data must be compared, classified, and analyzed; explanations of phenomena must be synthesized; and generalizations must be developed in the classroom. The social sciences are an excellent vehicle for rational-power development if they are approached from a problem-solving point of view and not as static bodies of information to be mastered. For a child to know that there are two major parties in his country's political structure is far less important than for him to analyze the events that led to the establishment of those parties. Knowing that a group of settlers called Pilgrims landed in North America in 1620 is not nearly as educational as analyzing why those people undertook the journey to a distant and unknown world. In gathering information about these and other historical events, many resources must be used. Historical records and textbooks are primary sources, but the historical novel is also a potential source of data. Gathering information from all kinds of human sources is important in studying the social sciences, and the laboratory of that discipline is the social, man-made world. *The information gathered, however, must be used to assist the learner in understanding a social issue and not as proof of a fact already presented.* Nor should information from the social world be presented simply to be remembered. How important is it today to know who was the twenty-ninth President of the United States or the sixth Chief Justice of the Supreme Court? If the word *science* in the term *social science* is properly used, information must be analyzed and used and not just remembered.

The concept of intellectual levels is vitally important in selecting representative ideas for use in teaching the social sciences. Such concepts as political parties and the monetary system are abstractions and fit only a few levels in the educational system. Elementary school children are primarily concrete-operational and, therefore, must have actual concrete experiences as a basis for learning. Hence, the representative ideas selected from the social sciences for that level should be those which the learners can experience directly. Every class is itself a social group. If students are led to perceive and understand interactions in the classroom, the home, and the school, they will have a basis for understanding interactions in the community, the state, and the nation. If that sequence is carefully considered, the primary divisions of the social sciences can be fitted into it, and if the learner is considered and an inquiry framework is employed, rational-power development will result. Furthermore, the learners will view experiences with the social sciences as relevant instead of as unrelated to their needs, as sometimes happens today.

The Vocational Arts

Throughout the educational history of this country, the responsibility of the schools to prepare students to function in a free society has been emphasized. In 1960 John Gardner, then president of the Carnegie Corporation of New York and Carnegie Foundation for the Advancement of Teaching, stated that responsibility this way: "Our schools must prepare *all* young people, whatever their talents, for the serious business of being free men and women."[16] Freedom to do what one wishes, to go where one likes, and to associate with whom one chooses are all part of being a free person. An extremely important ingredient of freedom, however, is freedom from want, and that freedom demands that a person be able to contribute to his own support. There are some people today who say that "society" should support them. Society, however, is the people, and in order for it to maintain itself, all its members must accept the need for self-support. There are, of course, some obvious exceptions: the very young, the infirm, and the old must be supported by society since they cannot sustain themselves. But for the majority of this country's citizens complete freedom is impossible and a myth without a parallel acceptance of the responsibility of self-support. For some, the period of self-support does not begin until after college. For many others, however, it begins immediately on graduation from high school. The design and implementation of programs for the latter group are our concern in this section.

The government of the United States has long been concerned with educational programs designed to help young persons become self-supporting. The Morrill Act of 1862 provided land to establish colleges to "teach such branches of learning as are related to agriculture and

[16] John W. Gardner, "National Goals in Education," *Goals For Americans* (New York: Columbia University, 1960), p. 100.

the mechanic arts."[17] The Hatch Act of 1887 provided $15,000 annually to each state and territory having an agricultural college. This act led to the establishment of agricultural colleges and experiment stations. Perhaps the best-known legislation for vocational education is the Smith-Hughes Act, which President Woodrow Wilson signed in 1917 which supplied funds for secondary schools to use in teaching "agriculture, home economics and trade and industrial subjects."[18] Distributive education, vocational guidance, and rehabilitation are all areas for which special funds have been provided. The vocational-education picture was described by the President's Advisory Committee on Education in 1938 as follows:

The Committee believes strongly that there are few educational problems now before the American people to which they should give more earnest thought than the need for sound and adequate programs of vocational education.[19]

The picture today is similar. The public understanding of the vocational arts is primarily at the level of teaching a student a specific job or skill that will enable him to secure employment. There is no doubt that much of the support for the vocational arts is based on the fact that the public believes them to be job training, with a heavy emphasis on the development of specific skills. Training a student for a specific job (office management, for example) or in a specific skill (such as typing) is an important goal of the vocational arts, but it is not the only goal.

The vocational arts are part of the curricula and hence should contribute in some way to the central responsibility of the schools, which is to lead students to develop their rational powers. That responsibility provides an operational definition of how the various vocational areas must be taught in the schools. If the students are to develop their rational powers, they must be given an opportunity to use them. In vocational subjects, as in the social sciences, that opportunity can best be provided by a problem-solving approach. In automobile mechanics, for example, rather than have the students inspect and memorize the parts of an engine, the teacher can give them problems that are representative of the types of difficulties en-

[17] Chris A. DeYoung, *Introduction to American Public Education* (New York: McGraw-Hill, 1942), p. 15.

[18] *Ibid.*, p. 16.

[19] Floyd W. Reeves, "The Federal Government and the Secondary School," *Bulletin*, Department of Secondary School Principals (Washington, D.C.: National Education Association, March 1938), pp. 29–30.

countered in the defective engines. Focusing the students on a particular problem gives them a goal to achieve. Obviously, they will have to learn the various parts of an engine and understand their functions before a particular difficulty can be diagnosed and corrected, but learning about a particular part of an engine is not an end in itself. In the foods and cooking phase of home economics, how much time is spent in learning to cook and how much is spent in learning to follow a recipe? Do you know what happens if soda or baking powder is left out of a cake? What function does yeast really serve? What would happen if you left the yeast out of bread? In learning how to cook (or to become proficient *in any vocation*), the functions of the ingredients (or elements of that vocation) must be understood. Every vocational arts teacher must be willing to let cakes fall, motors miss, radios not operate, and cards be punched incorrectly so that the students will understand both what they can and what they cannot do with the materials. Understanding the various materials of a vocation and how they function will lead the students to understand the structure of that vocation. They will not understand that structure, however, unless they can study both the positive and negative effects of the materials. Then, too, students entering the vocational arts in the secondary school are about to enter the formal-operational stage. Presenting them with representative problems from the discipline not only develops their rational powers but also directs them toward the acquisition of formal-operational ability. In addition, it gives them a greater degree of flexibility in their thinking about the vocation. In any vocational area the nature of a particular job may change. If the occupant of that job is not flexible in his thinking about his vocation, he cannot change when he finds himself unemployed; he has been trained only for a single job. Furthermore, since he no longer has job mobility, he is not truly a free citizen. If vocational education concentrates on specific job training or on covering specific material in a field, it is training its students for future unemployment. This is not only the antithesis of developing the ability to think but is also contrary to the notion that education sets men free. The most difficult task of the vocational arts teacher is planning the course so that the problems dealt with are representative of the field, the experiences of the learners match the intellectual level, and a functional understanding of the vocational art is developed.

Every vocational art has certain skills. In such areas as secretarial work, for example, the skills needed are obvious and should be taught first. A student cannot solve typing problems until he can at least operate the machine, however minimally. Students should be made aware that the acquisition of a minimum level of skill is necessary before anything else can take place. However, the teacher must conscientiously define the level of skill needed before the learning experience can be broadened to lead the learner to think in that vocation.

Mathematics

Before a child can learn anything about mathematics, he must conserve number. Only when he has developed this ability can he function in any type of mathematical system. The ability to conserve number carries with it the potential to serially order objects on some previously determined basis. When a child can serially order objects, counting takes on real meaning. Very young children can be "taught" to count, but whether they understand what they are doing is questionable.

Mathematics is often defined as a language, and that definition is partially correct. Languages, however, are designed and used by man principally for the purpose of communication. Mathematics, too, has a practical side, as we can see by walking into any of the marketplaces of the world. The ability to manipulate numbers efficiently and rapidly is often thought to be evidence of a good understanding of mathematics. Such is not the case. Adeptness in the practical aspects of mathematics such as number systems, counting, and number-manipulation systems has little to do with understanding the real essence of mathematics.

While the symbols used in ordinary language usually evolve within a community or linguistic group, the symbols of mathematics are artificial. Mathematicians, in fact, often avoid ordinary speech because of its lack of precision. The language of mathematics is a language of pure abstraction. Its symbols "can be more readily manipulated in reasoning processes than . . . the symbols of common language."[20] The history of mathematics will show, however, that its very abstract nature is what makes possible the development of mathematical systems that have wide applicability in all phases of the environment.

The foundation of all mathematics is logical consistency. Without logic there is no mathematics, for "the subject matter of mathematics is . . . *formal (abstract) symbolic systems within which all possible propositions are consistent with each other.*"[21] The structure of mathematics, then, is a series of propositions that, because of their nature,

[20] Phenix, *op. cit.*, p. 73.
[21] *Ibid.*, p. 74.

are logically related to one another and are discussed in an abstract language unique to the system. Not all these propositions are necessarily valid in the physical world (although in applying mathematics to the sciences, such a series is possible). Rather, *mathematics does no more than explain the relationship between propositions within a particular system, which is explained in abstract symbols.*

Mathematics usually begins by stating certain self-evident truths, called postulates or axioms. These axioms are the starting point for the development of a web of deductive inferences. At each point in the web, however, reaching the next point depends on finding an axiom to support the move. If no axiom can be found to support it, the track being followed by the investigator must be abandoned. When a series of axioms are used to prove a point, that point becomes a *theorem*, which can be used in making further deductive inferences. All these operations are in the realm of abstract thought, but the structure of mathematics is in that realm.

The placement of mathematics in our schools is a serious and important consideration. Our culture demands that young people entering the social world be able to handle computations. We expect such things as the repeating nature of our base-ten number system, the basic processes of manipulating numbers (addition, subtraction, multiplication, and division), and the fundamental nature of fractions to be understood by every graduate. However, the practical application of the products of mathematics is not mathematics. The true nature of mathematics is deductive inference, and making deductive inferences requires that the learner compare, classify, analyze, synthesize, and generalize—thus, developing the rational powers.

Just how much of the true abstract nature of mathematics (the essence of the discipline) can be taught to concrete-operational learners? As we saw in Chapter 4, research indicates that the majority of junior high school students operate at the concrete-operational level. The question is, of course, a curriculum question and must be answered by every educational institution. In answering it, the computational aspects of mathematics must be divorced from the postulational system. Also, the intellectual-development levels of the learners must be considered.

In recent years the concept of the set has become a dominant feature of modern mathematics programs. The set "is so central in mathematics (because) it embodies the principle of abstraction which is the essence of mathematical thinking."[22] Secondary school teachers

[22] *Ibid.*, p. 78.

must ask themselves whether their students are close enough to the formal-operational stage for an abstraction like sets to be useful as the foundation for a mathematics program. If the answer Yes, and if the teacher uses the inquiry method, most modern mathematics programs will allow students to achieve educational purpose, pass through the stages of intellectual development, and at the same time develop an understanding of the structure of mathematics. If the answer is No, then modern mathematics programs must be critically examined to determine whether there is a basic unifying concept, which can be presented using objects. Activities based on such a concept should be used until students reach a stage at which the abstractions underlying the modern programs can be comprehended.

Physical Education

The phrase physical education covers a multitude of activities and has different meanings for different people. Physical education, to many, is synonymous with competitive athletics; in reality, competitive athletics have little to do with a school's physical education program. Oftentimes, physical education is equated with physical fitness. There is no doubt that many learners would benefit from programs designed to get and keep their bodies in shape. The condition of a person's body can have a great impact on his self-image and hence on his entire attitude toward learning. If, however, physical fitness was the only goal of physical education, there would be little need to employ specially prepared persons as teachers. The best exercises for overall physical fitness are walking and running, activities that anyone can do without supervision. Thus the need for physical fitness alone is not sufficient justification for a physical education program.

For the physical education program to fit into the modern school system, it must make a contribution to the educational purpose.

TASK	*How can a physical education program assist the learner in developing his rational powers and simultaneously improve his physical fitness?* Before reading on, *jot down your ideas.*

Someday, try watching children who are not yet old enough to have learned to play only those games created by adults. Young children invent games of their own, and this is what learners of all ages need to be encouraged to do. A creative approach to physical education can lead learners to invent new games, rules, and scoring procedures and, in the case of older students, new exercises and sports. Creativity in any area develops the student's ability to think. Just as creative writing provides an experience in rational-power development that cannot be obtained any other way, creative physical education can too. And, since most games involve movement, another objective of the physical-education program (physical fitness) is also satisfied. Furthermore, the motivation that will carry the activity forward is inherent in the participant-created game. After an activity has been invented, the learners need to participate in it long enough to feel that no more changes from which they will benefit can be made in the rules.

One of the problems that can be expected to continue to confront modern man is what to do with an increased amount of leisure time. As the working day and week grow progressively shorter, more and more time is available for individuals to schedule their own activities. School physical education departments can make a contribution toward solving the leisure-time problem by introducing the precollegiate student population to activities such as golf, tennis, bowling, swimming, and badminton that can be continued after graduation from school. A school that does not have such facilities can often use public swimming pools, golf courses, tennis courts, or bowling alleys. Administrators need to accept the notion that the entire community, and not just the school building, represents the school's environment. But do these activities have anything to do with the development of rational power?

Before answering that question, let us look at a broader aspect of the physical education program. Do competitive sports such as football, basketball, baseball, and the various track and field events have any place in the schools? After all, not many persons take part in these sports, and fewer still earn their livelihood in this manner. Team sports are unlikely to be a convenient leisure-time activity because getting enough people together for a game is usually difficult. Nevertheless, a knowledge of team sports can help solve an emerging national leisure-time crisis. If a person understands baseball, he is liable to spend some of his spare time watching it. Understanding a sport is generally a prerequisite to becoming a devoted spectator, and this understanding is best gained through participation. School physical education programs can give all children an opportunity to participate in sports of their own choosing. Physical fitness is obviously fostered by both team and individual sports, but where does rational-power development enter in? In both cases, if the teacher uses a problem-solving approach, the learners will have an opportunity to use their rational powers; if he provides only instruction in the particular skill, they will not have this opportunity. Suppose, for example, you ask the students what happens to a golf ball when the driving force on the club is supplied from the right hand, as is the case for left-handed people, or what happens to a tennis ball that is hit from the top down? Not only does solving these problems require the exercise of the rational powers, but the solution is immediately relevant to the learners. Imagine that in a game of touch football the teacher changes the rules so that only three downs rather than four are required to gain ten yards. After several plays the teams can be assembled and the manner in which the style of play changed when the new rule was introduced can be analyzed. Opportunities for rational-power development are present in physical education, but the degree to which they are utilized depends on the creativity of the teacher and the degree to which he is willing to *permit* and *encourage* the learners to be creative. Do not be surprised if younger children are more creative than senior high school students.

Science

Within the past twenty years the disciplines of mathematics and science have probably had more attention focused on them and more funds made available to them than all other areas of learning combined. The spotlight became intense in 1957 when Russia orbited the first artificial satellite. The immediate reaction in this country was that the science and mathematics programs in our educational system were not adequate and that something needed to be done about them. Actually, orbiting a satellite was not a great scientific achievement, strictly speaking, although it was a great engineering feat. Newton outlined the scientific principles behind the launch in his *Principia*, published in 1687. The design of experiments and instruments to gather data from a space vehicle and the quantification and interpretation of those data represent the real scientific achievements of space exploration.

Nevertheless, in 1957 and the years following, considerable attention was paid to the science and mathematics programs of the schools in an attempt to close the "scientific gap" between Russia and the United States. (Actually, no such gap ever existed, although a small technological gap may have existed.) Congress passed such legislation as the National Defense Education Act and others to assist the public schools (and some activities in private schools) to upgrade their entire curriculum in order to prepare for the space race.

However, there was a basic flaw in the reasoning of those persons, mostly politicians, who reacted by criticizing U.S. education programs. If our schools emphasized programs to produce scientific manpower, the inherent assumption was that all students were going to become scientists. In fact, only a small percentage of the school population enters a scientific or science-based profession. Those responsible for all levels of science programs in our educational institutions recognized this fact. They began to question the potential of science for precollegiate students and to ask themselves how and in what grades science should be taught in schools, and even whether it should be taught at all. We shall try to answer some of these questions in the following paragraphs.

Thomas Kuhn has said that the study of history could change the image most people have of science. The current image, he believes, has been drawn (even by contemporary scientists) from a study of the scientific achievements recorded in textbooks. The purpose of textbooks, however, is to persuade, and "a concept of science drawn from them is no more likely to fit the enterprise that produced them [the textbooks] than an image of a national culture drawn from a tourist brochure or a language text."[23] The probability exists that the mental structure you have of science has also been derived from textbooks. But consider these responses to the question What is science?

Science has its origins in the needs to know and to understand (or explain), i.e., its cognitive needs.[24]

The primary purpose of science has little to do with weapons or washing machines: it is just to know and to understand.[25]

. . . rapidly moving fields [of science] are fields where a particular method of doing research is systematically used and taught, an accumulative method of inductive inference that is so effective that I think it should be given the name "strong inference."[26]

Another of the qualities of science is that it teaches the value of rational thought, as well as the importance of freedom of thought; the positive results that come from doubting that the lessons are all true.[27]

[23] Thomas S. Kuhn, *The Structure of Scientific Revolutions* (Chicago: University of Chicago Press, 1962), p. 1.

[24] Abraham A. Maslow, *The Psychology of Science* (New York: Harper & Row, 1966), p. 20.

[25] Russell Fox, Max Garbundy, and Robert Hooke, *The Science of Science* (New York: Walker, 1963), p. 3.

[26] John R. Platt, "Strong Inference," *Science*, 146 (October 1964), pp. 347–353.

[27] Richard P. Feynman, "What Is Science?" *The Physics Teacher* (September 1969), pp. 313–320.

The common theme of these quotations is that the principal concern of science is with the *process* of knowing, that is, with *inquiry*. The structure of science, then, is that which enables the inquirer to know something, to understand what it means, and to know *how* we found out something else related to it. Science, therefore, is a natural vehicle for achieving the central goal of education, the development of the rational powers.

In order for learners to benefit fully from interaction with the discipline of science, scientific inquiry must be encouraged from kindergarten on. It is up to the teacher to guide this inquiry by determining what from the discipline is to be taught. The content selected for a course must contain the important (or representative) ideas of the discipline. In other words, the integrity of the discipline must be maintained. The responsibility for content selection is vitally important to teaching science by inquiry.

There are two other factors, however, which the teacher must consider in selecting content. One of these is, obviously, the level of development of the learner. The abstract mathematical side of physics would be incomprehensible to concrete-operational children in the third grade. In addition, the material selected should be able to be understood through the inquiry process. This does not mean that terminology and concepts cannot be invented for the young investigators; they should be. Students may also need to be given assistance in formulating the plans for their investigations and provided with clues as to how those investigations can be carried forward. Often an investigation will yield all types of data that, when compared and categorized, provide ideas about a general phenomenon. There is no need for the science teacher to "fish" among the learners for a name for this phenomenon; he should invent the concept for them. When, for example, the learners have explored how, where, when, and what types of materials are attracted to a piece of metal but don't know the word *magnet*, the teacher should invent it for them. This exploration-invention-discovery method of inquiring has been used by Robert Karplus and his associates as the foundation for an entire elementary science curriculum.[28]

Earlier, we quoted four definitions of science, all made by scientists, and discussed how those ideas should be implemented by introducing learners at each intellectual level, through inquiry, to representative

[28] The project that developed the curriculum is called the Science Curriculum Improvement Study; it is thoroughly explained in Robert Karplus and Herbert D. Thier, *A New Look at Elementary School Science* (Chicago: Rand McNally, 1967).

ideas they can comprehend. If the teacher uses other criteria, if he includes topics just because they have always been taught, the learners will probably not develop an understanding of the structure of science as outlined by these four scholars. The teacher must remember that he himself is the best judge of the relevance of scientific content for his students. One twelfth-grade physics class may be perfectly able to inquire into the particle nature of light, while another may not be interested in going beyond light refraction with simple lenses. Both these groups are studying physics; the teacher has simply exercised his professional judgment regarding the relevance of representative ideas.

Science is a way of knowing about our environment, and in order to be true science, students must be taught not only what is known but how it is known. Unfortunately, education in the sciences often concerns itself only with what is known. Hopefully, the eventual result of the furor caused by Sputnik will be school science programs at all levels that focus on how things are known and how those things are related. Learning how things are related is, according to Bruner, "learning the structure of a discipline."[29]

The Importance of Structure

In this chapter each of the major disciplines taught in the secondary school has been examined in order to demonstrate how the *integrity* of any discipline could be maintained and how inquiry could be utilized to lead students to develop their rational powers. In addition, examining the structure of a discipline provides an understanding of how to select learning experiences that can be used at various levels of intellectual development. What you, the teacher, select from the basic structure of each discipline determines how the student's mental structure will be disequilibrated and changed. In order to do this, however, you must understand the structure of the discipline itself. Or, as Jerome Bruner said:

> . . . *the merit of a structure* [*that of the discipline*] *depends upon its power for* simplifying information, *for* generating new propositions, *and for* increasing the manipulability of a body of knowledge, *structure must also be related to the status and gifts of the learner.*[30]

[29] Jerome S. Bruner, *The Process of Education* (New York: Random House, 1960), p. 7.

[30] Bruner, *Toward a Theory of Instruction*, p. 41.

What Bruner is saying is that what is used from the structure of a discipline is that which enables the learner to simplify (compare, classify, evaluate, and analyze) the information he has collected, generate (imagine, synthesize, infer, generalize, and deduce) new ideas and data, and build a mental structure for himself. Bruner warns, however, not to forget the intellectual level (the gifts and status) of the learner. Leading learners toward these goals is possible if the teacher understands the true nature of his discipline and the learning potential it has for secondary school students.

As a teacher you must also be concerned with the philosophical and psychological aspects of teaching and with the organization of content for classroom use. In Chapter 6 we shall investigate the various curriculum patterns that can be used to achieve educational purposes.

6 Using Curriculum Design

The curriculum patterns in secondary education are classified according to the sources from which they were developed. However, it is difficult to determine whether this order of classification was determined before the development of curriculum patterns or was superimposed upon already-developed curriculum patterns.

To understand curriculum patterns we must first determine whether a particular curiculum type is the result of deliberate selection, of evolution, or a combination of the two.

It is important for you to understand the origins of curriculum types, the premises upon which they are based, and the reasoning behind them because the modern teacher plays a significant part in curriculum development and revision. Whereas, in earler times, the teacher was merely inserted into the curriculum pattern to perform a mechanical role, today he functions as an active participant in curriculum building and change. Because of this, each teacher should familiarize himself with each type of curriculum pattern and its rationale.

The Logical-Source Concept

A number of curriculum types that are directly related to what is perceived as a logical division among the various sources of content (subject matter) exist in secondary schools. In Chapters 1 and 2, we saw that the early American schools were skill- and content-oriented. Since that time, a variety of curriculum patterns, which may be identified as basically oriented toward skills, content, and discipline, and as having been derived from the logical-source concept, have evolved.

The separate-subjects curriculum

The separate-subjects curriculum is the oldest pattern of curriculum organization based on the logical-source concept. It is also the most widely accepted type of curriculum organization. Early examples of the separate-subjects curriculum can be found in the schools of ancient Greece and Rome, although the content covered was very different. Basically, this curriculum pattern divides the content to be taught into distinct areas of instruction. In its purest form it separates bodies of knowledge from one another and promotes instruction in a subject in isolation. The basic premise of the separate-subjects curriculum is compartmentalization; each discipline is treated as a separate entity. (In the purest form of separate-subjects curriculum, history is separated from the other social sciences and occupies a special niche in the instructional program.)

This type of curriculum makes no provision for the transfer of learning among content areas. Relationships between subjects are not sought, and as new content areas are developed, they are added to the local school program as independent subjects. The school day is divided into a series of periods, one for each subject. Furthermore, a great deal of attention is given to regulating the length of each period, the number of periods in a school day, the number of weeks in the school year, grading systems, and various other quantitative elements of measurement. Interestingly enough, both state and local requirements for high school graduation, as well as other requirements imposed on secondary education, were developed based on the separate-subjects curriculum.

When a new content area is added to the curriculum, it must be organized into a format for instruction. The scope of the subject must be defined and a sequence of instructional units appropriate to the various grade levels developed. This basic procedure is representative of the early attempts of educators to develop preplanned curriculum patterns. Even today, although a number of curriculum patterns have been explored, consideration of new subject matter for the curriculum follows this general procedure.

The separate-subjects curriculum, then, is highly compartmentalized, with content areas neatly wrapped into isolated packages. Within this curriculum, learning proceeds from the part to the whole, or from the simple to the complex. Practice, drill, and repetition are the basic tenets of the system, and student achievement is measured by the ability to recall factual information.

TASK	Before reading on, *jot down what you think are the shortcomings and strengths of the separate-subjects curriculum.*

The correlated curriculum

Although the separate-subjects curriculum has, up to now, been the most widely accepted curriculum pattern in the United States, it has also been widely criticized by educators. Obviously, it has some inadequacies, and it was perhaps these inadequacies that prompted the development of other curriculum patterns, among them the *correlated-subjects plan.* Correlated curricula are usually found at the junior high school level, but there are some instances of subject correlation in the high schools. Although the correlated pattern allows the skills normally associated with a subject to be retained within that disciplinary area, content that is applicable to more than one subject is selected. Probably the most common application in the junior high school is the use of a time block of two or more periods within which two subjects, such as English and American history, are related.

The rigidity of the separate-subjects approach produced a bias toward fragmentation in the school curriculum. Although the correlation concept makes some attempt to compensate for this fragmentation by showing relationships among fields, it has never had a very great impact on the subject curriculum.

TASK	Before reading on, *jot down what you think are the strengths and weaknesses of a correlated curriculum.*

The broad-fields curriculum

Another curriculum pattern based on the logical-source concept is the *broad-fields,* or *subject-area,* pattern, which goes a step beyond the correlation-of-subjects approach described above. The broad-fields concept attempts to relate not only content but skills. The curriculum divisions are broader; English courses become a subset of the language arts, and history, a part of social studies.

The area of language is developed by relating both the content and the skills contained in spelling, grammar, literature, reading, composition, speech, debate, and drama. The area of social studies is developed by relating the content and the skills normally identified with history, geography, sociology, economics, anthropology, psychology, and government. Previously, under the separate-subjects and correlated-curriculum approaches, little emphasis had been given to some of these content areas; thus, their inclusion marked a very real broadening of the areas of study in secondary schools.

Although it might be expected that broader areas of study would suggest longer class periods and fewer fragmented classes, the original pattern of separate subjects was so deeply entrenched that little change occurred in class schedules. Again, most of the changes were in the junior high schools, where the time-block concept had already become rather generally accepted. The broad-fields curriculum pattern did, however, encourage the transfer of learning between subjects. Furthermore, unit teaching flourished under the broad-fields pattern and gained in popularity, even in schools whose organization reflected a separate-subjects orientation.

TASK	*What do you consider are the strengths and weaknesses of the broad-field approach?* Before reading on, *jot down your answer.*

The integrated curriculum

The next curriculum pattern that can be traced to the logical-source concept is sometimes referred to as the *integrated curriculum.* A number of factors contributed to its development—the success of unit teaching, previous ventures in relating the content and skills of different disciplines, and new interpretations of the learning process itself. The concept underlying the integrated curriculum is the selection of a theme or problem that involves the utilization of skills and content from various subject areas. Although there are some applications of this curriculum pattern in American secondary education, the thematic-problems approach has met with the widest acceptance in the junior high schools, under the title *core curriculum.*

The core curriculum is a pattern that relates rather specifically to junior high school education. Although it relies heavily on the separate disciplines, we cannot categorize it as based solely on the logical-source concept, since it is to some extent student-centered.

Probably no other curriculum pattern is as misunderstood or misinterpreted as the core concept. Through the years, educators have used the term *core* to refer to almost any kind of junior high school program that varied from the separate-subjects curriculum. Often, the mere existence of a time block was considered sufficient justification by the local school administration to claim a core program, even though the time block incorporated two separate subjects whose only connection was that they were taught in the same room, to the same students, and by the same teacher.

Curriculum patterns referred to as core types range from simple time blocks, to unified studies, common learnings, and actual core programs. These plans often bear little relationship to actual core programs. Unified studies, for example, means merging two or more subjects into a single course. On the other hand, the common-learnings concept is based on the idea that there are certain general understandings that all students should have if they are to be prepared to participate in society. It has basically the same justifications as general education in the high school curriculum.

The core curriculum differs from other curriculum types in that it is based on a thematic, problem-solving approach. The problems (generally social problems), which serve as themes or central units for the core program, may be identified by either the teacher or the students, but the students play a vital role in both the planning and the problem-solving process. Although no specific content is prescribed, skills and content from the various disciplines are used as tools by students in studying the problems and reaching solutions and conclusions. Thus, although the core-curriculum pattern is not based on content, it does use content; and although it is not truly student-centered, it strives to answer some of the needs of young people by harnessing their interests and their desire to participate.

TASK	Before reading on, *jot down what you think are the strengths and weaknesses of the integrated curriculum.*

The preplanned curriculum patterns that have evolved from the logical-source concept, in the order presented, reflect a progressively more liberal attitude toward the transfer of learning among content areas, as well as a movement toward creating larger, broader curriculum areas.

There is one other approach to content, which may be associated with the logical source, that should be discussed here. With the development of the "new" mathematics and the "modern" science programs of the 1960s, there has evolved a concept of curriculum design based on the "structure of the disciplines." Although the idea that various subject areas have structure has been considered since the 1920s, the concept has been really explored and tested only in recent years.

This concept of structure differs markedly from the simple progression from part to whole and from the simple to the complex upon which other preplanned curriculum patterns are based. Structure, here, implies that generalizations exist within a content area; when the content is organized around these generalizations, the door is opened for both inductive and deductive learning.

Up to now, we have discussed various curriculum patterns related to the logical-source concept. Basically, these approaches have all been subject-centered. For simplicity in later discussions we shall refer to such approaches as Curriculum I patterns.

Student-Centered Approaches to Curriculum Development

There have been several attempts to develop patterns other than the Curriculum I varieties discussed above. These attempts have developed largely as a result of reactions against the subject-centered curriculum. In some instances, they may have been prompted by new developments in learning theory, educational sociology, and adolescent psychology.

Efforts to develop student-centered curriculum patterns have concentrated primarily on the elementary grades. However, they have had some effect on secondary school curriculum patterns. The work of John Dewey, Junius Meriam, Ellsworth Collings, and Florence Stratameyer focused the attention of educators on the child and the part the learner plays in the learning process. While the curriculum designs developed by these individuals enjoyed only limited success, their underlying philosophies at least gave educators reason to pause and reexamine existing school programs.

Conditions in early-twentieth-century America set the stage for some changes in the traditional subject curriculum, particularly for the early adolescent. First, the great waves of immigrants, who settled in the urban areas, brought with them large numbers of school-age children who spoke English poorly, if at all, and who lacked an understanding of our laws, customs, and citizenship. Compulsory attendance laws drew students from extremely wide and divergent backgrounds, and there was an obvious need to prepare these people, who were basically unqualified for the available job opportunities, to become productive citizens.

Second, it was becoming apparent that large numbers of students were not being promoted in the normal way, from one grade level to the next. The high percentage of students who had to be detained for more than a year at a particular grade level caused educators to wonder if part of the problem was the educational system itself.

Studies by several psychologists in the early years of the twentieth century contributed to this new, questioning attitude on the part of educators. Although it had long been recognized that individuals differed from one another in many ways, these studies indicated a tremendous range in individual differences—physically, emotionally, and mentally—especially during the early adolescent years.

As a result of these and other factors, the traditional organization of the elementary and secondary schools underwent some changes. After much study by a number of commissions, the last two years of elementary education (grades seven and eight) gradually emerged as a separate educational unit known as the junior high school. In some instances, the ninth grade was removed from the regular four-year high school and included in this newly organized school unit. In time, educators recommended that the junior high school become a separate school unit, set apart from both the elementary school and the associated high school.

All of these conditions contributed to a shift in emphasis in the curriculum. The philosophy of *life-adjustment education* appeared on the educational scene, challenging the logical-source concept. Although the subject-centered curriculum survived the challenge and remains strong even today, the life-adjustment philosophy had some effect. As you will recall, even the Seven Cardinal Principles suggested a gap between the American philosophy of education and education as it was applied in the schools. Not all the principles of education depended upon the acquisition of knowledge and skills, and educators began to recognize the needs of the individual student. This position was strengthened even more by the report of the Educational Policies Commission in 1938. Although life-adjustment education never enjoyed much success in the American high school, it probably contributed to the development of counseling and guidance services and played a part in broadening the course selection within a particular subject curriculum.

Despite a strong effort in the first half of this century to modify educational approaches to accommodate the needs of the individual student, life-adjustment education never managed to dethrone the subject-centered curriculum, which continued to flourish. Nevertheless, it made a strong impression on secondary education, and in ways that may have been unexpected. Evidence of the effect of the life-adjustment movement may be seen today in any comprehensive high school. Although the subject curriculum remains, course selection is wide. Many modern high schools offer instruction in everything from child care to automobile mechanics, from cooking to careers, from music appreciation to cosmetology. The life-adjustment philosophy also increased the status of school activities and brought about their inclusion in the curriculum. Once considered extra-curricula, school activities programs have been promoted to a position of near equality with coursework. What was once viewed as the frills of education became a junior partner. Although the activity programs were a tremendous victory for advocates of the student-centered curriculum, they have several weaknesses, the greatest of which is that they still occupy a secondary position. In addition, (1) student participation is voluntary, (2) it may be expensive, (3) many who need to participate do not, (4) activities are scheduled after the end of the official school day, and (5) success in school remains based on the academic curriculum.

For purposes of clarity, we shall refer to approaches that emphasize the student and his needs as Curriculum II patterns.

TASK	*Why do you think a school curriculum should not be student-centered?* Before reading on, *jot down your answer.*

Administrative and Organizational Innovations

The time block

Many administrative and organizational innovations that influenced curriculum patterns have been developed and expanded in the past fifty years. One of these is the time block. (As mentioned earlier, a time block is simply a class period equal in length to two or more regular class periods.) Time blocks have been justified for varying reasons. It was claimed that junior high school students needed help in making the transition from the self-contained elementary school classroom (in which they had contact with one teacher for several hours daily) to the highly departmentalized high school (in which they might encounter six or seven different teachers for relatively short periods of time). Many educators believed that students should spend two or more normal class periods with one teacher, as at the junior high level, so that they would have a teacher to identify with. Presumably this would lessen the possibly traumatic effects of passing from a somewhat personal student-teacher relationship to the more impersonal, subject-centered high school environment.

Time blocks have been developed in some schools, on the other hand, because educators believed that the nature of various courses made a 50- to- 60-minute period inadequate and impractical. As the emphasis on laboratory work increased, this was especially true in the general area of the sciences. Longer periods became a prime concern of many science teachers because of the problems they encountered in arranging and preparing apparatus, conducting experiments, and cleaning, dismantling, and putting away equipment.

Another application of time blocks emerged with the increase in vocational specialization in the upper grade levels of the senior high school. Students who intend to start work directly after graduation can spend two or three hours daily doing concentrated work in a specialized skill in order to prepare themselves for the job market.

Team teaching

A second administrative modification of the curriculum pattern is the team-teaching concept. Under this system two or more teachers may work together in planning and implementing activities for a particular course or class. This idea is not particularly new and has been adopted in secondary schools for various reasons. Teaching teams are often justified on the basis that some teachers possess certain talents to a greater degree than others. One teacher may excel at presenting material to students in an interesting way, while another may be exceptionally good at stimulating interaction among small groups. Various other arguments have also been advanced in support of the team-teaching concept, among them that two or more teachers can provide a variety of teaching techniques, an opportunity for increased teacher-student relationships, and a depth of classroom experience that would not be possible with only one teacher. On the other hand, experience has shown that the mere appointment of teachers to a team may not improve the classroom situation. Too often, teaching teams are an attempt to deal with overcrowding or have been developed because it was considered the thing to do. Sometimes, when teachers are not prepared to work together in a classroom, team teaching can be detrimental to the learning environment. In too many cases, one member of a team becomes dominant, leaving the other members as passive participants in the learning process.

Grouping students

Because of wide ranges in student ability, achievement, performance, and command of learning skills, some schools attempt to group students in such categories as high achiever, slow learner, and average performer. This grouping may be based on the subjective judgments of teachers, counselors, and administrators; on classroom performance in various subject areas; on scores on standardized tests; and even on student attitudes toward school. Grouping techniques are normally applied only in academic disciplines such as language arts, the sciences, mathematics, and social studies. Grouping also occurs in a natural way in the elective portions of the curriculum, in that students will decide to take or not to take an advanced course based on their success or failure in the basic course. A student who did not do too well in algebra I is unlikely to choose algebra II as an elective.

The grouping of secondary-school learners has encouraged authors to develop textbooks dealing with content in a designated subject at different levels. For example, in a particular high school three textbooks may be used for teaching world history—one in accelerated classes; another, less sophisticated, in regular classes; and a third for classes of slow learners. On the other hand, the availability of textbooks of varying degrees of difficulty has promoted the concept of grouping in some schools and has contributed to its perpetuation in others.

There is much disagreement among educators about the value of grouping. Undoubtedly, there are some disadvantages, as well as advantages, for students. Possibly because of the lack of unanimity on the part of educators in regard to grouping techniques, a tendency is developing today toward a limited stance, which advocates the grouping of students in all academic subjects except social studies. The reasoning behind this position is that social studies provides a framework for exposing students to real life, and thus to the social problems that arise from cultural and individual differences.

Track programs

The track program is still another administrative innovation found in secondary education today. "Tracks" were originally developed to assist students who were able to identify their fields of specialization early enough to select courses that would be appropriate to their later careers. In schools that have such programs, we commonly find three or four almost standard types of tracks. The college-preparatory track contains coursework recommended for students who plan to pursue college degrees and stresses advanced work in mathematics, science, the language arts, and social studies. The general-education track is designed for students whose education will end with high school and who are not specializing in a particular field. The business or commercial track is also common in secondary schools and consists of courses designed to prepare students for jobs as office clerks or secretaries. The fourth track, found in many schools, is vocational, with commerce sometimes included under this general heading. Although track programs are not synonymous with grouping techniques, student abilities and aptitudes have some influence on track selection and participation.

Although track programs are somewhat limited in depth and scope in many schools because of limited facilities, the opportunities for student specialization during high school have been enhanced in recent years by the creation of special vocational-technical schools in many urban areas. In rural areas the opportunities for specialization have been increased by the development of area vocational schools, attended by students from different districts in a particular area. Such efforts in the vocational portion of the curriculum have made it possible for schools to offer a much wider variety of coursework.

Modular scheduling

An administrative innovation that has had considerable effect on American secondary education in recent years is *modular*, or *flexible, scheduling*. Teachers and administrators have long questioned the reasonableness of the assumption that all subjects can be taught in a 55-minute period, five days a week, 36 to 40 weeks of the year. Many educators believe that the factors involved in the learning process in a particular content area should be the primary determinant of length and frequency of class meetings. Modular scheduling breaks down the traditional 55-minute period, redesigning the schedule in terms of the objectives of each subject, the kinds of activities involved, the needs of the students, and the methodology of the teacher. Educators who support this approach advocate large and small groups for various activities, special laboratory groups, and opportunities for independent study. Schedules, they believe, should be manipulated to support the learning process rather than to restrict it.

State and regional requirements

Our examination of curriculum patterns would be incomplete if we failed to discuss the effects of the various accrediting agencies on the secondary school curriculum. State departments of education have established minimum requirements for graduation from schools within their borders. These minimum requirements deal with the total number of credits that must be earned in certain areas, and they are based on the judgments of established educators concerning the kinds of general understandings, content, and skills all students should have in order to be adequately prepared to participate economically, politically, and socially in our society. While exposure to a unit in mathematics does not ensure that the student will develop the arithmetical skills needed to function in society, the state requirements do establish guidelines for minimal investigation on the student's part in subject areas that are believed to be essential to his future well-being and productiveness.

Regional accrediting agencies also impose requirements on member secondary schools, but they do so through the respective states. Their requirements deal with the curricular qualifications of member schools, rather than course requirements for individual students. The regional accrediting agencies provide guidelines for the scope and sequence of curricular areas; standards for schools in all areas of the curriculum, organization, and administration; and standards for qualifications of teachers. Class size, teacher workloads, and supportive school facilities also come under the scrutiny of these agencies. Through their standards for membership, such organizations have exerted considerable influence on the curriculum.

Teacher-preparation institutions

Another influence on the secondary school curriculum has been the teacher-preparation institutions. In the fact that a college or university establishes required courses—aligned with state teacher-certification requirements—for those preparing to teach in a particular field (and if we recognize that teachers tend to teach as they have been taught), we can see how the institutions of higher education affect the high school curriculum. Teachers graduating from these institutions see themselves as trained to work primarily in a specific field.

Social Needs and Curriculum Patterns

Although much has been written about social forces and their relation to education, they have probably had little real influence on curriculum design. For example, much attention has been given to the need of the ordinary consumer for adequate mathematical skills. If, however, you were to visit a consumer-mathematics class, you would probably find most of the emphasis being placed on the mathematical side of the course. Thus, the *consumer* aspects of mathematics have had little impact upon the design of mathematics curricula.

Social needs have had some effect, judging by administrative and organizational adjustments, on some elements of the local curriculum. Frequently, grouping techniques, the selection of curriculum materials, and the emphasis on vocational subjects reflect attempts to meet social needs. Sometimes specific courses in areas not a part of the normal curriculum, such as black history or vocational agriculture, are developed in particular schools. In other instances, efforts to attain acceptable standards of desegregation create organizational changes. Still, social forces have had little overall effect. Societal values have received wide publicity and much lip service through the years, but their influence has been felt only within the framework of established curriculum designs.

An Analysis and Synthesis of Curriculum Patterns

We have established that subject-centered, student-centered, and administrative organizational patterns determine the direction of curriculum development. Of these determinants the subject-centered approach has been dominant, and it has received considerable support from various administrative modifications. Student-centered curriculum patterns have met with limited success and have not succeeded in really challenging subject-centered structures. In fact, the effect of Curriculum II approaches has been observed primarily by the absorption of some of its concepts into aspects of Curriculum I patterns.

In several earlier chapters we discussed two criteria that are considered essential for the elements of secondary education. The first of these was the development of the individual student's rational powers; the second was suitability to the student's developmental level.

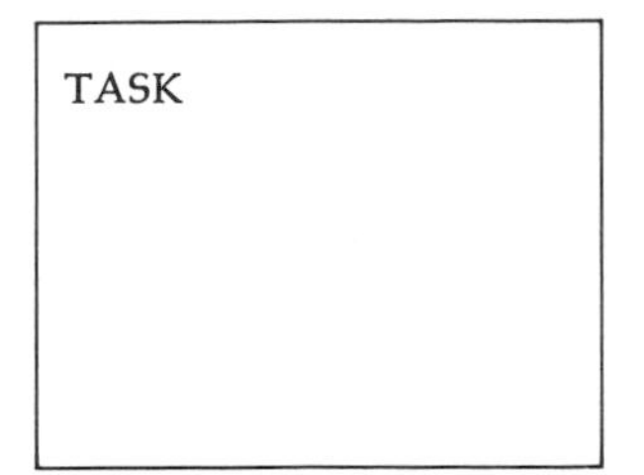

TASK

How do you think the subject- and student-centered curriculum patterns discussed in this chapter measure up to the two criteria, rational-power development and suitability to developmental levels? Give reasons for your answer.

Neither of these criteria seems to have been met by the curriculum patterns described here. Curriculum I patterns have consistently promoted a factual orientation that encourages students to memorize selected items from established bodies of knowledge. The scope and sequence of content within the framework of these patterns have ignored even the possibility of the existence of developmental levels. The selection of content is geared to grade levels or chronological ages rather than to the students' intellectual development. On the other hand, the student-centered Curriculum II patterns do little to encourage critical thinking. Although they purposely emphasize student needs and interests, nothing is done here to indicate attention to the individual's level of development either. The administrative organizational innovations in recent years have done little other than reinforce Curriculum I patterns by providing alterations and modifications to existing forms. They too have failed to meet the criteria of rational-power development and suitability to developmental levels. They are aimed basically at developing more efficient means of achieving the objectives of Curriculum I patterns.

Over the years the patterns of Curriculum I, Curriculum II, and administrative organization have gone through a process of evolution. Weaknesses and flaws have been eliminated, strong points retained, and modifications added until a new curriculum pattern emerged.

This evolution is clearest in the changing perspectives on skills and content within Curriculum I patterns. The pure form of the subject curriculum isolated the content and skills of each discipline. The correlated patterns attempted to show relationships among content, but considered the skills of each subject as unrelated. The broad-fields patterns created broader subject areas, within which both content and skills were related. In the integrated-curriculum patterns themes and topics were selected that allowed the skills and content of even broader subject areas to be related. There is an apparent trend toward interrelating subject content in larger and larger units, moving away from subject independence toward interdependent content fields. Despite this, each content area has maintained certain elements of structure. Does this mean that each discipline has its own basic structure, and will a study of that structure lead to a greater understanding of the discipline?

In all fairness, it should be stated that more and more attention is being focused on the central aim of American education. Educators and teachers who participate in curriculum building and revision are becoming increasingly conscious of the inadequacies that exist in secondary-school curriculum patterns and appear to be striving to correct them. Increased attention to the central purpose of education in teacher-preparation institutions, in in-service school programs, and in the literature of the profession seems to be having some effect. We are making some progress, then, in using the curriculum to achieve the central purpose of education—the development of the rational powers. Could we not accomplish even more if equal attention were paid to developmental level and its relevance to the curriculum? Curriculum selection may be weak unless aligned with a meaningful purpose and philosophy, but unless the intellectual level of the learner is considered, it is almost meaningless.

Curriculum patterns based on the logical-source concept are concerned with the transfer of learning. Within Curriculum I the transfer of learning may depend on the ability of the learner to relate the skills and content of one subject area to those of another independent subject area. Or, in view of the structure of Curriculum I, we might define transfer of learning in terms of the student's ability to generate new content and skills from those he has mastered. In either case, the transfer of learning is skill- and content-oriented. Curriculum I fails to explain what takes place in the learner between the internalization of skills and content and the growth of the rational powers, which is the end result of the transfer of learning.

In Chapter 5 we saw that all disciplines are related in that they require the use of the rational powers. It was also suggested in Chapter 5 that the process of learning a discipline is content-free, in the sense that different disciplines utilize a similar process of generating new knowledge. If we assume that the transfer of learning takes place because of the rationality of the learner and the disciplines, then it is the rational powers, not content, that are the vehicle of transfer. Following this line of reasoning, the purpose of Curriculum I should be to present a subject (or to select content from a discipline) in a way that emphasizes the basic rationality of the discipline, thus encouraging and reinforcing the development of the rational process.

The student-centered Curriculum II patterns, on the other hand, were evolved without applying the criterion of rationality to learning or to the learners. Their relevance depends on the concept of developmental levels, which supplies some basis for understanding the abilities of the learner, the perceptions that guide his behavior, and the function of involvement in the learning process.

Preplanned and Dynamic Aspects of the Curriculum

Every curriculum has two phases—the *preplanned phase* and the *dynamic phase.* The preplanned curriculum provides the framework for the dynamic curriculum. It contains the basic, fundamental experiences essential in any curriculum and is designed to meet the needs of students as a group, rather than as individuals. Teacher participation in the development of this preplanned curriculum is necessary to ensure that it reflects what each teacher views as the minimum of experiences needed by his students. Furthermore, without a thorough understanding of the preplanned curriculum, the teacher is ill-equipped to apply maximum creativeness in developing the dynamic curriculum.

The preplanned curriculum also provides for the articulation and continuity of learning experiences within the local school. Since it allows for a progression of experiences in a vertical sequence, it is sometimes referred to as a *spiraling curriculum.* It also provides for a reapplication of past learning at various points within the vertical sequence, to accomplish new learning, promote readiness for future learning, and encourage retention of what has already been learned. An understanding of the spiraling curriculum is essential if the teacher is to interpret correctly any portion of the preplanned curriculum and to provide continuity for his students.

In other words, the preplanned curriculum is the common element to which all students are exposed. It provides the framework within which all teachers of a particular subject can communicate and interact and a basis on which to construct a dynamic curriculum that will accommodate the needs of individual students.

In Chapter 7, we will examine how classroom procedures may be used to accomplish learning. A knowledge of curriculum patterns is of little value to the teacher unless he also understands classroom procedure and methodology.

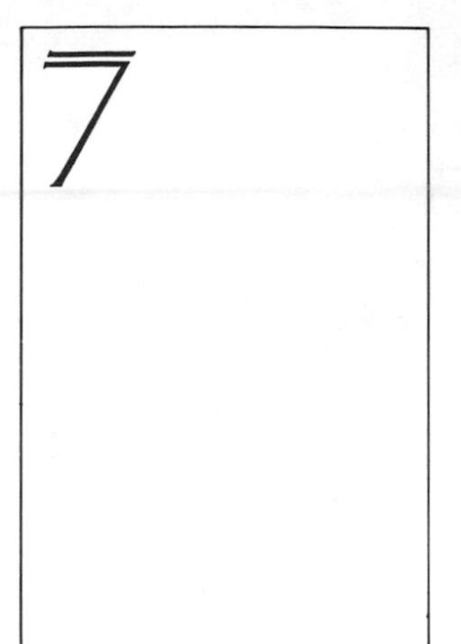

7 Using Classroom Procedures

In the following pages we shall examine how three criteria—development of the rational powers, Piaget's concept of developmental levels, and attention to individual needs—can be used to formulate strategy for the selection and creation of classroom procedures. We believe that selection of classroom procedures is a function of the kind of learning and learning environment desired, that these three criteria are the essential elements of a good learning environment, and that if the right kind of learning environment is established, teaching approaches will be applicable to all curriculum areas.

The fact that we can identify a common instructional strategy does not mean that the relationships involved in a learning environment are absolutely stable. Because they are not stable, we cannot prescribe any procedure with complete confidence. On the other hand, the teacher need not depend on trial and error in developing classroom procedures; it is possible to approach the development of a methodology that combines various techniques and procedures in a logical fashion.

The Classroom Environment

There are several aspects of the classroom environment that need mentioning before we become too deeply involved in the actual teaching-learning procedure. One of these has to do with human relationships. To be truly effective, the teaching-learning process requires two active participants—the teacher and the student—who are able to, and want to, communicate with and relate to each other. For a classroom atmosphere to be conducive to learning, there should exist a mutual respect between the teacher and the students. As we suggested in Chapter 3, the teacher can do much, simply by example, to produce an honest, cooperative attitude on the part of the students.

In addition to encouraging cooperative student and teacher attitudes, a good classroom atmosphere allows room for each student, regardless of his lack of ability, to enjoy some measure of success. This, of course, cannot be accomplished unless the teacher is able to tailor the curriculum to individual needs. No one likes to fail, and many students have developed learning disabilities as a result of exposure to dictatorial teaching procedures geared to levels beyond their comprehension. The teacher must be sensitive to such learning disabilities and through his classroom stance and attitude lead these "victims" of our educational system to participate successfully in the classroom experience.

TASK	*What do you think is the ideal learning climate for a classroom?*

It is important that the classroom house a relaxed and comfortable climate for the learning process. Students do not function well in a sterile or an unrealistic setting, or in a classroom that reflects tensions and pressures. The teacher should strive to achieve a classroom atmosphere free of fear, resentment, distrust, or uncertainty. Although the learning process itself requires disturbing the students' intellectual equilibrium, for efficient results this procedure must take place in an emotional environment that is secure, consistent, and sincere. In this kind of setting students can become involved in learning.

TASK	Before reading on, *see if you can recall two or three outstanding teachers in your own past. What attributes did they possess that caused you to classify them as great teachers?*

As early as 1846, a benevolent disposition, good health, a pleasing appearance, and a genuine and earnest sympathy for the young were considered essential for effective teaching.[1] Traditionally, teachers have been considered "successful" or even "outstanding" based on

[1] Paul Witty, "Some Characteristics of the Effective Teacher," *Educational Administration and Supervision*, XXXVI (April 1950), p. 193.

such criteria as personality, friendliness, congeniality, firmness, fairness, and even ability to maintain order. Often, such judgments were based on evaluations of the store of knowledge accumulated by a teacher's students. If a student has had exposure only to teacher- or content-oriented classrooms, he too is likely to base his opinion of teachers on their personal traits or on his own success on examinations

In looking back over your own school years you probably remember certain teachers because of their honesty, sincerity, fairness, ability to explain or describe, openness, or personableness. This is not unusual; it is even normal. In an educational system that is based primarily on telling students things, one's frame of reference is necessarily somewhat restricted. If almost all your classroom experiences are of this variety, then you might very well view any other as strange. School districts historically have experienced much difficulty in distinguishing between good and bad teaching, and between effective and incompetent teachers. Part of the problem is identifying the characteristics of good teaching, or good teaching performance. Although it is easy to identify teachers who are exceptionally well prepared as far as a knowledge of subject matter is concerned, identifying teachers who can function effectively in the classroom is much more difficult.

Educators have struggled with the problem of identifying good teachers and good teaching for years, and often have turned to students for help in making this identification. In the late 1940s, for example, Witty questioned students in his sample about the traits of teachers who had been most helpful to them. Most students felt that teachers should work toward the development of classroom environments which foster understanding, security, and mutual respect and that teachers should contribute to the development of emotional stability in their students.[2]

The criteria for teacher selection used by school-district personnel is also revealing. Generally, little tangible information on an applicant is available. Decisions are based on the candidate's college transcript (which attests to his studiousness and competence in a particular subject), a personal interview (which gives the interviewer a brief glimpse of the candidate's appearance and personality), a statement of his educational philosophy (which undoubtedly reflects the indoctrination of whatever training institution he attended), and references selected by the applicant that attest to his emotional stability, moral fiber, and initiative. Clearly, from such information, the school dis-

[2] *Ibid.*, p. 195.

trict cannot hope to predict with any degree of validity which teachers will be successful in the classroom arena.

By the same token, educators have been just as much at a loss in attempting to evaluate teaching performance. School districts have struggled for years, with little apparent success, to develop instruments for accurately evaluating classroom performance. Almost without exception, the instruments that are devised are constantly under revision. All of this attests to the basic uncertainty about what makes a successful teacher. As long as a severe discrepancy exists between purpose and practice in the educational system, there will be some difficulty in determining which teachers are effective.

It is because we have had no better criteria that we have fallen back on such traits as fairness, firmness, honesty, integrity, good judgment, and personableness in evaluating teaching performance. In 1969, Cassel and Johns listed eleven characteristics of the effective teacher: (1) He is competent in his subject area. (2) He gets along well with others. (3) He understands children. (4) He makes learning activities meaningful. (5) He has a dynamic personality. (6) He helps students evaluate their progress. (7) He interprets the school program to the community effectively. (8) He is intelligent and exercises sound judgment. (9) He uses discretion in speaking of his colleagues or the school. (10) He uses the democratic process continuously and effectively. And (11) he has teacher belongingness and identification.[3]

We do not wish for a moment to create the impression that these qualities are not important for successful teaching. Quite the contrary! Considering what we know of adolescent characteristics, the personal traits of the teacher cannot be lightly dismissed. No student relishes the thought of being taught by a vindictive, dishonest, or deceitful person, who is not to be trusted. The teaching profession is based on the idea that the teacher is someone a parent can depend on to work with his child and who takes the place of the parent during the school day.

Thus, the personal qualities of the teacher are of the utmost importance. As we stated earlier, the teacher must strive to establish a classroom climate free of such elements as suspicion, fear, and uncertainty, a condition that is difficult to achieve if the teacher is not trusted or respected. Because the teaching-learning process involves a two-way relationship between the teacher and the student, the importance of basic concepts of human relations must not be underesti-

[3] Russell N. Cassel and W. Lloyd Johns, "The Critical Characteristics of an Effective Teacher," *National Association of Secondary School Principals Bulletin,* XLIV (November 1969), pp. 120–123.

mated. Nor can we ignore the importance of admirable personal characteristics.

Perhaps the heart of the puzzle for most administrators is the fact that an individual may be highly competent in an academic area and still not be a good teacher. Some of our greatest thinkers, theorists, academicians, and philosophers have excelled as scholars and failed as teachers. A good example might be an outstanding professional athlete who fails miserably as a coach. The fact that an individual completely understands a particular subject does not necessarily mean that he is capable of communicating that understanding or, more important in an inquiry-centered classroom, leading someone else to explore, invent, and discover things about that subject. Similarly, a person may have a wonderful character and personality, but fail in the classroom because of his inability to help others develop an understanding of a subject area.

Probably few teachers would argue against the thesis that a relaxed and friendly classroom atmosphere is superior to one that reflects fear, anxiety, uncertainty, and insecurity. Human elements contribute much to a successful curriculum, and little real learning will take place until an appreciable level of acceptance or rapport is established between student and teacher. This does not mean that there is necessarily an order of priority in the classroom, that good rapport must be established *before* learning occurs. It is more logical to believe that rapport and understanding develop together, and that successful teaching reflects the satisfactory combination of these two elements.

To summarize, the pivotal element of human relations in the classroom appears to be *perceived congruent behavior,* which may be defined as a consistent and parallel relationship between motives and actions, as perceived by the teacher and his students. Apparently, students will tolerate teacher actions that normally would be considered arbitrary or inappropriate as long as they perceive a consistency between the motives and behavior of the teacher and his treatment of them and their classmates.[4] Student perceptions play an important part in the relationship between the teacher's motives and his actions, as does the teacher's own perception of these relationships. When both the students and the teacher perceive identical relationships between his motives and behavior, the classroom en-

[4] Joseph Luft and Harry Ingham develop a model of the possible relationships involved in congruent behavior in *Group Processes: An Introduction to Group Processes* and *Of Human Interaction* (Palo Alto, California: National Press, 1963).

vironment is the most desirable one possible. However, when the perceptions of the teacher and the students do *not* correspond, student insecurity and uncertainty may develop. The teacher should strive to achieve an open and honest stance toward developing perceived congruent behavior and should recognize that students' perceptions of the relationships between his motives and actions may at times be more accurate than his own. Thus, if the classroom climate is sometimes not as conducive to productive learning as you would like, is it because you are looking at things only from your viewpoint as a teacher and not from the viewpoint of your students? A teacher should utilize the differences and similarities between his and his students' perceptions to maximize the impact of his behavior. If you as a teacher are sensitive to relationships and perceptions, then you are well on the way to developing healthy human relations in your classroom.

The Characteristics of the Learner

Many instructional approaches used in the classroom seem completely unrelated to what we know about the learner. Content is selected because it is considered appropriate for certain grade levels or age groups, and procedures are chosen because they are convenient for the transmission of information. The interests of the learners, both as a group and as individuals, are disregarded. Yet the content that is selected through the teacher's efforts is expected to bring about some change in the student. Before going further, let us examine some of the things we know about learners.

1. *An individual does not learn unless he experiences some urge to learn.* The student does not automatically "learn" that which he is exposed to. He learns as a result of some urge to participate, an urge that may be based on personal need, a feeling of challenge, curiosity, fear, or some other emotion. The urge to learn is sometimes referred to as *motivation,* and the more the motivating force comes from within the learner, rather than from some external source, the more effective and efficient the learning process is likely to be.

2. *An individual will learn most efficiently that which has real meaning for him.* A student may be exposed to content and commit it to memory, but if that content has no meaning for him, he has not learned it—he has only memorized it. It is possible for an individual to memorize long lists of nonsense syllables, but because those items have no meaning, no real learning takes place. When the student can

see meaning or value in a skill or an activity, the motivating force that encourages participation is more likely to come from within.

3. *Students are different in many ways.* In any group of students there is a tremendous range of differences in the degree of preparation, experiential background, and skill proficiency. Since a great many skills, experiences, and abilities are necessary for success in learning, it is foolish to expect individuals at any level to react identically to packaged content.

4. *The individual responses to success.* When a student experiences failure, he is likely to become discouraged, and this discouragement may lead to disillusionment, frustration, and further failure. Punishing those who fail does little good and is more likely to create resentment than incentive. On the other hand, a successful, satisfying learning experience may inspire the student to greater effort, and hence to further success.

5. *Emotional tension interferes with the learning process.* Various aspects of the classroom climate, as well as of content and of the learning process itself, can produce tensions in the learner. When an individual functions under conditions of strain and tension in the classroom environment, his participation in the learning process is likely to be impeded.

6. *An individual learns through participation.* Reading or hearing about a concept has only limited value; a student *learns* as a result of performing or participating in a learning activity. As learning activities progress from the simple to the more complex, the mental processes involved became increasingly intricate. If the individual is allowed to participate actively in rather than simply observe an activity or exercise, he is more likely to learn from it. The degree of active participation is also important if the individual is to profit fully from the experience. If he is actively involved in only a small part of the learning activity, he is less likely to gain a full understanding of a concept than if he were actively involved in the entire activity.

7. *An individual's intellectual level does not necessarily change as he moves from one grade level to another.* There is no magical gain in intellectual development from year to year as the student progresses through the various grade levels. Neither does a student automatically and mechanically leap from the concrete-operational stage unto the formal-operational stage when he reaches a certain age. As we pointed out in Chapter 4, intellectual development is a gradual process. If a student is not properly prepared to participate in learning activities at a given level because of inadequate skills, he cannot be expected to become involved to any appreciable degree in the learning process. It

cannot be assumed that a student is adequately prepared for participation simply because he has been promoted from the previous grade level or has been exposed to a certain content.

8. *The student has a better chance to participate successfully in the learning process when he is allowed to use two or more senses simultaneously.* Too often, we assume that when a student is told about or reads about a concept, this exposure is synonymous with learning. Instead of just reading or listening, the student should be allowed to exercise as many of his senses as possible during the learning process.

The principles enumerated above are only a few of many that have been gleaned from years of research on the learner and learning process. Add to this list any ideas you have developed as a result of your own experiences as a secondary-school student that might bring a student to want to participate in classroom learning activities.

If you added such items as (1) gearing content selection to the interest levels of students, (2) making the classroom experience come alive, or (3) designing classroom activities that are realistic rather than false or artificial, you are on the right track. These are some of the things you should consider as you approach the problem of developing your own classroom curriculum, Curriculum III. By recalling your own negative experiences as a student, and putting yourself in the place of your pupils, you can gain some insight into the complexity of developing a classroom approach that considers the *learner*.

Selecting Classroom Procedures

The creation, selection, and implementation of teaching procedures is an extremely demanding task, yet one that can be approached logically by applying the three criteria of rational-power development, suitability to the developmental stage of the learner, and attention to individual needs.

The criterion of rational-power development demands that we seek techniques and procedures designed to bring into operation *all* aspects of the rational powers. Consideration must be given to all procedures that will allow use of the full range of the rational powers, in an ordered or unordered way. Furthermore, the evaluation techniques used must be compatible with the teaching procedures and also designed to assess rational-power development and use.

The criterion of suitability to developmental levels does not necessarily preclude procedures that require students to use all their rational powers. A concrete-operational learner may generalize, analyze, and synthesize. However, this criterion does regulate and determine the kinds of stimuli the learner can accommodate or assimilate. A concrete-operational learner does not have the cognitive structure to accommodate perceptions of a logico-mathematical nature. Each procedure or technique should be analyzed in terms of what it asks the learner to do and what can be expected of him at a particular developmental level. The selection of appropriate stimuli is a direct function of the learner's developmental level.

The criterion of attention to individual needs is related to a number of generally accepted educational concepts of primary concern to the teacher. Some of these are:

1. All individuals differ in many ways—physically, mentally, psychologically, and emotionally.
2. Students learn by doing, rather than by simply observing.
3. Students differ in the extent to which their background has prepared them for participation in a course.
4. Students who participate actively in the classroom curriculum will develop an understanding of what they are doing; similarly, students who understand what they are doing are likely to participate in a classroom activity.
5. Students differ in the amount of incentive, drive, ambition, and motivation they have.

In considering the factors that influence the selection of procedures in the classroom, some attention should be given to "teacher-talk." Verbalization, as employed by the teacher, often has much to do with the nature of the classroom environment and the extent to which the learners involve their rational powers. Generally, teachers talk too much and allow their students to talk too little. However, teacher-talk can be an important and constructive element in the learning process. For example, when teachers pose questions at only the recall and recognition levels, we may assume that just these aspects of the rational powers are being developed; on the other hand, when they pose questions that encourage student involvement at higher levels of the rational powers, they have provided for the learners the opportunity to engage in responses at all levels. (See the section on convergent and divergent questions in Chapter 3.)

Another element in the classroom environment that influences the selection or creation of procedures is the learners' vocabulary. Actually, the learner has four vocabularies: for listening, for speaking, for reading, and for writing. The techniques normally employed by teachers emphasize these vocabularies to varying degrees. The learner's reading and listening vocabularies are avenues through which he receives inputs of new information and experiences. If the teacher limits the learner to the input of listening and the output of writing, he may be restricting the student's performance.

Other considerations important to the selection and creation of classroom procedures include (1) the method of inquiry, (2) the nature of information giving, and (3) intrinsic or extrinsic motivation. Consider the method of inquiry, which we have said is the methodology for the development of the rational powers. Inquiry has three phases: exploration, invention, and discovery. Exploration occurs when the learner is experiencing, manipulating, or observing the actions, operations, or objects to be studied. During the invention period he begins to invent classifications, hypotheses, and explanations, and to label, cluster, and explain events or situations. In the discovery phase he develops a system for verifying and utilizing his inventions. In selecting classroom procedures, the teacher must consider which phase of inquiry is appropriate for the learner.

Other terms that may be aligned with exploring, inventing, and discovering are seeking, self-selection, and pacing. *Seeking behavior* occurs as the learner explores his environment. The learner will naturally seek those experiences in his environment that are appropriate to his level of maturity and needs and will ignore those that are meaningless or uninteresting. *Self-selection* occurs as the learner chooses activities that are appropriate to his developmental stage and explains events or situations within his field of perception. *Pacing* describes the tendency of the learner to progress at a rate commensurate with his ability. Specific classroom procedures should provide this sequence of activities and involvement for the learner.

Now, let's take a closer look at inquiry. We have said that inquiry has three phases—exploration, invention, and discovery. How does inquiry differ from classroom procedures, such as lectures, demonstrations, reading assignments, discussions, and simulations, normally associated with teaching? If you look closely at these procedures, you will see that *each is a technique for helping the student explore the content area.* Notice that we say explore. The differences among these

FIGURE 7–1
Exploration can be a lively and interesting phase of the learning process.

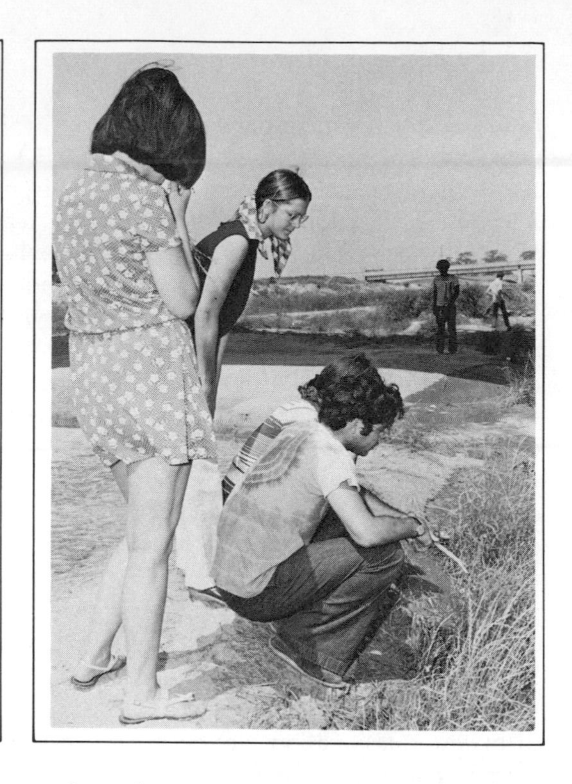

techniques lie in the degree of involvement of students and teachers. In a lecture the teacher explores for the student, who is a passive, or inactive, participant in the learning process. In a demonstration either the teacher or a student explores while other students watch and listen. Again, the exploring is being done for the majority of students. Reading assignments require students to participate in exploratory activities on their own, without the aid of the teacher. Discussions, which are normally based on questions posed by the teacher, promote exploration and sometimes review information or data already collected through lectures, reading assignments, or demonstrations. Simulation is a form of exploration, which usually actively involves students to a greater degree than either lectures or demonstrations.

Many teachers who reject the inquiry method as inappropriate for their content fields are actually actively involved in the first phase of inquiry, under the guise of such activities as lectures, demonstrations, and discussions. They are constantly involved with various techniques designed to help students investigate (or find out) data. *This is exploration;* this is inquiry, in its initial stage. One could say that any teacher who is engaged in the learning process with students is participating in at least an incomplete variety of inquiry. Teachers normally attempt to help students explore a topic, but without encouraging them to move on to the invention and discovery phases. This is unfortunate, for exploring content implies the finding and accumulation of data but not necessarily an *understanding* of it.

In light of this discussion, then, lecturing is not really a teaching method, but rather a classroom technique for moving into the first stage of inquiry. This could also be said of the other techniques mentioned above. But notice we have said that these techniques have been used by teachers to help students explore. *They may also be used to assist students in the phases of invention and discovery,* but they are not because too many teachers assume that a student's exposure to the exploration phase automatically brings with it an understanding of content and promotes intellectual development.

Inquiry is more than a teaching method; it is a teaching philosophy. Teachers use it only when they become convinced that learning how to learn is the primary task of the student and that this task can be accomplished only through individual involvement with content. We should sound a note of caution here, since we are treating techniques within the framework of inquiry. Although reading assignments may be legitimate approaches to some aspects of the learning process, the teacher should exercise care in the use of textbooks. Textbooks that have as their purpose the outlining of the facts of a discipline to be memorized (as most do) are not suitable resources for inquiry teaching—they do more harm than good.

At this point, we would ask that you turn back to Chapter 3 and reread the section on teaching the Constitution through inquiry. Teachers often use a graphical representation of the Constitution because it makes the basic elements of that document "easy to memorize." When facts are laid out in this fashion, students tend to see the exploration phase as finished and may not feel any need to do further research. On the other hand, when students are asked to search out, interpret, classify data, and become involved in the exploration, they can build their own models and do not need this done for them.

Now let us look at the second phase of inquiry, conceptual invention, as described in that example in Chapter 3. After the exploration phase students must be encouraged to share their information and make generalizations. (Many teachers do not even encourage students toward this higher level.) If the students can formulate the concept of the Bill of Rights from an analysis of their own generalizations about constitutional amendments, their understanding of it will be much greater than if they were simply told about it.

The third phase of inquiry, in this example, involves students using the understandings they have developed to make judgments—to *dis-*

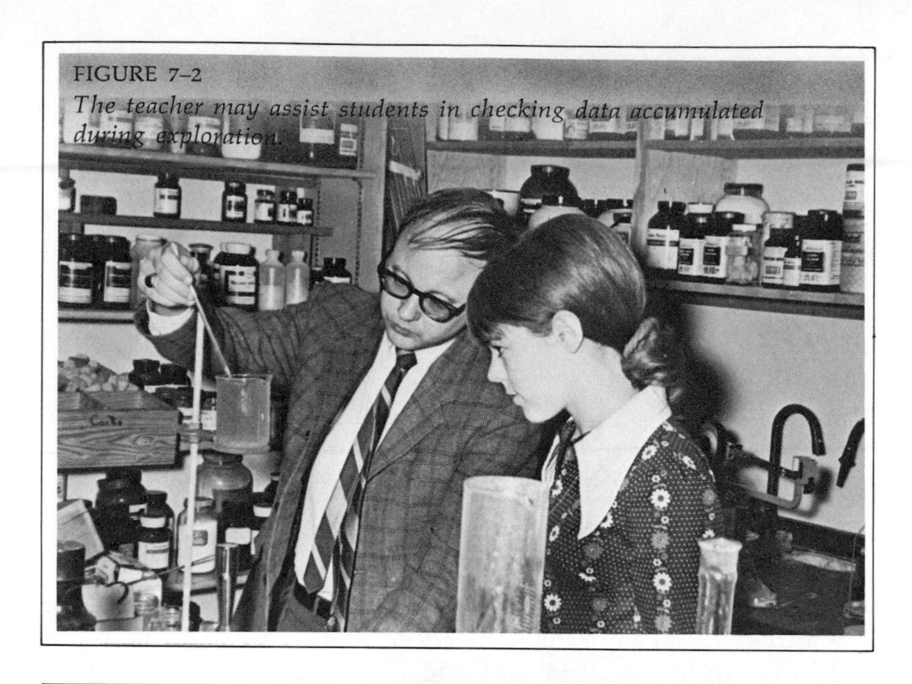

FIGURE 7–2
The teacher may assist students in checking data accumulated during exploration.

FIGURE 7–3
A good learning environment is one that permits inventions.

cover factors relative to their understandings that may be related to aspects of government or citizenship with which they have daily contact. Contrast this level of student participation and involvement with that found in classrooms where the exploration phase is considered the terminal point in the learning process.

Procedures for Presenting Information

The presentation and provision of information are necessary, legitimate, and vital functions of the teacher. They can be accomplished through lectures, discussions, demonstrations, or reading assignments (as well as many other specialized techniques) or through a combination of techniques. Each of these techniques may be useful. However, it is essential that the teacher be able (1) to use all these procedures, and (2) to determine when one technique is more appropriate than another. For example, a lecture may be harmful if it is totally a substitute for the exploratory phase, yet it can be extremely valuable as a means of showing students how some of their inventions might be verified. A lecture can also be valuable as a preliminary to pupil exploration. Demonstrations are a little more flexible than lectures in that they not only can be used more often as part of the exploration, invention, and discovery phases but also can be used to involve students in these phases. Demonstrations have another advantage over lectures in that they give the teacher an indication of the appropriateness of the task to the students' developmental levels and the level of involvement of their rational powers. Discussions have even more flexibility than demonstrations, and they too may be used in all three phases of inquiry. During the exploratory phase, a well-led discussion can elicit, emphasize, and pool the groups' information in ways that may result in new information and insights for each student. During the invention phase, as various students present their ideas, each student has an opportunity to compare, revise, and adapt his own conceptual inventions.

Whatever technique is used to present information, the content as well as the procedure should help to simplify, to cluster, and to be generative. To *simplify* means (1) to tailor the material to the developmental level of the learner, and (2) to reduce the complexity of the data so that the possibility of order is apparent. To *cluster* means to present related ideas. The learner, in order to maintain or sharpen his equilibrium, perceives new learning as additive to that which he has already acquired. He resists requests to learn unrelated items, either by resorting to rote memorization or by developing a logic-tight compartment to separate the unrelated items from his present clusters of knowledge. Too, the learner is constantly grouping and regrouping his knowledge experiences. Teaching procedures should recognize, support, and encourage this clustering activity. Content and procedures are *generative* when they provide the learner with additional power to use what he has learned and to learn what he has not yet learned.

Generating Intrinsic Motivation

If we were to overstate and oversimplify two generalizations from our selected criteria, we could suggest that learning contributes to further

FIGURE 7–4
Until the student has experienced success in the learning process, the teacher cannot depend on intrinsic motivation.

learning, and development of the rational powers contribute to further development of the rational powers. However, these statements are made without considering the phenomenon of motivation. When the learner focuses the full range of his rational powers on actions or operations appropriate to his developmental level, energy is generated. This energy rewards the learner and inspires him to repeat and continue the cycle of exploration, invention, and discovery. Teaching techniques that foster these activities tend to generate intrinsic motivation. On the other hand, techniques that do not take advantage of this cycle cause the learner to need support from some extrinsic system of encouragement. However, while the effects of the inquiry cycle on student motivation are very real, the system is a cognitive explanation of motivation and may not account for the impact of affective domain factors. There is also the danger that the learner may be conditioned to distrust or be suspicious of the opportunities provided by the inquiry cycle. He may lack confidence in himself as a learner or in the teacher as a guide. As a teacher, you must be ready to capitalize on any energy, need, or drive you perceive in the learner to produce the initial motivation to participate in the inquiry cycle.

At this point, some additional comments concerning motivation are probably appropriate. For example, the time between the learner's initial entrance into the learning cycle and his personal recognition of progress toward a goal is a very important factor in maintaining, reinforcing, and promoting subsequent motivation. Generally speaking, the longer the time lag, the greater the difficulty in maintaining, reinforcing, or promoting further motivation. The teacher must be sensitive to the time lag experienced by his students, for during this period they need all the encouragement and attention he can give them.

Too often, teachers identify reward and punishment systems with motivation. These tools may be dangerous if not used very carefully. Within each classroom a set of rewards and punishments is established that reflects desired student behavior. If a student does not value the reward and punishment system, the teacher has two alternatives. He can exclude the student, or he can apply rewards or punishments that are perceived by the student as important. The teacher must exercise caution in applying punishment, for the student's energy may become diffused. Motivation is an expression of previous learnings. The student who exhibits "unmotivated" behavior is displaying learned behavior, as is the student who exhibits motivation. Motivation is not something the teacher can provide for or to the students.

Equilibrium and Disequilibrium

Piaget's concept of equilibrium and disequilibrium are also important considerations in the selection and creation of classroom techniques and procedures. The student strives to stay in equilibrium and to use new learning experiences to sharpen, support, and extend that equilibrium. He will resist disequilibrium, although student tolerance of this state varies. The teacher should consider the purpose of classroom procedures as he selects and refines them. It is important to determine if a technique or procedure tends to reinforce a present state of equilibrium or create a disequilibrium; procedures selected to do either will begin with similar activities. In the exploratory phase the learner identifies his present system for clustering, generating, classifying, and comparing. But in the invention phase the techniques designed to support or disturb equilibrium differ. Techniques designed to create disequilibrium must contain elements that do not fit the constructs of a previous equilibrium state. If these elements are appropriate to the learner's developmental level, he will have the option of rejecting them or inventing a framework that will accommodate them. Another difference existing in the second phase is that techniques chosen to support a previous state of equilibrium may make use of previous inventions. In selecting techniques that encourage disequilibrium, the teacher must be conscious of the increased anxiety level of the student whose state of equilibrium is threatened. He should provide additional positive and effective reinforcement during the period in which disequilibrium is introduced.

Diagnostic Skills

Any discussion of classroom procedures would be incomplete without some attention to the diagnostic skills that traditionally have been considered to fall within the realm of teacher responsibility. For example, teachers are expected to be able to diagnose the level of difficulty of reading material, the skill levels of students in specific curriculum areas, potential mental and physical impediments to learning, and various other problem conditions. Such skills are unquestionably important in meeting the criterion of attention to individual needs. But to function fully with the three criteria introduced here, the teacher needs to develop a new set of diagnostic skills.

First, he must be prepared to assess a student's position relative to developmental levels so that he can adjust the learning environment to the student's level of readiness for objects, actions, and operations. This assessment should be continuous and should not cease after a student has been identified as preoperational, concrete-operational, or formal-operational. The response readiness of the student as well as the stimuli of the learning environment must be continually assessed and reassessed in terms of his developmental level. The diagnosis of reading skills, group relationships, and problems that impede the learning process is important primarily when viewed as a supplement to the analysis of the relationship between the learning environment and the student's developmental level.

Another diagnostic skill of primary importance is the teacher's ability to assess the student's range, quantity, and degree of complexity of utilization of the rational powers. Since this is a function of developmental level, it is very helpful if the teacher has already accurately assessed the student's position in relation to developmental levels. The range and quantity of the student's rational powers are important because their utilization is a cumulative phenomenon. Bloom suggests that for a learner to perform at higher levels of the rational powers, he must already have the ability to perform at all previous levels pertaining to the knowledge experience. Still, this does not mean that the learner must always proceed from the simple to the complex, or from recall to recognition to application. Through divergent thinking, he may proceed to higher levels of analysis or synthesis, and then through deduction, move back through the lower levels.

It may be a good procedure for the teacher to deliberately vary the deductive and inductive movement of the learner through various levels of the rational powers.

During the conceptual-invention phase of inquiry the learner has usually utilized some of the rational powers beyond the lowest level, recall. At this point diagnostic procedures are needed to help the teacher judge whether the learner needs to move toward knowledge and comprehension or toward higher levels in rational-power application. Quantity is also important in that it takes many experiences at the lower levels of the rational powers to generate the ability to cluster and invent—indications of a movement toward a higher level. Although Bloom's thesis is not identical or even completely parallel to the Educational Policies Commission's statement of the central purpose of education, his work on the taxonomy of educational objectives is useful in preparing diagnostic procedures for assessing the range, quantity, and degree of complexity of the student's involvement in rational-power development.[5]

Finally, it goes without saying that a teacher must have the diagnostic skill to determine what point each student has reached in the inquiry process. To use the exploration-invention-discovery cycle, the teacher must be able to locate accurately a student's performance within a phase so that instructional procedures can be adapted to that phase and the student encouraged to move on to the next phase. While the classroom techniques we have discussed may be used during any of the three phases of inquiry, they must be properly adapted to each phase.

We have not attempted here to analyze individual teaching techniques, but rather to look at techniques as they might be incorporated in the overall learning process. Many new techniques are being developed that may make valuable contributions and add depth to the learning process. As you develop procedures of your own, keep in mind our comments concerning the three criteria for the selection and creation of classroom methodology.

[5] Benjamin S. Bloom, ed., *Taxonomy of Educational Objectives, The Classification of Educational Goals, Handbook I: Cognitive Domain* (New York: Longmans, Green, 1956).

Understanding Complicating Factors

The individualization of the learning process is basic both to successful instructional methodologies and to curriculum design. It is a complex enough task in itself, but it becomes even more involved and frustrating when you consider the various factors that can complicate the learning situation in the classroom. Emphasis on the individual student has been generally accepted in American public education since the early 1900s and has progressively received more recognition. Studies by early-twentieth-century psychologists such as Cattell, Thorndike, and Hall revealed extremely wide ranges in intellectual, emotional, and physical characteristics of adolescents. The results of these studies, together with numerous other factors, contributed to the eventual development of the junior high school. The junior high school in itself was an expression of the need felt by educators for a type of education designed especially to meet the needs of adolescent students.

Although the necessity for attention to individual differences among students has long been recognized and accepted by educators, many teachers pay only lip service to this concept. Over the years, countless means have been employed to provide individualized instruction in classrooms. But many of these efforts have become the object of controversy, and few educators (even though they may endorse an idea or procedure) have appeared truly satisfied with the results. Thus, public education continues to search for procedures that will permit emphasis on the individual student. The inquiry method, which does permit the teacher to focus on the individual, has been used in some schools for quite a long time, but, unfortunately, it still has not really replaced the more traditional approaches.

Even though the inquiry method, where it is adopted, may provide a legitimate vehicle for achieving individualization in the learning process, there are still a great many variables operating both within and outside the school that can adversely affect what goes on in the classroom. There are basically three elements involved in the learning process—the teacher, the student, and the curriculum content—and we can use these three elements to classify factors within the school that may interfere with learning. Before discussing these internal sources of conflict, however, we shall examine conditions outside the school that can complicate matters. Environmental conditions in the local community, in particular, have a strong influence on what takes place in the classroom.

Students differ not only in their physical, emotional, and intellectual makeup but in other ways that have to do with cultural, subcultural, and environmental factors. In order to understand each of the students in your classroom, you must take into consideration those aspects of the individual's background and experiences that contribute to his attitudes, personality, and performance in a formal learning situation. Furthermore, you must keep in mind that many of the differences among students are not necessarily discernible through observation of an individual's conduct in the classroom or his general performance.

The term *disadvantaged* has been overused in recent years and perhaps has lost some of its meaning. Basically, it refers to students who are inadequately prepared to participate in the learning situation. Such inadequate preparation may result from any or all of a variety of environmental factors. Certain aspects of these environmental conditions affect students in almost any community, and thus we find students who are disadvantaged (for one reason or another) at all levels and in all types of schools. Even those schools that are considered average, with students whose standards and values are considered middle class, have students who are disadvantaged in one or more categories. However, because most problems tend to be accentuated in schools in poor areas, more can be learned by probing the sources of resistance to learning in these schools than by attempting to analyze the factors that operate as barriers to learning in the more stable middle-class schools. Furthermore, it is very likely that the factors that complicate the learning process in an inner-city problem school exist to a lesser degree in the "better" schools.

Negative Aspects of the Inner City

Even a superficial examination of the inner city of any major urban center will reveal the obviously unpleasant circumstances of its environment. The entire atmosphere of the inner city reflects the overcrowding, poor living conditions, filth, and disease that are part of the everyday life of the inhabitants. The smoke, soot, and dust of industry are inescapable and hasten the degeneration of homes and apartment buildings. Families that can financially afford it flee from these uncomfortable conditions and move to the suburbs, where they find more adequate housing, larger yards and playgrounds, better shopping, and healthier living conditions. Families that cannot afford to leave the inner city are trapped in an atmosphere of hopelessness and despair.

Sometimes the impression is created that persons who spend their lives in such depressing circumstances do not really care about such things as cleanliness, neatness, and healthful conditions. This is not necessarily true. Fine families are often found residing in the inner city. These are people who have never been able to earn enough to adequately feed and care for their large families. They remain, therefore, where rent is low and where the unskilled can find extra work. Necessity, not desire, is what keeps many people penned up in the inner city.

Of course, the inner city is also a refuge for many who do not really care how they live. It is a haven for degenerates, winos, bums, and the nonproductive, as well as for those who capitalize on the miseries of the "downs-and-outs," such as loan sharks, fences, and pimps. More than anything, these overpopulated areas resemble a jungle, with the defenseless prey for the merciless. From the dimly lighted streets to the shadowy alleys, the failures of the world's greatest society shuffle their way through a hopeless existence.

Physically, the inner city reflects all the ugliness and unpleasantness of decaying civilization. Its boulevards show the effects of heavy industrial traffic, while the gutters and alleys overflow with trash and litter. Buildings stand in a state of disrepair, paint peeling and shrieking for attention. Small patches of yards contain a wide variety of junk and weeds, with hardly a suggestion of grass. There are few playgrounds in the inner city, so youngsters have no choice but to play in the streets. Overcrowded conditions at home cause them to seek recreation elsewhere. The absence of organized programs encourages them to roam the streets and alleys aimlessly, often manufacturing games out of their own imaginations, always looking for someway to pass the time. Strom reports that inadequate space in the home causes family members to take to the streets, where they see and hear the activities and language that accompany gambling, narcotics, prostitution, and drinking.[1]

[1] Robert D. Strom, *Teaching in the Slum School* (Columbus, Ohio: Merrill, 1965), p. 8.

The economic condition of the inner city closely resembles its physical condition. Families residing there represent largely the lower strata of American society, the semiskilled and unskilled work forces. In addition to having lower-than-average incomes, inner-city families are not too knowledgeable (or sensible) about budgeting and handling wages. Welfare families are common, and broken homes are far from unusual. Poverty or near-poverty conditions normally ensure hopelessness in the inner city. The people trapped there eventually become resigned to their fates, realizing that they will probably never enjoy better living conditions. The hopeless attitudes of parents are, in time, transmitted to the children, who sooner or later accept the same resigned outlook on their lot:

The depressed-area child is involved in a world culturally different from the non-depressed-area child. His neighborhood is accented by filth and punctuated by violence. He must learn to cope with these conditions if he is to survive.[2]

The constant exposure of inner-city youngsters to degeneration, hopelessness, despair, and failure in the home and community environment sets the stage and pattern for their future development. The absence of ambition and motivation to succeed in most inner-city inhabitants gradually conditions youngsters in this environment for future failure. The inner city breeds irresponsibility and violence and prepares its young people to be suspicious of society, its laws, and its institutions. It is this kind of environment in which the inner-city school exists.

Probably no educational institution has received as much attention and publicity in recent years as the inner-city school. Although problems have existed in these urban localities for a long time, education in the inner city has become a prime concern because of what may be achieved through it toward the broad goal of racial integration. The inner-city school has come to be regarded as one in which extreme problems are encountered, both within and outside the classroom. The problem school is characterized by destruction, vandalism, and violence, and is a focal point for animosity, obstinance, and suspicion. The very term *inner-city problem school* connotes low teacher morale and poor school spirit. Unsuccessful and discouraged teachers have called this educational environment both impossible and dangerous. Teachers have repeatedly denounced inner-city education, focusing on student attitudes. Criticism has also been directed toward

[2] George Henderson and Robert F. Bibens, *Teachers Should Care* (New York: Harper & Row, 1970), p. 61.

FIGURE 8–1
Lack of regard for school property and acts of vandalism are common in the inner city.

school administrators and patrons. Patrons and students, on the other hand, as well as some school administrators, often believe that much of the blame for unsuccessful inner-city education rests with the teachers. There are others who feel that the schools' curricula are at the base of the problem.

Merely attempting to place the blame, however, is not productive. The important thing is to identify the problems that exist in the schools, to investigate their effect on the curriculum, and to explore alternatives for correcting those conditions. In any school the most obvious complicating factors are students, teachers, parents, content, facilities, and the administration.

Students as Complicating Factors

Projecting the inner-city environment into the area's schools allows us to understand most of the reasons for negative student attitudes. Too often, the schools have failed to really "educate" inner-city youth. Over the years, residents of these areas have grown to distrust public educational institutions. Because of the lack of understanding between teachers and various elements in the community, the school seems to many people to be operating on a level apart from and unconcerned with the needs of its students. Kimball Wiles points to the real concerns and needs of youth: to be successful, to achieve, to be self-directing, and to be accepted.[3]

The nation's schools generally reflect an approach to learning that is teacher dominated and content centered. This stance has been particularly accepted as a good procedure in middle-class areas, which produce most of our teachers. However, this acceptance of content-centered technique does not mean that youngsters even in the middle-class schools have "learned" the material to which they were exposed or have progressed in the development of their rational powers.

Acceptance of this type of procedure is an indication that the presentation of material or content has come to be regarded as "teaching" by both teachers and students. Students from basically middle-class backgrounds have learned to accept the rules and play the game in the classroom. Memorization of content has become almost synonymous with learning, and teachers attempting to use another technique may be rejected as different or unusual. These attitudes, then, represent the frame of reference of most middle-class teachers.

Because of the general attitudes encountered in inner-city schools, great numbers of teachers have hesitated to accept positions in those institutions. Often, staff members seek transfers to other schools "where students want to learn." Many teachers, however, find considerable satisfaction in their relationships with students in the inner city. In this section we shall investigate how some of the negative attitudes found in the inner city can be turned to advantage in the learning process.

The restless student is not an unusual phenomenon in the depressed-area school. When a youngster does not understand what is going on in the learning process—either because his reading ability is several levels below that which is expected of him or because he does not have the skills needed to work with learning materials at a given grade level—he should be expected to be restless. *Perhaps restlessness under such circumstances is indicative of a normal rather than an abnormal student, in middle-class, suburban districts as well as in inner-city schools.*

Students in inner-city classrooms often have short attention spans, and their interest wanders easily. If a pupil does not understand the material being explored, and especially if he believes that it is beyond his comprehension, he is not likely to concentrate on the lesson for very long. Any interest he may have in classroom activities will wane

[3] Kimbal Wiles, *The Changing Curriculum of the American High School* (Englewood Cliffs, N.J.: Prentice-Hall, 1963), p. 53.

FIGURE 8–2
Some students are easily distracted.

if he does not, or cannot, comprehend what is being taught. If the student does not gain at least some satisfaction from the learning process, that process, for him, will be meaningless and unproductive.

Unprepared students are also common. Homework assignments are often neglected, and many students seem unable or unwilling to participate in class activities, perhaps because they have not mastered the skills needed for successful participation. Some young people so dislike the school environment that they will rebel against any assignment connected with the institution. Many of these individuals are capable and can be led to profit from the educative process if their teachers are alert enough to assess the situation properly and respond to their needs. However, determining which students can and which cannot (or will not) perform successfully at a specific grade level is a difficult task.

Those young people who have already decided that participation in school affairs is undesirable are quite adept at driving the teacher to distraction. Harassing the teacher is a game, almost a science, for some students. One of the most difficult problems is the student who is determined to be disorderly. Often, he has had several years' experience in how to annoy teachers effectively.[4] If the classroom situation is basically unpleasant for students, they may try to make it equally unpleasant for the teacher, to the point where they are "rewarded" by being removed from class because of their uncooperative attitudes and behavior. Unfortunately, once a student is removed from a class, you no longer have an opportunity to influence his behavior.

[4] Melvin Keene, *Beginning Secondary School Teachers Guide* (New York: Harper & Row, 1969), p. 122.

Problem students are often considered by teachers to be the greatest barrier to successful classroom instruction. Time and again instructors are heard to remark, "If I could just get rid of one or two of my students, I could teach." Often the teacher feels that it is necessary to spend much of his time on matters pertaining to control and discipline. The fear of encounters with problem students can harm a teacher's position with and attitude toward his students. Differentiating between those who are unwilling participants in the learning situation and those who are maladjusted or disturbed is a difficult problem, and one you may need help to solve.

Part of the problem is that the difference between the emotionally unstable child and the normal adolescent is a matter of degree. However, an emotionally unstable student is more likely to get into a rage over things, while the normal adolescent, for the most part, maintains adequate control of his emotions.[5] A great many students in the classroom show some degree of maladjustment, from less severe withdrawal symptoms to more serious cases of rejection and violent overt reaction. The normal climate of the classroom may be more than some students can handle, and when the pressure becomes too great, they may react in an undesirable fashion.

Classroom pressures are created not only by the teacher but by the students themselves. Student pressure on an individual class member, for example, can cause a great deal of classroom unpleasantness. Educators have long recognized the power of the peer group to control the behavior of adolescents. A student is in the presence of the teacher only briefly; he spends much of his day in the company of his fellow students and neighborhood friends. He is likely, therefore, to be more concerned with what other students think of him than with winning the approval of the teacher. Thus, when a student is faced with a choice between pleasing the members of his peer group or his teacher, it is understandable that he may place a higher priority on the approval of those in his own age group. Regardless of the cause of social failure with less disadvantaged age-mates, the unsuccessful individual may seek acceptance from others suffering from status deprivation.[6]

Much has been written about peer-group relationships, and yet they are one of the least understood aspects of adolescent behavior. The power of the peer group and its effect on the individual is not hard to understand when it is placed in the proper perspective. The

[5] Solomon O. Lichter *et al.*, *The Drop-Outs* (New York: Macmillan, 1962), p. 23.
[6] Sandra A. Warden, *The Leftouts* (New York: Holt, Rinehart & Winston, 1968), p. 102.

teacher often ignores the influence of the peer group on the individual student and perceives behavior in the classroom in terms of teacher-established expectancies of student performance. However, just as the teacher is responsive to the values of his peers, so too is the adolescent conscious of the code, the expectancies, even the dictates, of the group of which he is a member.

The peer group of a student may have its foundation within the classroom, within the society of the school, or outside the school setting. Regardless of the bases for selection, and even though its organization may be extremely informal, the individual member is acutely aware of the attitudes of other group members. Because he has a need to belong and not to stand alone, he has a strong tendency to want to please his group. He behaves as they expect him to behave in order to win their approval. In the classroom a conflict situation may arise when the teacher puts pressure on a student in the form of a reprimand. The student may feel that he cannot "lose face" with his friends, and therefore responds to the teacher's admonition with a display of defiance. This is only an isolated example of the influence of the peer group in the classroom. Sometimes student animosity may take the form of an organized resistance toward the teacher that involves all students in the room to some degree. In such instances, although a student may not be a member of a specific group, he may hesitate to alienate those who are members by ignoring their stance toward a teacher.

The teacher cannot afford to disregard peer-group influence. He must be familiar with how it operates and be able to avoid unnecessary conflict situations. In this way, he will not only be able to avert peer-group opposition but may even be able to use peer-group influence to further the learning process.

Another problem that teachers face is the student with a legitimate physical disorder. Often, a student's physical defects are unknown to the teacher; in fact, it is sometimes quite difficult for the teacher to get any information about the student's health. This is particularly true in inner-city schools. Even though the schools technically may require physical examinations for students, enforcing this policy may be almost impossible. Actually, understanding why parents in the inner city might want to avoid an annual physical examination for their children is not difficult. The principal reason is the cost; many parents believe, perhaps logically, that the family would do better to spend the money in other ways.

Nevertheless, there are some things that a teacher should know about a student that only a physical examination will reveal. Knowing which students suffer from allergies, diabetes, heart and muscular disorders, could enable the teacher to prevent considerable embarrassment, or even disaster. The teacher should also be familiar with such student problems as epilepsy, seizures, and fainting, which excessive classroom pressure can aggravate. One problem that is easily recognizable in time but might go undetected in a child with introvert tendencies is stuttering. Insisting that a student who suffers from a speech disorder perform orally may cause him to resent both the teacher and the learning process.

One of the chief reasons for the difficulty in obtaining needed information about students in inner-city schools is the high degree of family mobility within depressed geographical areas. It is not unusual for a family to move from neighborhood to neighborhood and from community to community within the inner city. Financial problems often force a family to move from one apartment to another. In addition, students who become involved in some difficulty in one school sometimes enroll in another school to evade the attention of school authorities. This kind of thing is made possible by the large number of split families and broken homes and the complexities of close and distant family relationships. Sometimes a student prevents detection of his legal home address by moving in with friends who live in another district. All such moves further complicate the problem of obtaining adequate background data on students.

Of course, one great difficulty in teaching inner-city children is coping with excessive absenteeism. For years teachers have complained, "We can't teach them if they won't come to school." Although family financial problems sometimes interfere with regular school attendance, this is not the only reason for absenteeism. Certainly, some students are not overly enchanted with their participation in the school program, and many develop a hearty aversion to almost everything for which the school stands. Often, children avoid what they consider to be unpleasant experiences in the classroom (because classroom experiences have failed to give them satisfaction or success), even though their parents want them to participate fully in the educative process. On the other hand, it is not unusual for the parents themselves to doubt the legitimacy of the school program *and* the school staff. Children from such families quickly detect their parents' lack of confidence in the school and its teachers. Absenteeism in such cases tends to be very high, with parents as well as children using all sorts of excuses for missing school. Some individuals find classroom confinement so distasteful and frustrating that skipping school is worth the risk of detection and punishment. Certainly truancy accounts for some student absenteeism, and the line between legitimate and illegitimate absence is often a fine one. As long as some students consider school work irrelevant and are unable or unprepared to participate in the learning process, the outside environment will appear more inviting.

In addition to inhibiting the learning process, student absenteeism complicates teaching. When students are absent on different days, the teacher must take into account which students may fall behind because they missed an important part of the lesson. Not giving those who have missed a class the opportunity to catch up by taking time to work with each student who needs special attention only makes the learning process seem more unfair.

Countless things can and do interfere to varying degrees with the learning procedure. Yet the teacher is expected to be constantly equipped and prepared to direct classroom affairs, control behavior, and respond in a constructive way whenever a situation occurs that may prevent the achievement of the central goal, rational-power development.

Although teachers spend a great amount of time attempting to deal effectively with discipline problems, there are many who believe that the emphasis on discipline in the school and in the classroom is self-perpetuating and has had negative results. There is a strong trend in modern educational theory away from an emphasis on rules and punitive measures and toward a positive and constructive stance. One of the greatest differences between what might be called the traditional and the modern classroom is the interpretation of discipline. Although we tend to think of classroom discipline in terms of student behavior, a more appropriate approach might be to focus on the teacher. We shall deal with this approach to discipline in the next section.

Teachers as Complicating Factors

In many cases, when children encounter difficulty in learning, we find parents blaming teachers; teachers blaming students, parents, and administrators; and the administrators blaming a wide variety of conditions that impede intellectual achievement. Probably the blame for a student's failure to learn cannot be placed on any single element of a particular educational situation. Yet each of us, as a student, parent, teacher, or administrator, has probably observed teachers who have contributed to rather than alleviated classroom problems. In this section we shall examine how the actions, attitudes, and procedures of teachers complicate the learning process.

Unprepared teachers are a serious problem in the modern classroom. To evaluate the degree and kind of preparation that is necessary to produce a successful teacher involves considering a variety of competencies and understandings. Adequate preparation for teaching is often thought of only in terms of competency in a particular subject. While the importance of other elements may be recognized in theory, in practice the aspects of the complete teacher frequently take a back seat. The uncertainty with which educators through the years have given weight or priority to subject-area preparation is illustrated by the debate over whether a teacher's advanced degree should be in a particular subject or in education. Some educators prefer teachers to do most of their advanced work in education, while others insist that graduate study in a particular subject is preferable. To become too involved in such an argument at this point would not be profitable. It is sufficient to point out that something more than just proficiency in a particular subject is needed to make a successful teacher. Too many teachers have been highly successful as teachers in areas outside their own specialty for us to accept the notion that subject competency is the *only or even the primary* key to satisfactory classroom experiences. A secondary school teacher, in particular, needs to be adequately versed in adolescent behavior, learning theory, human relations, and teaching procedures.

Characteristics of the teacher other than preparedness in these areas can also contribute to success or failure in the classroom. Self-confidence, sensitivity to responsibility, and emotional stability cannot be learned from textbooks or lectures, yet they are essential qualities in a teacher. To some extent, these teacher attitudes and sensitivity qualities can be developed in the college classroom, but they really require actual contact with learners. If, as often happens, the student-teaching experience does not provide sufficient involvement, some degree of unpreparedness in inevitable. A teacher who is unprepared in one or more facets of the teaching art will have difficulty establishing and maintaining a successful learning environment, which can also have a detrimental effect on other teachers because of the carryover in student attitudes and behavior from one classroom to another.

One aspect of a teacher's performance that normally receives little attention pertains to how he is viewed by others. A teacher's effectiveness is undoubtedly related to the expectations held by students, parents, administrators, and other staff members as to what he should do and how he should behave. Each person, professional or non-professional, who has contact with the classroom curriculum has his own preconceptions as to what constitutes acceptable teacher performance and behavior, and the teacher may discover that his efforts are contained to some extent by those notions. Certainly, he cannot help but be conscious of such expectations.

Traditionally, the teacher has not been overly concerned with student evaluations of his performance. Since the approach to instruction was teacher-centered, it was easy for him to dominate the class and control their behavior. However, although this system did force the students to participate, at least mechanically, in the learning process, the teacher could not control student attitudes.

Over the years, students receptive to conditioning received in school and at home accepted the teacher-centered instructional system and played the roles prescribed for them. Even though a student might not like a particular teacher, he would carry out the functions of his role in accordance with the rules of behavior and performance prescribed for the entire class. Although many students rebel against this kind of classroom procedure, the system has survived. In spite of its ineffectiveness, *the telling-memorizing system is still the most practiced teaching methodology in the American public schools.* Since students have had universal exposure to this procedure, they tend to expect it and to expect the accompanying teacher behavior patterns.

Something in the present system causes many students to lose interest in school, and perhaps to drop out. Yet it is generally accepted that even problem students get along well with one or two teachers, and it does not appear to be because of the subject area. Some teachers just have the knack of working with all kinds of students. We are not sure just why some teachers appear to have a magic touch with their students, but we can identify some teacher characteristics and behavior patterns to which students react unfavorably. Teachers who possess these characteristics seem to have difficulty in functioning in the classroom.

First of all, let us examine what learners expect from a teacher. Students expect their teacher to be honest, sincere, and straightforward with them. A teacher who gives his students the impression that he is a sneak, and is trying to trap them, or catch them off-guard, will probably never obtain their respect. This, of course, is why students often rebel against teachers who give "pop quizzes."

Inconsistency on the part of the teacher is another negative attribute that dispels the students' faith in him. There is some security in having confidence in a teacher's behavior and conduct, whether in regard to the conduct of a lesson or his handling of disciplinary problems. Inconsistent behavior by the teacher indicates to his students that they can anticipate shaky and uncertain classroom conditions. Such classroom circumstances create an uncomfortable atmosphere in the classroom and set the stage for potential discipline problems. It is certainly not an environment that promotes inquiry.

Another teacher attribute students are very quick to detect pertains to fairness. Students expect a teacher to be fair in his treatment of them and to refrain from showing favoritism to any student or group of students. While the tendency to respond more favorably to students who put forth maximum effort is only natural, the teacher cannot allow it to control his behavior if he wishes to retain the respect of his other students.

Teachers in the inner city need to be especially alert to control these traits. Whereas students in a relatively stable, middle-class school will dislike these characteristics in a teacher and grumble among themselves about him, they understand what they must do in order to curry favor with him, the school, and possibly their parents. If a high mark in a class means enough to them, they will play along with him.

In the inner city, however, the situation is quite different. Inner-city youngsters, too, realize that the teacher is expected to be fair, honest, sincere, and unbiased. When faced with the evidence that he is not what he is supposed to be, they may react in ways that are extremely unpleasant. Most middle-class students will reject the teacher who pretends he is something he is not; even fewer students in the inner city will tolerate a fake. Also, since fewer students in the inner city experience any success in school, they feel little obligation to please the teacher, if that teacher appears to be something other than what he should be.

The teacher with a middle-class background who attempts to teach in the inner city needs a special kind of preparation and depth of understanding. Without this, he himself is a complicating factor in the classroom. He may find the handling of disciplinary matters particularly troublesome, especially since standard disciplinary procedures used with apparent success in middle-class schools often prove completely useless in the inner city.

In the middle-class school, teachers commonly use warnings and threats to produce desired responses from their students. The middle-class youngster understand that if he does what the teacher wants him to do, the warning or threat will be nullified. In the inner city, however, a threat may be taken literally by a student, and viewed as a challenge. Instead of complying or, as he sees it, knuckling under as a student in a middle-class school might do, the inner-city student may meet the threat head on.

Each of us, without straining his memory too much, can recall negative characteristics of teachers with whom we have had contact. Negative characteristics on the part of teachers can repel students to the point that they do not want to participate in certain classes or courses. We know that students like to work with some teachers and reject others. This in itself should be sufficient to make us recognize that teachers often contribute to learning difficulties.

Many energetic and dedicated teachers have had their enthusiasm dampened by encounters with established members of a teaching staff. It is an unwritten law in schools that seniority among teachers be respected. New teachers understandably look to older teachers on a staff for information concerning the local "system" and policy. Unfortunately, it often happens that a few teachers, because of their long affiliation with a school, assume positions of false authority. They are given a measure of respect by newer teachers, and this politeness is reflected in their election as heads of departments. In some schools the department heads exercise a good deal of control over other teachers through their system for handling such things as materials and supplies. Under such circumstances, a teacher may find it very difficult to include any flexibility in his classroom approach, because his performance is geared to the decisions made by another teacher in the same building.

The new teacher who reports to his first assignment full of enthusiasm for exposing his students to new and different classroom experiences may find his methods frowned upon by other staff members. Although a teacher is normally allowed a great deal of latitude within his own classroom in matters pertaining to his approach to the learning process, he must be alert to the possibility that an effective but different methodology may alienate other staff members.

Unfortunately, over the years the idea has developed that a teacher improves automatically with age. Thus, a teacher who has spent several years in a school may feel (and others may agree) that he has become an authority on his subject area and on the students served by that school. Even though such teachers may have performed ineffectively for many years, it may be unwise for a new and untried teacher to challenge their procedures.

Sometimes certain teachers in a school dominate the local school administration and employ almost bullying tactics to gain their ends. This situation often develops following a change in the local school administration, when the new administrator tries to get along with solidly entrenched staff members. Once an administration allows itself to become dominated by certain elements of the teaching staff, its power to lead the school in directions that conflict with the ideas of those teachers is seriously undermined.

Content as a Complicating Factor

The third primary element in the classroom, after the student and the teacher, is the subject to be taught—the content. Just as some students are "turned off" by certain teachers, we find that not all students are equally receptive to the various subject areas. Think back to your own lack of enthusiasm as you faced a semester in which you were required to study history or some other subject you did not like. Individuals seldom have the same enthusiasm for each of the disciplines; they like some subjects better than others.

There are, of course, reasons why we develop preferences for certain subject areas. We shy away from a subject which previous experience has warned us is boring and uninteresting. Generally, we tend to judge an area in terms of the satisfaction it brings us. If a learner's exposure to one social studies course has been negative, he will probably not look forward to subsequent courses in that area.

Sometimes a negative attitude toward a subject is caused by a bad experience with a specific teacher; we have a tendency to associate subjects with the teachers who teach them. If a learner intensely dislikes the way a certain teacher conducts a class, and if that teacher is a member of the science department, he may categorize all science classes in terms of that particular teacher and select subjects other than science in the future.

Then too, many students avoid classwork in certain subjects simply because they lack a basic understanding of the discipline. A student without a legitimate foundation in a discipline generally realizes that further work in that area is a losing proposition. It is not unusual for a student to do fairly well in one subject and do poorly in another. When curriculum requirements force students to take further courses in such an area, then content can become a complicating factor in the learning process.

Part of the problem is the degree of reverence with which teachers view such standard equipment as textbooks and curriculum guides. Teachers commonly assume that the material outlined in the curriculum guide must "be covered" in the normal course of the semester's work. This assumption suggests that students (and teachers) are not individuals; that they do not learn differently, at varying rates and with differing degrees of comprehension. It also suggests that any student at a given level is "ready" to accomplish the work spelled out in the text or curriculum guide. Were content really this sacred, we would be able to do away with teachers altogether, for there are many more economical ways of exposing a learner to content than through a teacher. "Covering" material in the classroom suggests that exposure to information is synonymous with learning. It also implies that dispensing information is the same thing as teaching. Too strong an emphasis on content, to the point that the individuality of the learners is disregarded, also makes it a deterrent to the learning process.

Sometimes content is arranged in a particularly uninteresting way that is a barrier to learning. The arrangement of material in guides and textbooks does not necessarily represent the best way to approach a particular class. Teachers who rely solely or too heavily on such materials are abrogating their responsibility to their students.

Parents as Complicating Factors

Another aspect of the teaching situation that normally receives little attention involves the parents of students. Although teachers consider their primary concern to be their students, parents cannot be just ignored. The power of parental pressure is evident in the methods some teachers use to avoid contact with them. Giving a student an unsatisfactory grade may result in an unpleasant confrontation with an irate parent. To avoid this experience, some teachers search for ways of rationalizing student performance so that unsatisfactory grades need not be awarded.

No one enjoys the unpleasant aspects of his job, and the teacher is no exception. Through the years, he has learned that most contacts between teacher and parent develop when the student is not performing well in school or has become involved in some problem situation. Because parent and teacher contact has so often been negative, each element tends to avoid contact with the other.

A hostile parent can interfere with the teacher's efficiency in a number of ways. He can harass the teacher without ever coming face to face with him by complaining to the school principal or circulating rumors about him in the community.

There are countless reasons why parents develop hostility toward teachers. For example, parents (like students) have certain expectations pertaining to teacher performance. When a teacher's performance does not conform fairly well to these expectations, the parent may begin to doubt the teacher's ability. This doubt may change to suspicion or conviction if his child does not do well in the teacher's class. The teacher must realize that all parents are potentially hostile and will react unfavorably if they think the teacher is acting in a way that is unfair or detrimental to their child's chances of success.

Part of the problem associated with teacher-parent relationships is caused by lack of contact and poor channels of communication. Parents are normally poorly informed about what actually goes on in the classroom; most of their information is gleaned from their children and from what they hear around the community. Usually, the only indication the parent has of his child's progress is a periodic report or grade card. Since a child is usually not anxious to report unsatisfactory progress in a subject, the parent may assume that the child is doing all right, until he receives a bad report card.

It is even more difficult for the teacher to communicate with parents in the inner city than those in middle-class suburban areas. Here, many parents specifically avoid contact of any kind with the school; their own experiences with such institutions have often been unsatisfactory or at best questionable.

Concerned that their children get a good education, lower class parents are sensitive about their own lack of achievement in school. Both those who did well and those who did poorly in school feel as if they are outsiders and that their opinion about education would neither be appreciated nor respected by the teachers. It is understandable that lower class parents view a parent-teacher conference as a time to discuss only problems of discipline or student failures.[7]

Often they are quite distrustful and fearful of the school and its staff, and their children's failure simply confirms what they have always believed about schools and teachers.

We know that students sense the attitudes of their parents, and often reflect those attitudes themselves. Whether a parent is openly hostile, then, is not the real point. His lack of confidence in the school, or in a teacher, may create as many problems for the child in the classroom as if he were openly hostile.

[7] Henderson and Bibens, *op. cit.*, p. 108.

Physical Facilities as Complicating Factors

Probably few teachers have not at some time experienced problems caused by inadequate supplies, equipment, or facilities. Certainly, we expect parents, school administrators, school-board members, and other interested persons to want to provide those conditions which allow the teacher to perform most effectively in the classroom. And yet, the reality of limited funds has caused more than one teacher to do without classroom materials he considers essential for accomplishing the objectives of the course and the educational system. Often, teachers are granted some small amount of money annually, against which they may charge needed supplies. However, even under these circumstances, the teacher may have to do without certain supplies until too late if he does not order them far enough in advance.

Some of the most frequent criticisms voiced by teachers have to do with textbooks. Generally, the text chosen for use in the classroom is adopted during the preceding year, sometimes by those who are not involved in its actual classroom application. Sometimes a textbook is selected by teachers who expect to use it but who are reassigned to other grade levels or subjects before the materials are delivered.

Some standard objections by teachers concerning adopted and approved classroom materials are that (1) the materials are out of date, (2) they are inappropriate, (3) they are insufficient, (4) they are too limited in scope, (5) they are unavailable when they are needed, (6) the teacher was uninvolved in their selection, and (7) they do not require learner involvement.

Some teachers solve the problem of inadequate or inappropriate classroom equipment and materials by using their own private funds to purchase items they consider necessary. This, however, is not the teacher's responsibility. Furthermore, the strides taken in media hardware and software in recent years make it impossible for teachers to afford the financial strain of supplying and equipping their own classrooms. This matter is the responsibility of the local board of education. On the other hand, it is unfair to expect the school administration to equip and reequip classrooms whenever there is a turnover in the teaching staff. Requests for additional equipment and supplies must be well founded and adequately presented to the administration if they are to deserve any significant priority.

Certainly, one of the greatest complaints of teachers has to do with outmoded and ancient facilities. It is not unusual for teachers to find themselves assigned equipment that is almost inoperable. A standard joke among shop teachers is that they are given machines cast off by industry twenty years before, and for which essential parts cannot be secured. Yet, with that equipment the shop teacher is expected to produce young people who can function in up-to-date workrooms. Old school buildings in urban areas are often used even though their plumbing, heating, and electrical facilities are no longer adequate. Even the greatest teacher would have his work cut out for him if he were required to hold the attention of his class when its members were preoccupied with the problem of keeping warm.

Crowded buildings in urban areas have contributed to the problem of already unpleasant learning conditions. When existing buildings are asked to take care of exploding school populations, teachers are forced to jam additional desks into rooms designed originally to handle only a certain number. In crowded classrooms the inadequacy of teachers aids such as chalkboards and screens becomes a real problem. When seating problems force teachers to place students where they cannot adequately observe or participate in learning activities, the teacher's job is truly complicated.

Another bitter complaint often heard from teachers has to do with their inability to secure desired and available equipment when they need it. Although many schools have a qualified audio-visual specialist available to serve the teachers, this duty is more commonly a collateral task assigned to an already busy teacher. Even a very responsible and dedicated teacher will have difficulty in properly fulfilling his teaching responsibilities if he is given the added duty of attempting to coordinate the use of equipment among teachers and keeping available equipment located and in good operation. The teacher who has planned a full and complete learning experience for his students, and who is relying on the availability of a filmstrip and projector, may find that his carefully detailed approach must be drastically altered at the last moment. The lack of supportive services in the school may thus also have a detrimental effect on the quality of the instruction.

New teachers in a school building are often confronted with a problem for which they are completely unprepared. It is a fact of life in many schools that the new teacher accepts the role of "traveling instructor." Because more teachers are required than there are classrooms, some teachers find themselves in different rooms throughout the entire school day. When schools become overcrowded with students and teachers, it is not unusual for an English teacher to find himself in classrooms outfitted for mathematics, science, sewing, or

FIGURE 8–3
Crowded conditions and student disinterest impede classroom instructional procedures.

drafting. Chemistry and physics teachers may find themselves in classrooms where there is not even a sink with running water. The teacher who needs certain kinds of specialized materials in each of his classes may find that they are located in rooms to which he does not have access. Truly insurmountable physical problems are faced daily by some teachers in their efforts to do a creditable job with their students.

Of course, many teachers complain that they are never contacted concerning the type of equipment they desire. Many a piece of equipment has aged in a school storeroom simply because a well-intentioned person in a position of authority thought he was ordering the right thing. A truly conscientious administrator will consult members of the teaching staff before purchasing materials and equipment.

The School Administration as a Complicating Factor

Teachers are often disappointed in their local school principals, and sometimes feel that the administrator is not too concerned with what they are attempting to accomplish in the classroom. In some instances, the local administration is actually a barrier to more effective teaching; more often, problems between teachers and administrators are explainable if time is taken to analyze the circumstances.

Nevertheless, the teacher may experience difficulties within the classroom as a result of an unhappy relationship with the school principal. In all fairness, the teacher should understand the complexity of the principal's role and his responsibilities before condemning him for apparent lack of effort or support. Traditionally, the principal has been the instructional leader of the school and teaching staff. And teachers judge a principal's performance on the basis of how well he handles problems pertaining to the curriculum and teaching problems.

This attitude on the part of a teaching staff may be logical, but it fails to take into account many modern-day demands on the local principal's time. When being a principal meant heading the instructional staff in a small and isolated school district with a small student body from a limited geographic area, it was very possible for a man in this position to maintain relatively close personal contact with both teachers and students. He might even be personally acquainted with the parents of students. But with the development of bigness in education, principals have lost this close contact with teachers, students, and parents. They have had to take on numerous other responsibilities: membership on curriculum committees and various school and community councils; increased involvement with community pressure and staff administrative groups; and increased involvement in federal school programs and with state and regional accreditation agencies.

Unfortunately, many principals are administrators first, and instructional leaders second. Whether this situation reflects the expectancies of teachers and administrative superiors, or is simply the principal's adherence to behavior patterns established by other administrators under whom he has worked, is not certain.

Certainly, colleges of education have done little to define the role of principals as administrators and school leaders. Requirements for administrative certification tend to stress administrative trivia and theory and neglect those aspects of leadership having to do with human relationships and educational problems. School administrators are still being trained as though the authority of the office they will occupy is sufficient to ensure success. Too many school principals continue to measure their annual success in terms of whether they have avoided any major confrontations with teachers, students, or parents. Too often, administrators (and teachers) consider a principal to be successful as long as classes are held regularly and with a minimum of confusion.

Most school administrators want to do a good job and make the maximum contribution possible to their schools. The problem is that a principal often inherits a role that precludes any real involvement in matters pertaining to the improvement of instruction. He is likely to find himself fully occupied with such matters as equipment repair, building repair and maintenance, teacher schedules, student schedules, classroom utility, district reports, accreditation reports, reports on federal programs, PTA meetings, student disciplinary actions and reports, pre-enrollment estimates, coordination of testing programs, the ordering of present and future classroom materials, coordination of activity programs, and scheduling of assemblies and faculty meetings. With all these activities the responsibility of the local principal, he is indeed a busy individual. In addition, he is expected to maintain peaceful relations with the community and handle the complaints of unhappy parents. There is little wonder, then, that the principal may experience some difficulty in finding the time to concentrate on such things as improving the quality of instruction in the school and evaluating teacher performance.

Perhaps one reason the principal often fails to concentrate on classroom instruction is that he realizes how difficult it is for any one individual to be adequately qualified in all areas of instruction. It is only when attention is drawn to a teacher or rumors of problems in that teacher's classroom reach the principal's ears that it becomes necessary for him to bring himself up to date on the teacher's activities and performance. This condition provides the teacher with some assurance of autonomy within his own classroom. As long as matters in the classroom appear to be progressing satisfactorily, little interference may be expected from the principal.

We may assume that before hiring a teacher, a principal is satisfied that he is qualified in his subject area and, if provided with textbooks and instructional materials, will be able to alter his instruction to meet the ability levels of students in his various classes. For this reason, and because it is so difficult for the modern-day principal to find the time to oversee matters in the classroom, a teacher who wants to use a different approach in his classroom (one other than reading the text or telling the students the facts of the lesson) may encounter little opposition. But he may have a problem in securing the principal's backing in obtaining instructional materials, devices, or equipment not normally ordered by the school.

It is not uncommon for dissatisfied and unsuccessful teachers to malign the administration. Many a principal's reputation has been assaulted in the teachers' lounge. This does not mean that the teachers' lounge is necessarily a bad place. It is often one of the healthier aspects of the school, but it is also a place where teacher frustrations, anxieties, and tensions find an outlet. The new teacher should be careful not to accept everything he hears from other teachers and reserve his judgment of the principal and his performance until he has legitimate evidence on which to base his evaluation.

It is all too easy to blame the principal if things do not go well in your teaching. And since it is the principal's job to help you accomplish your mission in the classroom, perhaps he should shoulder some of that responsibility. However, teachers themselves are often the reason for a principal's hesitation to play too active a role in matters relating to instruction. Some teachers react to suggestions from the principal about classroom teaching procedures by saying, "He's trying to tell me how to teach English (or whatever their subject is) and he doesn't know a thing about teaching English." On the other hand, if the principal attempts to leave classroom procedure to the teacher, we may hear, "He isn't interested in what goes on in the English classes."

If the principal does not appear to play as active a part in setting the classroom curriculum as teachers feel he should, perhaps much of the fault lies with the teachers. Teachers often find that when they approach the principal with an idea, he is most receptive and even appreciative of their concern and interest. Too often, teachers keep good ideas to themselves because they don't believe the school administrator would be interested. Teachers should be encouraged to use their initiative and creativeness. Instead of separating themselves from the school administration, they should give this teaching partnership a chance to work.

Correcting Complicating Factors

With all these complicating factors, can the teacher even hope to be able to perform successfully? Many teachers are successful even though they are confronted with all these problems. Let us look at some of the things successful teachers do to make the learning experience productive for their students. One of the fundamental concepts implemented by successful educators is the idea that the teacher is, ultimately, the only person who can exercise legitimate and positive control over the various factors that contribute to the learning climate: "One of the first prerequisites for a smoothly functioning class is that the students feel welcome and accepted. Without a doubt, the teacher is the key person in establishing the atmosphere."[8]

Regardless of how diligently he tries, the school administrator can-

[8] *Ibid.*, p. 98.

not effect actual and positive control in each classroom. The teacher is the only person who has daily contact with both students and content. Ultimately, then, it is he who is responsible for the curriculum to which his students are exposed. No matter how beautifully designed the educational program may be, the classroom experience will be no more effective than the teacher makes it.

Often the various factors that hamper the teaching-learning process cannot be isolated and dealt with separately. Complicating classroom factors generated by problems related to inadequacies in the school plant, facilities, and student or teacher attitudes are all inextricably bound together in the classroom experience. One problem may contribute to the existence of a second problem. The only person who has the opportunity for direct contact with all the various elements at the classroom level is the teacher.

Because the teacher is in a position to control his own behavior, and because teacher performance contributes to student behavior, he is a logical starting point in our search for ways to overcome the complicating factors described here. The teacher is the focal point in the classroom experience. It is his responsibility to assess properly the positive and negative aspects of the learning environment and to arrange, manipulate, and adjust these elements in such a way that productiveness will result.

All of us have certain ideas about teachers. A teacher is supposed to be honest, sincere, and fair. He should be unbiased and unprejudiced, with almost godlike qualities. Of course, teachers are human, and we cannot expect each person who is placed in charge of a classroom to be perfect. However, the teacher, whether or not he wants to be, is a living and observable model for his students at all times. He must constantly demonstrate and practice the kind of behavior he expects of his charges. If he wants the respect of his students, he must exhibit respect for them. A teacher once observed, "If a teacher treats each of his students exactly as he would want his own child treated in a classroom, he cannot help but be successful." Some teachers fall into the trap of forgetting that their students are individual human beings, and not inanimate containers for content.

There are many interpretations of what a really disciplined classroom should look like. However, most teachers would probably agree that the ideal classroom is one in which all the students are actively involved in the learning process, each student is interested in participating in the various learning activities planned, and there are no distractions or behavior problems to interfere with classroom procedures. In many classrooms discipline is closely connected to effectiveness, as we pointed out in Chapter 3. When the teacher is concerned with "control first and teaching later," he is liable to find that he must spend much time controlling and has little time for teaching. Storen suggests that students need to be given a part in decision-making and that if they are gradually given responsibility by the teacher, self-discipline will develop.[9] An approach to discipline that has proven quite successful for teachers interprets "discipline" as *a cooperative classroom atmosphere in which teacher-student relationships reflect mutual involvement in the pursuit of common goals.* The ideal, then, is movement toward student self-control and self-discipline. As long as the teacher dominates the classroom and makes all the rules, he will find himself occupied with enforcement problems. However, when students are truly involved in what is going on in class, they will themselves provide the measure of control necessary for productiveness.

It seems reasonable that students who are potential troublemakers would be less likely to create problems in the classroom if they perceived themselves as achieving and making progress, instead of merely sitting in class because of their inability to participate. The teacher who concentrates on helping each of his students enjoy a successful learning experience, and does not become preoccupied with punitive measures, is contributing to a constructive teaching atmosphere. There is always a link between teacher and student behavior. The student who has been marked as a troublemaker because of his past failure to achieve is a potential problem for all his teachers. Yet, when such a student finds that a teacher is truly concerned with him and his progress, his potential for causing a problem is lessened. We often hear that teachers create many classroom discipline problems themselves. Perhaps it would be more accurate to say that all teachers have exposure to potential discipline problems, but some teachers do not create problems from this potential.

Certainly, many of the difficult situations that develop in the classroom could be avoided. To some extent, the teacher-oriented philosophy tends to invite discipline problems. Students are essentially good potential doers and extremely poor watchers and listeners. Yet,

> *For some reason, and no one seems to know why, the attitude has developed that the quiet classroom is the classroom in which learning is progressing most rapidly. Perhaps this attitude developed in the educational past when books, charts, films, filmstrips, slides, and all*

[9] Helen F. Storen, *The Disadvantaged Early Adolescent: More Effective Teaching* (New York: McGraw-Hill, 1968), p. 20.

other types of educational materials and proper learning activities were so scarce that if the learner was to find out anything he had to listen to the teacher.[10]

If the teacher wants good results in his classroom, he must design his approach to include students, to *involve* them in the learning process. The vast majority of potential student-discipline problems will never materialize if the teacher concentrates on involving his students in the work at hand.

Of course, some students will never be reached by the teacher. They simply are not able to participate, for reasons ranging from deep personal difficulties, psychological problems, and severe social maladjustment to problems relating to basic mental limitations. When the proper kind of classroom climate has been established, however, even these extreme cases are less likely to interfere with the learning process. A very small percentage of pupils are actually extreme cases, and when the classroom atmosphere is pleasant and productive, the potential explosiveness of any situation is lessened.

We have seen how the teacher *can* exercise some degree of positive control over student attitudes and behavior through his own attitude and stance toward his students. So, he has the capacity for affecting his own attitude (the first element in the learning process) and he can also affect student attitudes (the second element in the classroom experience). In regard to the third primary element in the learning process—the content to be explored—many teachers feel extremely restricted. But if we were to take a realistic look at content, we might be pleasantly surprised by what we found. It is true that there is an abundance of textbooks and curriculum guides, which tell the teacher just what is expected in a subject area at a particular grade level. However, instead of recognizing these materials for what they are—indications of *expected* curricular effort—teachers tend to regard them as the final word and follow them to the letter.

The textbook may well be one of the greatest detriments yet invented to good teaching. Too often, it is accepted as containing everything the child should know about a particular subject at a particular grade level. This concept, in itself, is in direct opposition to what we say we believe learning really is. If a textbook is treated by teacher or students as a repository of facts to be memorized, it is being used improperly. Learning consists of much more than merely memorizing facts. Properly utilized by the teacher, a textbook can be a valuable

[10] John W. Renner and William B. Ragan, *Teaching Science in the Elementary School* (New York: Harper & Row, 1968), p. 233.

resource that helps students tackle problems encountered in the learning process. It is a guide designed to assist the teacher in developing his approach to the curriculum.

The well-known curriculum guide is more than just a framework of guideposts for the teacher. It contains a wealth of material that can prove helpful in the classroom. However, such content as is found in the curriculum guide represents little more than suggestions for the teacher of the kinds of teacher and student activities that might be incorporated in the classroom curriculum. There is no reason for the teacher to assume that he cannot expand the lists of activities and resources, nor that his initiative as the classroom leader should be suppressed to the degree that he dare not vary from the procedures outlined.

The teacher must realize that it is his *duty*—his *responsibility*—to develop classroom activities that will help his students become involved with and develop an understanding of classroom curriculum. The teacher who attempts to indoctrinate his students with the material found in the textbook or curriculum guide is not *teaching* anything. The students can read this material themselves, and a teacher is not even necessary in the classroom, except to maintain order. When a teacher receives his certificate, he is expected to understand both his subject area and the learning process. If he cannot then develop materials and activities in this area that are representative and commensurate with his students' level of development, he is not really prepared to teach.

The teacher who bemoans the fact that a large percentage of his students are failing needs to refocus his attention on what he is doing in the classroom. Those who observe that "if little learning has been accomplished, little teaching has taken place" are often right. We must never forget that students are people, and people do not enjoy failure. Instead of testing his students' retention of the subject matter they have been exposed to, the teacher might do well to reexamine his purposes. The teacher who can "teach" his students how to understand and use rather than "memorize" and "know" data will be an asset to any school district. He will also have become much more than an expert in an academic field; he will be a successful and highly respected TEACHER.

We have discussed how the teacher can exercise control over the three primary elements in the classroom curriculum: himself, his students, and the lesson content. With these principal ingredients in the learning situation he has direct contact. Other forces that can have an undesirable influence on the classroom curriculum, he has contact with only indirectly. One of the most potentially unpredictable and dangerous of these forces is parental attitudes. Teachers appear to fear parental contact and often shy away from much exposure to the parents of their students. Yet, if they only realized it, parents possess an even greater fear of the teacher.

Both the school and the individual teacher are in a position to do something about potential problems caused by hostile parents. Up to now, educators have allowed contact with parents to be predominantly negative in nature. The only really positive attempt to bring parents and teachers together has been the PTA type of organization, which unfortunately seldom attracts the kinds of parents who most need to develop some kind of contact with school personnel.

Just as it is important for the school to recognize that each student is a human being, with human feelings and emotions, we must accept the fact that parents are human too. Regardless of their cultural background, parents respond favorably to those they perceive as being interested in and concerned about their children.

The mistake commonly made by both teachers and administrators is to contact parents only when forced to do so. The teacher who is wise enough to make contact with each parent periodically is responding to the parent's emotional need to know how his child is doing in school, and not just at the time report cards are sent home. Also, parents are drawn to those teachers who notice the good things their children do.

Any experienced teacher knows the kinds of difficulties that can arise with hostile parents. An alienated parent is capable of stirring up problems, both within and outside the school environment. Still, although most teachers have been required to study child and adolescent psychology, few have been encouraged to do any research on parental psychology. The teacher must recognize that his dealings with a student will have some kind of effect on that student's family. We cannot treat students as though their only identification is with the class in which we encounter them. The teacher's success is partially dependent on his acceptance by students and the community; he cannot ignore the effect his relationships with community elements may have on his effectiveness in the classroom.

Probably one of the most effective methods of developing a satisfactory relationship with parents, both hostile and otherwise, is to help them to understand that you as a teacher have the best interests of their children foremost in your mind. Parents are not likely to become abrasive with persons who have demonstrated a very real interest in their children. Normally, parents receive a report of student grades from the school about every six to nine weeks. Other than these reports, there is little contact between the school and home unless the student has become involved in some difficulty or trouble. The teacher who takes the time to telephone periodically the family of each of his students to inform them of some small bit of progress the student is making, is demonstrating to those parents that he is interested in and concerned about his students. And, that teacher is ensuring a cooperative attitude on the part of the parents. Strangely enough, *parents rarely hear about it when their children are performing adequately in school.* Often a little bit of initiative on the part of the teacher will remove the fear of teacher-parent contact and will result in a more healthy classroom attitude on the student's part.

Teachers must realize the role they play in the area of public relations. Little goes on in a classroom which does not find its way into the community. Because the teacher is on daily public display, he is an open target for any community critic. For this reason, it is of the utmost importance that he be able to convince both parents and children that he is dedicated to the task of assisting each of his students in the learning process and that he accepts their failures as indicative of his own lack of success as a teacher. The teacher who reflects this philosophy and attitude will experience little difficulty with either problem students or hostile parents. Instead, he will find that his students and their parents will defend him to the very end.

We have examined some of the problems caused by staff and administrative attitudes and by the inadequacy of physical facilities. Although many teachers experience a sense of frustration and helplessness when faced with these conditions, there is much that can be done. Unfortunately, teachers often feel almost as if they are fighting a war with the administration, that the principal is not interested in their teaching problems.

Just as most teachers would like to be successful in the classroom, probably the great majority of school administrators would like to see their institutions reflect the highest standards of educational achievement. A teacher who assumes that the school administrator is uninterested in what goes on at the classroom level and ceases to attempt to improve the classroom experience because of this, is adopting an indefensible stance. Although the school principal cannot possibly be constantly conversant with what takes place in each classroom each hour, he is interested in good education. He is interested in helping teachers perform in as fine a manner as possible. But the teacher cannot overlook his own responsibility to keep the principal informed about his needs and problems. If the teacher is realistic in assessing his needs and sufficiently persistent in asking that something be done about them, he should not have too much trouble in getting the support of the principal. When a principal recognizes a teacher as having real ability and a high degree of commitment to the teaching-learning process, he is likely to pay heed to that teacher's assessment of classroom needs. And the successful teacher is exceedingly easy to identify —not so much by his teaching methodology as by the classroom climate, the students' attitudes, and their overall productiveness. Few principals can resist the teacher who will leave no stone unturned in his efforts to make the maximum contribution to the teaching-learning process.

In other words, reasonable and dedicated teachers determine, to some degree, how involved the principal becomes in the instructional program. By their initiative in keeping him informed of curriculum suggestions and material needs, they help him to focus on the instructional program. Strangely enough, teachers want the principal to be their instructional leader, yet they often circumvent his participation because they fear they may lose some of their classroom autonomy. The truly committed teacher will lose nothing through efforts to get the principal involved in the instructional program and harnessing his assistance.

The teacher's own commitment has much to do with the way parents and other staff members feel about him. Parents and other teachers alike respect the successful teacher, the teacher with whom students willingly cooperate, participate, and learn. Even complicating factors such as limited physical facilities and equipment seem to affect very little the effectiveness of a truly great teacher. Students know when they are involved in the learning process; they appreciate the satisfaction they enjoy from educational achievement. Parents and other teachers will have no legitimate quarrel with the teacher who is able to develop such an attitude in his students.

But what does all this have to do with our three criteria of rational-power development, a curriculum suited to the learners' developmental levels, and attention to individual needs? Consider for a moment this rationalization. Every one of the complicating factors we have discussed can be mitigated by leading students to a greater depth of understanding of the educative process as well as the content contained within that process. By recognizing the teacher as the focal point in the classroom, you are putting your finger on the pulse of the learning process. If students are really to achieve and succeed in this process, it must be through the teacher's efforts. Through his approach to the classroom curriculum, he can choose to involve students in the learning process or let them remain passive. He can develop procedures appropriate to their stage of development, or he can "teach" the content assigned for that grade level. He can focus on each of his students as individual human beings with human feelings, needs, and emotions, or he can simply "throw out content to his classes and hold them responsible for its memorization and recall. The teacher can work toward providing the optimum classroom program by enlisting the cooperation of other staff members, administrators, and parents, or he can act alone, disregarding the external factors that affect his performance.

In considering the complicating factors in the classroom, the criterion of suitability to the students' developmental levels is of the utmost importance. Ultimately, the students' achievements hinge on their ability to comprehend the learning process. If the instructional materials and course content for their grade level are designed basically for learners in the formal-operational stage, and if the students are concrete-operational, they will inevitably be frustrated in their attempts to participate actively in the learning process. This does not mean that the general content outline for the preplanned curriculum is wrong. However, that content must be interpreted in terms of your students' backgrounds and developmental levels. In practice, this approach necessitates a certain amount of attention to individual needs because your students will probably be at various points in a particular developmental stage. If a teacher is really concerned with his students' success, his first step is to determine their developmental level, and then select and adapt content so that it is possible for each student to participate actively in the learning process.

We, as teachers, often view a student's lack of cooperation, interest, or participation in the learning process as evidence of lack of ability, inadequate background preparation, or even obstinance; in reality, it is often our *expectation* of student performance that is the error. If content in the formal-operational classification is used with students in the concrete-operational stage, they may fail regardless of how hard they try.

It is possible for a teacher to come to grips with the complicating factors, both internal and external, that interfere with the learning process if he has the proper attitude, commitment, and approach. A truly successful teacher has met these complicating factors and conquered them through consideration of his students' needs and the three objectives of the educational system.

In Chapters 7 and 8 we investigated classroom procedures and factors that hamper the learning process in terms of the three criteria: rational-power development, the intellectual-development level of the learner, and attention to individual needs. In Chapter 9, we will introduce the media that can be used to complement and supplement the inquiry approach developed by the teacher.

9 Using Media

Although the concept of educational media is relatively new, classroom instructional aids have been around for a long time. Aspects of these aids have had a negative connotation in the past for teachers, parents, and school administrators. Today, although a wide variety of media are available for use in the classroom curriculum, they still get a somewhat negative reception in some quarters.

As recently as the late 1950s, the teacher could normally expect to find a rather limited supply of media in the average school. It was unusual to find more than a token number of specialized pieces of equipment in the school, and an even smaller supply of materials to be used with them was available. The 16-mm movie projector, along with a sprinkling of filmstrip and slide projectors, was probably the most common piece of audio-visual equipment. Equipment of this kind was often considered too costly and an extravagant use of public funds. The "software" to be used on such machines was also in short supply, which contributed to their disuse.

However, the philosophy of educators in the 1940s and 1950s also contributed to the lack of media development and use. One favorite instructional aid, especially for mathematics and language teachers, was the workbook. Often, teachers who relied on the workbook were considered to be weak in preparation and ability, and were criticized for using a "crutch" to cover up poor teaching methodology. Some urban school districts even forbade the use of workbooks in their schools, and subject-area consultants checked up on teachers to see that they did not use such materials.

Even today, the position of the audio-visual specialist is relatively new in the schools. For years, all audio-visual duties were taken care of at the school level by a teacher who did extra or collateral duty in this area. The teacher who received this assignment saw to it that forms were distributed to the staff for ordering films for their classes. He also kept an inventory of working equipment and was responsible for seeing that the equipment was inspected during the summer months, so it would be ready for operation at the beginning of each school year. He was in charge of collecting films to be returned to the distributor and distributing new films to teachers when they arrived. Sometimes he received some small financial payment for his extra work. More often, though, he did not. If his duties were considered sufficiently important to warrant it, he might be released from one class hour of his regular teaching assignment. The audio-visual chores had to be performed by someone, but were not important or complex enough to warrant hiring a special person to perform them.

Although a few teachers continue to use film and tapes in lieu of teaching, thus causing educational media to retain some of their negative connotations, their usefulness in the instructional process is generally accepted. It is not uncommon today for a prospective teacher to be required to demonstrate proficiency in the handling and operation of a number of pieces of media equipment in order to qualify for a teaching certificate. Further evidence of the gain of media in education may be found in the amount of software developed for classroom instruction during the 1960s. Educators seemed finally to recognize that professionally prepared materials add something to the classroom curriculum.

A note of caution must be sounded, however, lest we fall into the same trap that initially gave media a questionable reputation. *We must not attempt to make media a substitute for the teacher in the learning process.* Educational media can make a very real contribution, as long as they are used to complement and supplement instruction. By placing too much reliance on them, we are abrogating our responsibilities as teachers. This, of course, was one of the errors associated with educational television in its early years. Students and teachers alike rejected this use of the medium because of its impersonality.

Probably there is nothing in the classroom curriculum that deadens student interest or destroys it as quickly or effectively as a 55-minute monologue. We know a number of things about the learning process and about learners, but we have not demonstrated a willingness to apply what we know to our classroom methodology. In classrooms across the country, teachers continue to "tell" their students what they want them to "know" about the subject being studied. Most of these teachers apparently believe that if they "tell" their classes something, and repeat it often enough, their students will "learn" it. Of course, this procedure almost completely excludes the learner from the learning process. When he becomes a listener or an observer, day after day and hour after hour, he is forced sooner or later to resort to memorization in order to take part in classroom activities.

As we have said before, experience with students has established that youngsters are good doers and poor listeners. Yet, we continue to use a classroom approach that ignores this basic fact. We go further than that. We know that the average adolescent cannot sit still for long periods of time. Yet some teachers and administrators insist that a good classroom is one in which the students sit quietly in their seats, listening to the teacher, and prepared to respond to each of his directions or commands. We know that the normal adolescent has a relatively short attention span. Yet we choose a 55-minute period for almost every course and expect him to automatically and dutifully tune in to the lesson.

We have, in our development of secondary education, attempted to fit each subject's content into a rigid schedule. We assume, apparently, that time is the important element in the learning process, and that it takes the same length of time for *all* students to learn something, regardless of the nature of the course. Again, we ignore a basic characteristic of the learner. Research has established that students learn at different rates and in different ways. The present system completely disregards individual differences and seems to suggest that any student at a given grade level will reach a certain level of achievement in a specific period of time.

Why is it so difficult for us to recognize that understanding a teacher's verbalization of a concept requires a student to perform a series of abstract operations for which he may not be prepared? Why are we so hesitant to use any other approach? *We know that all the senses are or can be used in the learning process.* Yet many teachers seem to regard oral explanations as the only means at their disposal for communicating with students.

Certainly, media can be used in a variety of ways and for a variety of purposes in the classroom. Some of these uses are more legitimate than others, in terms of the instructional program, but the validity of any application depends on the teacher, his purpose in using a particular medium, and how he uses it. There are many obvious uses of media; it is even possible for two teachers to use the same medium, hardware and software, for different purposes and have each usage be entirely appropriate. For example, models can be used to supplement instruction. Allowing students to observe, compare, and feel objects is obviously a more effective method of acquainting them with the properties of those objects than by telling them about them. It would be most difficult to verbally describe in a classroom what students could learn very quickly for themselves through direct experience. On the other hand, a teacher could use these same models simply to provide a change of pace and add a bit of variety to the classroom presentation. Any application of media in the classroom is useful to the degree that it assists the teacher in helping his students to accomplish objectives in the learning process.

There are a number of appropriate uses of media in the classroom. One of these is to stimulate the interest of students by providing something tangible and concrete for them to focus on. When this is the goal the teacher should choose materials that appeal to the interest levels of his learners. Materials should be designed to get and hold the attention of viewers, and should be sufficiently provocative to make them want to investigate further. Care must also be exercised in the selection of interest-grabbing material to ensure that it is not just entertaining but is related to the content about to be encountered.

Another use of media is to lend realism to the class discussion. Sometimes, it would be most advantageous for a social studies class to take a field trip to view a city council or a state legislature in action. When this is impractical, because of the distance, time, and expense involved, the teacher may decide to include a film that shows what the class would see if they could visit these governmental chambers. In this instance, the medium of a film is more convenient, and perhaps more efficient, since students can concentrate on the materials without the distractions provided by an actual trip.

In the applications of media discussed thus far, the student has been simply an observer. There is nothing wrong with this, as long as the teacher recognizes that these uses of media exclude the student from active participation and that participation involving the concept being taught must follow at some point in the lesson. When these uses of media help the teacher achieve educational objectives, they are probably being effectively selected and implemented. Just as lectures or demonstrations have their uses in instruction, so too can media be used to present and clarify concepts. But the teacher must always keep in view the fact that media may be misused or overused. Using media only to present facts in a way that excludes the participation of students is as inappropriate in the classroom as is reliance on "telling" students what you want them to know in any other way. The techniques employed by the teacher determine whether a medium effectively complements his methodology. When a medium is used in a way that requires students to interact with the supplemental material, it can produce intense student involvement.

Regardless of how good special material prepared for use with media may be, its effectiveness is entirely dependent on the teacher's skillfulness in manipulating the three basic classroom elements: himself, his students, and content. Media and associated materials simply add another dimension to content. That added dimension can have the effect of confusing and complicating the classroom curriculum if the teacher is not constantly aware of his objectives in using media. Media should *not* be used as a filler. Its use should always be carefully planned to contribute to the learning process.

Perhaps one reason many teachers have hesitated to use media to any great degree is because they have had bad experiences with it. Sometimes the teacher plans to use a very appropriate media material and then finds that it is unavailable whenever he needs it. Because of such frustrating experiences, some teachers prefer not to become too dependent on outside materials. The procedures for ordering and securing special materials can also be a discouraging factor. Some school districts require teachers to order "prepared" media materials at least two weeks before they are needed. This creates a problem for the teacher because he has no way of knowing, perhaps for a number of days, whether or not his request can be filled, since other teachers may have already requested the identical materials. In a large school district, if teachers of a certain subject follow a curriculum guide at all, they may all need certain materials at approximately the same time. However, the greatest difficulty created by the delay in securing special materials is that the materials are often unavailable at the particular point in the learning process at which they can make their greatest contribution. Good teachers have learned that it is almost impossible to plan in detail exactly what will happen in each classroom session. Of course, if a teacher uses the straight lecture method, he can completely control the schedule for covering material, but when students are included, as they should be, in the learning process, this kind of predictability is necessarily forfeited.

This does not mean that the teacher cannot predict or anticipate at approximately which point in the learning process certain materials could greatly enhance the classroom experience. It simply suggests that the teacher needs to be sensitive to the response and progress of each student and flexible enough to take advantage of indications that a student is ready to interact with a concept or a piece of instructional material. The kinds of complications that may be created by such a classroom approach are obvious. The teacher cannot possibly, under such circumstances, predict two weeks in advance a readiness that may develop during a single hour. Because of this, many teachers plan in a general way for the utilization of professionally prepared media material, estimating approximately when their students will profit most from studying such materials. In addition, a great many teachers attempt to develop their own special materials (sometimes together with other teachers in the same school unit), so that they can have them immediately available for their students.

Developing one's own materials is not as complicated as in years gone by. For example, modern man has learned to produce and reproduce materials in so many ways that there is little excuse for teachers not to use some form of visual aids. Experimentation with inexpensive plastic-sheet material has encouraged many teachers to produce a wide variety of homemade visual aids.

However, once again a note of caution should be sounded. Teachers may get so involved in the production of visual materials for classroom use that they again fall into the trap of discouraging student involvement. A visual presentation may seem adequate to the teacher, yet contribute little or nothing to a student's understanding of a concept. Students today have been indoctrinated with a wealth of professionally prepared media material outside the classroom, such as professional television productions, and the teacher's efforts may seem pitifully amateurish in comparison. Even the student who has failed to make satisfactory progress in his schoolwork may be rather discerning and even critical of the teacher's comparatively puny efforts. The American student, in other words, has developed a sophisticated eye for quality in visual productions. If the teacher's efforts are inadequate in terms of professional quality, they well may evoke more mirth than understanding in students.

The teacher must attempt to avert such distractions in the learning process. Certainly, the degree of rapport a teacher is able to establish and maintain with his students has much to do with how they react to or interact with his efforts. When a student recognizes a teacher's competency in a content area and accepts the fact that the teacher wants to assist him in the learning process, he is likely to overlook rough or crude designs drawn by the teacher to help him understand a concept. This is especially true if the teacher has developed the facility of constantly using convenient and familiar examples to which the student can relate. If a few quick lines on the chalkboard can help students "see" the meaning of a concept more clearly, the crudeness of the design is irrelevant. Such efforts will be accepted by students as long as the teacher does not attempt to dazzle them with chalkboard art.

The teacher who can use a variety of media to help his students gain an understanding of a concept demonstrates a depth of responsiveness to both his students and content. The mere fact that he is sensitive enough to assess his students' lack of understanding contributes to a classroom atmosphere in which students are likely to overlook deficiencies in his mechanical illustrative ability. There are two fundamental principles in the application of media: (1) No medium should be misused, and (2) a variety of media contributes to an interesting and effective classroom experience. The latter principle assumes particular significance when we consider the characteristics of the learner. Unfortunately, although we have been familiar with these characteristics, we have failed to develop classroom approaches compatible with them. In the next section we shall take a brief look at some characteristics of secondary school learners and see how media can help the teacher take advantage of those characteristics.

Learner Characteristics

The teacher is almost forced to assume that his students will have relatively short attention spans. It is difficult for an adolescent to concentrate on anything for very long, probably because he is not yet formal-operational. Although some students at this age may have longer attention spans than others, since the teacher is responsible for the progress of all his students, he must also consider the student whose span of attention is extremely short. A teacher who "talks at" his students for long periods of time, without providing a variety of items for them to focus their attention on, is disregarding a primary consideration in working with adolescents.

The adolescent learner is a notorious daydreamer. This does not mean that he deliberately attempts to circumvent the learning process. He simply has difficulty in keeping his mind from wandering and from thinking about a number of different things. Not only is his span of attention relatively short but his ability to fix his attention on a subject or topic and give it his full concentration is somewhat limited. Because of this, the alert teacher will attempt to provide a classroom experience that is interesting for the learner. Talking at students for long periods tends to dull their receptiveness to what is being communicated and may create the kind of monotonous background noise that encourages daydreaming. A multimedia approach to the classroom experience can compensate for the student's inability to keep his mind from wandering. Since there is a tendency for the student to refocus his attention whenever the teacher uses a different teaching aid, the use of a variety of media, hardware and software, creates changing conditions in the instructional scene.

Of course, one of the greatest complaints of teachers concerns the restlessness of students. Yet we know that the adolescent, because of his irregular growth patterns, often finds it impossible to sit still or be quiet for very long. Students are likely to fidget, squirm, twist about in their seats, tap their pencils on their desks, shuffle their feet, or knock their books on the floor. Although this behavior is normal, it is distracting to many teachers. It may also be detrimental to the learning process if the learners become bored. A teacher would need a fantastic personality to be able to hold the attention of adolescents for an entire period simply by talking. Certainly, anything that keeps the students interested, helps the learning process; anything that causes students to focus their attention on the lesson, contributes to the nullification of distractions and interruptions created by student restlessness.

Perhaps one of the most irritating characteristics of the adolescent pertains to his emotional makeup. He may be extremely susceptible to the development of tensions in the classroom, and at times his behavior may be unpredictable and erratic. Often, he is easily embarrassed, quite self-conscious, and hesitant about drawing attention to himself. If he should not comprehend some portion of what the teacher attempts to explain, he may withdraw temporarily from personal involvement in the lesson. He may focus his attention on some other activity that is taking place in the classroom, or he may create a disturbance that could be interpreted as misconduct. Another frequent reaction of adolescents is the nervous giggle, which is sometimes produced by a combination of fear, uncertainty, insecurity, and distracting conditions. It may occur, for example, when several adolescents in a classroom become lost at some point in a teacher's explanation. As student attention dissipates, a giggle may start and spread through the classroom like an epidemic. Such uncontrolled and seemingly irresponsible behavior may unnerve the most experienced teacher. Once the pattern for uncontrollable mirth has been started in a class period, almost anything that occurs may intensify the general hysteria. Rather than attempting to control such student behavior, the teacher should plan his classroom approach so as to provide a sequence of interesting events that students can follow. In this way, tensions are lessened, cases of wandering attention fewer, and distractions are kept to a minimum.

Teachers often overestimate the adolescent's capacity to concentrate on one thing by shutting out what goes on around him. A youngster in this age group is easily distracted; and once his attention has strayed, he may have great difficulty in refocusing it on the lesson. Properly selected pieces of media, skillfully manipulated by the teacher, can bring his attention back to the lesson. Although media have the potential to encourage more productive involvement of students in the classroom, they are not a convenient solution to an unproductive learning experience. If the teacher does not have a real understanding of his students, their interests, and their behavior, and should he not comprehend how to properly gear his approach to his students, it is probable that little real learning will take place. In other words, *if the teacher does not know how to teach, media will not help him.*

Reading—A Barrier to Learning

One primary reason for considering the use of media in the classroom curriculum relates directly to the reading ability of students. In Chapter 8 we discussed some complicating factors that relate both directly and indirectly to the classroom curriculum. One of the greatest barriers to instruction at the classroom level is the inability of many students to read and comprehend material prepared for a specific grade level. Teachers assume that a student in the eighth grade has the fundamental learning skills needed to understand and use the materials developed for that level. Unfortunately, this is an assumption they cannot afford to make. We know that students differ from one another greatly in a number of respects. It is ridiculous to believe that all students at a particular grade level will have developed equal and identical proficiency in all subjects.

The wide ranges of ability, even in a grouped classroom, make it highly improbable that all students will gain the same understanding from reading a specified piece of assigned material. We cannot even assume that all students will attempt to read an assigned passage or chapter. Students who reject the learning situation (and the school environment itself) simply will not do the background work needed to make their participation in the learning process easier. It is foolhardy to assume that all students like such assignments or will attempt to complete them thoroughly and efficiently. On the other hand, it may be a tragic error in judgment for teachers to assume that students avoid reading assigned material simply to spite or challenge them.

Experiences in the field, as well as the investigations of reading specialists, have demonstrated rather clearly that several problems in our educational process are specifically related to reading skills and proficiency. First of all, education in the American public school has been geared traditionally to the skill of reading. Although some change is perceptible in this condition today, teachers still assign reading material to students and follow that assignment with questions, discussions, or tests. The teacher, historically, has considered two avenues available for the transmission of information: (1) the student reading what the teacher wants him to know, and (2) the teacher telling the student what he wants him to know. Either of these approaches, or even a combination of the two, has definite limitations as far as the learning process is concerned, especially when we consider what we know about adolescent reading ability.

Second, students differ greatly in their reading ability, reading proficiency, reading comprehension, reading speed, and reading level. If we are to be truly honest in our attitude toward the learning process, we must admit the absurdity of assuming that all students in a specific classroom will gain the same understandings from exposure to identical reading material. Surely we do not believe that this is true; yet, year after year, this procedure is used in classrooms across the United States as a legitimate teaching method.

Third, textbooks selected for a particular grade level or for a special group of students within a grade level may be appropriate for the average student in the group, but are not at all appropriate for students who are either above or below average. We then teach the material in these textbooks to all students, even if it is boring to the fast learners and confusing to the slow ones. Furthermore, we assume that textbooks prepared and published for a specific grade level are of appropriate difficulty and that there are specific and identifiable levels of difficulty for students at each grade level.

Fourth, all students are not equally prepared for or skilled in reading and interpreting data from a textbook. Frequently, only a small percentage of students has sufficient reading skill to be able to deal effectively with grade-level textbooks without assistance from the teacher. A great many students, because they can obtain neither satisfaction nor understanding from reading the text, either do not do the assignment or do it in a shallow and superficial way. Is reading really that important? If a student cannot read well, does that mean that he cannot learn? Historically, teachers have hesitated to accept bases for learning other than reading. Yet individuals who cannot read a word can learn to perform highly skilled tasks.

In 1967 and 1968, the Midwest Roofing Contractors' Association sponsored a project to develop apprenticeship training materials for the industry. Apprenticeship programs and associated training materials were already in existence but had proved unsuccessful. An examination of these programs revealed that much of the labor force was partially illiterate. The training programs had failed not because the curriculum or the materials were inadequate but because the trainees could not read and comprehend them. New materials that placed little emphasis on the printed word were prepared; instead, they were highly dependent on media materials and trainee involvement in practical work laboratories. One training program was selected to implement the new approach. This program was highly successful, but the other programs continued to fail miserably. Previous programs had been designed to run for three years, and the dropout rate was approximately 90 percent. The experimental program ran for one year, the apprentices learned the skills required, and approximately 90 percent successfully completed the program.

Teachers simply cannot assume that all students have the reading skills necessary to perform successfully with materials designed for their grade level. Somehow we must develop classroom approaches that provide opportunities for all students to participate in the learning process. To do this, we cannot rely on reading material; nor can we rely on the teacher's ability to verbalize concepts. If we want equality of opportunity for all students, we must consider all the ways we can assist students to get the most out of the classroom curriculum. In doing this, we will also be providing the opportunity for rational-power development. In the following pages we shall explore some of the varieties of media available for use in the classroom and suggest how these materials may be used to help students who are deficient in learning skills.

Types of Media

The textbook

Without a doubt, the most common medium used by the classroom teacher is the textbook. It has had almost universal acceptance in the public schools of the United States. As we have seen, however, it has limitations in that it does not take into account individual differences but assumes that all students at a given grade level can make identical use of its contents. Although the textbook and its frequent companion, the workbook, is still commonly used, there is a growing tendency to rely on it not as the source of all content knowledge for a course but only as a reference to which students may turn when they or the teacher feel that consulting it would be productive. Used in this way, the textbook can be a useful tool for the student.

While the textbook may be regarded as a primary resource book for the teacher, he often uses other materials as supplementary references and resources. Having a variety of printed material to which students may turn for needed information contributes to their desire to find out things for themselves. When printed resources are too limited, the student may assume, erroneously, that the existing textbook contains everything he needs to know in a course.

There is a growing tendency toward the production of textbooks that promote and even require the student's involvement with their content.

TASK	*How do you feel about such textbooks?* Before reading on, *jot down your reactions to this idea.*

This movement away from the traditional way of presenting content is a result of the increased scrutiny being given to classroom procedures. We are nearing the point at which educators will not accept the traditional concept of a textbook as the final authority for the teachers and students.

Visual aids

Probably few teachers or students in this technological age have not had some exposure to such pieces of media hardware as *filmstrip* and *slide projectors*. Teachers realize that they can use these visual aids to bring an element of reality to the abstractions the student reads about or hears the teacher talk about in the classroom. Some students may not grasp a concept that is discussed in class, but will have little trouble understanding it when they see it come alive on the screen. Visual aids are especially meaningful for the concrete-operational adolescent, who is object-bound. The value of these aids for the learner cannot be overemphasized. They provide a frame of reference, an element of reality, and a concrete image upon which the student can focus his attention.

Although much software has been produced in the area of slides and filmstrips, many teachers find it more useful and interesting to develop their own materials. Relying completely on professionally prepared slides and filmstrips may limit the teacher somewhat in maintaining flexibility in the classroom curriculum. When he makes his own slides and organizes them to help his students accomplish certain classroom objectives, what he may lose in professional preparation and composition, may be compensated for in the beneficial effect on his students. By developing his own specialized materials, the teacher is brought closer to his students and to what they are trying to accomplish, since he must consider their needs in his development of those materials.

One of the most widely used and generally accepted pieces of media equipment in the modern secondary school is the *overhead projector.* Although large numbers of teachers still do not use it, it has become a very popular and extremely dependable instructional aid. It can be used in so many ways and for doing so many things that it makes the chalkboard almost obsolete. Great quantities of quality materials in a variety of curricular areas have been produced for use with the overhead projector, but the chief attraction of this machine for the teacher is its versatility. It can be used in any number of ways, and its effectiveness is limited only by the teacher's skill in using it.

Models and *mock-ups* are often particularly helpful visual aids at the classroom level. Many students find it extremely difficult, if not impossible, to work with abstractions. And although filmstrips and transparencies may be very useful, they are only two dimensional, and a three-dimensional model has a realism surpassing that of pictorial reproductions. Unfortunately, many teachers give up the idea of using such a medium because limited finances prohibit the purchase of professionally prepared models. However, many models may be constructed by students themselves as projects; model building is a perfectly legitimate function for any department in the school. In other instances, the teacher may be able to fashion a reasonable and effective model from items he already has on hand. Often, if the teacher is alert, he will have at his fingertips the equivalent of models in materials he has not even considered. For example, talking about or drawing diagrams of the circle and its parts is not nearly as meaningful to students as using the bottom of the classroom wastebasket as a model. All students are familiar with wastebaskets and, hence, have already had direct experience with circles. The teacher need only point out this fact to them to get his point across in a very real way.

Chalkboards, flannelboards, and *drawing charts* are all media for explaining concepts through pictorial representations. A wise teacher will avoid overusing the chalkboard in order to keep some variety in

FIGURE 9–1
Models are useful in demonstration teaching.

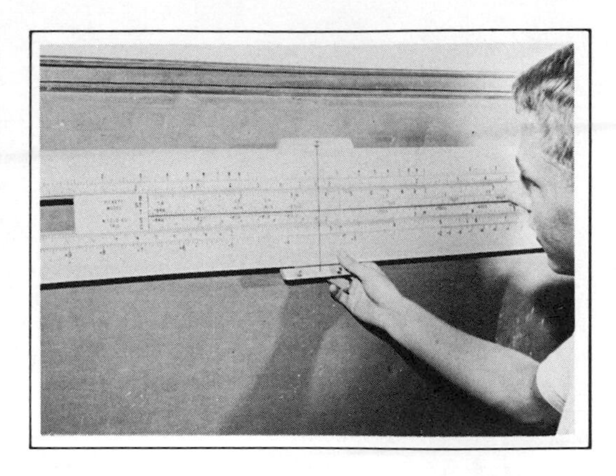

his approach. These media are restrictive to some degree, as they permit only two-dimensional reproductions; their effectiveness is further limited by the teacher's ability to draw accurate pictures.

Programmed materials

Whereas many forms of media used in the classroom have been available for years, programmed materials are a fairly recent development. There are basically two kinds of programmed materials, *printed* and *mechanical*. Both varieties have been developed to assist slow learners and are based on the principle of leading the student to select proper responses to conditions or questions. Programmed materials are designed so that the student can proceed at his own pace, working toward very short-range goals. They are of extremely limited value in an inquiry-centered classroom because they lead the student by predesigned steps toward already-established "answers" or conclusions. They make a contribution in that they enable a student who has seldom if ever experienced success in school to realize that he can participate individually in the learning experience. Programmed materials resemble textbooks in that they "tell" the student things, although they do "involve" him to the extent that he must choose "right" answers (as the teacher involves the student in a question-and-answer session). Some programmed materials present data with which the student must interact and which he must consider before forming a conclusion. However, all these materials have the same drawback; they reinforce the notion that education is simply a process of finding "correct" answers.

The mechanical forms of programmed instruction probably hold more interest for students than printed programs. Students appear to enjoy for a while manipulating a mechanical device. Mechanized programmed instruction is either linear or branching. *Linear programs* take the student in a single direction. He is exposed to a certain content and then asked to respond to a question about that content. If he answers correctly, he is asked to proceed to the next bit of content and the next question. If he selects an incorrect answer, he must repeat the exercise until he picks the correct answer.

In the *branching* variety of programmed instruction, the student who selects the proper response to a question may be allowed to skip a number of items in the lesson. If he picks an answer that is not correct but is not altogether incorrect, he may be given different content to study, which will help him to choose the "right" answer the next time the question is asked.

In any type of programmed material, however, the student is prompted to select a "pat" or correct answer. The content he studies contains the answer, and if he pays attention to it he will be able to make the correct response.

Instructional television

Instructional television is a prime example of the misuse of a medium in the classroom curriculum. Although some school districts have carefully developed plans for using televised instruction, these programs have normally enjoyed limited success. The selection of an outstanding lecturer from the instructional staff to make canned presentations may harness desirable talents of certain teachers, but the result is still a presentation or demonstration in which the students participate only as observers. When the television presentation is designed to stimulate the interest and participation of the viewing audience and is followed by a carefully coordinated follow-up program using "live" teachers, this approach has more legitimacy. One drawback of televised instruction is the need to gear each class to the progress of a number of groups. Unless all classes that participate in the program proceed at the same rate, successive lessons become impossible or meaningless to those who have fallen behind. Strangely enough, the profession of education has not yet thought of using television to present problem situations, followed by information useful in solving the problems, which students can then handle on their own or with the aid of the teacher.

Films

Films enable the teacher to bring a commonality of background experience and knowledge to his students. A well-organized and pro-

FIGURE 9–2
Simulation can be used to involve students in the learning process.

fessionally prepared film can add much to the classroom curriculum; the element of movement provides a depth of realism that is impossible to achieve with many other types of media. However, there are pitfalls in using films in the classroom. It is not unusual for students to become so interested in the story that they miss the point of the film. The entertainment aspects of films may actually distract students from the focal point of the learning experience. Before the teacher uses a film, he should prepare his class carefully for the viewing experience by asking them to look for evidence related to the problem under study, interactions that are already under way, and clues to ramifications of the established problem. Afterward, the students should be led, through inquiry, to investigate further what they have seen. Without this kind of preparation and follow-up film may be a waste of instructional time.

Videotape

A medium that has developed very rapidly in recent years is *videotape*. It has approximately the same advantages as motion pictures and is much more flexible. Although a film may be used to great advantage in the classroom, it has certain limitations. It is costly, and once the film is made, it cannot be altered. Videotape can be erased, edited, and rerecorded. But its greatest advanatage is that it can do all the things a film can do, *and* it can also provide a vehicle for student participation. Whereas students can only view a film and discuss it, they can produce their own film with videotape. Uses for videotape facilities are limited only by the teacher's imagination, and they are especially valuable in simulation.

Simulation

Simulation is not new to the classroom, and it certainly is not strange to students. At a very early age the student begins to pretend, to act, and to play out the roles of others. Secondary school teachers have concentrated so much on telling students facts that they have gotten away from simulation. Students have a tremendous capacity for playing roles and accepting the conditions and limitations of a position. We already know that students learn more by *doing* than by *listening*. Recently we had the opportunity to observe an American history class in which students took on the roles of congressmen from various states. Each student was responsible for being informed daily about anything reported by the news media pertaining to "his" state. This class was living testimony to what can be accomplished through simulation. The students' own participation in debates, filibusters, and the formulation of legislation made contemporary history become truly meaningful.

There are many types of simulation, some of which a teacher will find more appropriate and useful than others. Any type of simulation that allows the students to become part of and directly involved in the learning activity is valuable.

Criteria for Selecting Media

Including a section in this chapter on criteria for selecting media is very nearly presumptuous. *No one can judge what is proper media for a given class except the person teaching it.* There are, however, some criteria that should be considered. In selecting media, ask yourself the following questions:

1. *Is the medium constructed in such a way that it encourages the learner to inquire?* Many materials require only direct reiteration of certain facts; from our frame of reference this is an undesirable characteristic. Media that encourage inquiry contribute to the development of the learner's rational powers.
2. *Does the medium involve the learner in some way, or is he just an observer?* In other words, does the student learn by interacting

with the medium, or does he just sit passively? Motion pictures are particularly guilty of "doing the learning to" the student.

3. *Does the level at which the media is pitched match the intellectual-development level of the learner?*
4. *Is the activity made possible by the media essential to the achievement of the course objectives,* or is it a "fun" activity designed to enrich the learning experience by telling students things about the subject that are "nice to know"? Do not be apprehensive about using a fun-type medium.
5. *Does involvement of the student with the media increase the student-student, student-media, student-teacher interaction and decrease the teacher-student interaction?* In an inquiry-oriented learning experience the primary responsibility for initiating interaction lies with the student. Media that increase the opportunity for interaction help to achieve the central purpose of education.
6. *Does the medium lead to further investigations, or is the lesson over once it has been used?*
7. *Is the medium sufficiently flexible for each student to become involved, and interact, with it?*

Certainly, great strides have been taken in recent years in the development of media and in their application to the classroom curriculum. When properly selected and applied, classroom media can add much flexibility to instructional strategies. Media materials in the hands of a skillful and alert teacher can also help many students bridge the learning gap. The verbalization of concepts is simply not enough. Media may be used unimaginatively simply as an extension of the traditional approach to teaching, but they can also be used to accomplish other objectives. However, the fact remains that there are several limitations to procedures that involve basically listening and reading rather than doing and participating.

We have long accepted the fact that some students are more capable than others of working with abstractions and abstract concepts. Thus, there can be no argument about the need for appropriate media materials in junior and senior high schools. If even a *few* students are concrete-operational, the teacher is not concerning himself with their needs if he does not complement his instructional procedure with media materials that will help them to participate in and understand the learning process.

Should we pursue further the concept of individual differences, we find additional justification for the inclusion of media materials in the curriculum. We know that all students in a classroom do not profit equally from, or share in the same way in, an educational activity. Nor are all students equally prepared by their background experiences to participate in the learning process. Media, together with special attention and help from the teacher, give the classroom experience a depth that can contribute much to a student's understanding of a topic. Any vehicle that allows a student to see, touch, or otherwise interact with materials, rather than listen, can help him relate more completely to the planned experience. As a teacher develops the capacity for involving each student in the learning activity, he will discover that the various media provide almost limitless means for interesting his students and even manipulating their thinking.

The criterion of developing the individual student's ability to think is of the utmost importance in considering the appropriateness of various media applications. Even the organization of the traditional classroom suggests that some students perform well, some fairly well, and others not so well. Knowing what we do about individual differences and about how individuals learn, we can recognize the impossibility of attempting to teach thirty or more youngsters anything by exposing them to identical content. With the traditional approach, about all the teacher could do was aim his lecture at the average student, even though he realized that the more alert students might become bored and the slower learners (usually) completely lost.

Students cannot become true participants in a classroom curriculum unless they have adequate background and preparation for the learning experience as well as some proficiency in the tools required for participation. It is ridiculous to expect interaction between a student and content if the student has not developed a frame of reference that permits this interaction. Students who say, "I want to ask a question, but I'm not sure what I should ask," are indicating to the teacher that their experiences have not given them the necessary tools, content background, and rational-power development for participation, and that he, the teacher, has not provided activities suitable to their individual needs.

Media have the potential for providing an element of realism that is often absent in the learning process. They provide a means for exposing students to aspects of subject-area content that only a few might realize from reading the textbook or listening to the teacher. In addition, they provide an opportunity to exploit all the student's senses, not just his hearing. Thus, they provide the teacher with the means for developing a fuller and richer classroom curriculum, one that allows each student, rather than just a select few, to participate.

But media alone cannot accomplish this. To be really successful, the teacher must understand his students' limitations and capabilities and design his approach to the learning process so that media materials are used to their best advantage and in ways that complement his classroom procedure.

10 Using Evaluation

In this chapter we shall not investigate evaluation in the usual way, that is, in respect to the development of testing procedures, directions for making up tests, or principles for selecting testing devices. Instead, we shall examine how student evaluation may be used by the teacher to facilitate the learning process.

Probably one of the most dreaded and misunderstood tasks of the teacher is the evaluation of student performance. We believe that teachers dread this task because it arouses a number of personal anxieties. For example, a teacher may realize that his evaluation, at best, is an inadequate judgment of the student's intellectual growth; the evaluation techniques normally used are teacher-centered. In addition, many teachers feel an intuitive uneasiness about using testing devices that make evaluation an end in itself.

Through practice, evaluation has come to be regarded as almost synonymous with testing, an interpretation that has been accepted by students, parents, and educators. The reverence paid to testing is attested to by the fact that many school districts set aside periods of time for midsemester and final examinations. Testing students has become the thing to do; tests have become the vehicles for terminating secondary school courses and for determining what each student has accomplished by his semester's work.

Probably most teachers and students, at some time during their formal schooling, have studied for a test by reviewing factual information. This is how one prepares for the traditional, teacher-made tests that have become so much a part of American education. In addition to teacher-made tests, there are the formal, standardized tests designed to measure the students' aptitude, interest, intelligence, reading ability, and academic achievement (as well as many other things).

The results of these tests are used and misused by educators throughout the students' educational careers.

A third type of test found in American secondary schools consists of those instruments devised by outside authorities, such as textbook authors. It is not uncommon for a textbook writer to construct examinations designed to measure student achievement in terms of the content investigated in his published materials. Such instruments are used at the classroom level together with teacher-made testing devices. The degree to which an individual teacher uses author-constructed examinations depends upon his faith in such tests, his lack of faith in tests he constructs himself, and the availability of other testing instruments.

Types of Testing Instruments

Standardized tests

We shall spend little time here in discussing IQ and achievement tests, for our purpose is to explore how evaluation can be used by the teacher at the classroom level to measure the achievement of educational objectives. Certainly, standardized tests have been and are used in some school districts to help school personnel group students according to their ability and to encourage or restrict participation in certain advanced courses. When properly interpreted, standardized tests may reveal important information about the individual student. Unfortunately, the results of standardized tests are often used to stifle student interest, initiative, and participation.

Probably the standardized tests most misused and misunderstood by teachers are those designed to measure intelligence. For years, educators justified a student's lack of achievement by pointing to his low IQ, as established by a standard device. On the other hand, educators have had great difficulty in explaining low levels of achievement among students with high measured IQ's. Current measures of intelligence may mean very little, both because they depend heavily on reading ability and because they are oriented toward middle-class students. Students who are disadvantaged educationally, culturally, or economically are unlikely to perform well on an IQ test, yet there may be nothing wrong with their capacity for learning. Performance on achievement tests is similarly dependent upon reading ability. If a student suffers from a reading disability, he may perform quite poorly on an examination. But his low score may be an indication of his poor reading ability, not of a low level of achievement in the area in which he is being tested.

Since achievement in American secondary schools has traditionally been dependent upon reading ability, perhaps one of the more legitimate elements of standardized testing pertains to identifying reading problems and disabilities. Reading specialists can do tremendous things in the area of diagnostic testing to determine the type and extent of students' reading disabilities. Although great strides have been taken in this particular area, how many really effective programs exist in the schools for correcting reading disabilities? A high school counselor once commented, "We have no difficulty identifying students with personal problems, or problems with the basic tools of learning and fundamental skills. We identify the same students year after year; it's just that we don't help them after we identify them." Unfortunately, teachers have often accepted the low measured intelligence of an individual student as an indication that little could be done for him. Scores on standardized tests are valuable only insofar as they help the classroom teacher help his students to participate in the learning process. If they cannot make this kind of contribution to the teaching-learning process, or if the teacher does not understand what the results of standardized tests really mean, then they are of little value.

A final and more important criticism of many standardized tests is that they do not measure the growth in the students' rational powers and fail to take into consideration developmental levels. Thus, in this regard also, they are of little value.

Published content examinations

Since an author is more familiar with his own material than someone else, he should be in a better position than the teacher who plans to use that material to develop a relevant testing device. However, such published tests have several questionable aspects. First, the teacher who uses such an instrument assumes that all students learn at the same rate and in the same way. He assumes that if his students know the answers to the questions, they have learned the material. And he apparently assumes that a test instrument can be a valid evaluation device, without taking into consideration the individuality of the learners. Many teachers avoid using published tests but use them instead as guides in developing their own tests. Other teachers prefer to develop tests that reflect their particular approach to the teaching-learning process and their interpretations of content.

Teacher-made tests

Certainly, we recognize that teachers feel a need to test their students. Not only do teachers accept testing as a way of determining student achievement, they are conscious of the many pressures that demand student testing. Once a teacher has accepted the idea that he must test his students on the content of his course, he must make some hard decisions about testing, and face some very real problems. Probably every teacher has asked himself these questions:

1. How do I determine which questions will accurately measure student achievement?
2. What should be the minimum level of student accomplishment on the test for a passing grade?
3. How can I word the questions so that there will be no vagueness or ambiguity?
4. Should I develop an objective or a subjective test?
5. If I construct a subjective test, how can I grade it fairly?

There is more to constructing a test than simply sitting down, looking at the main points in the lesson, and framing questions that will elicit a reasonable response.

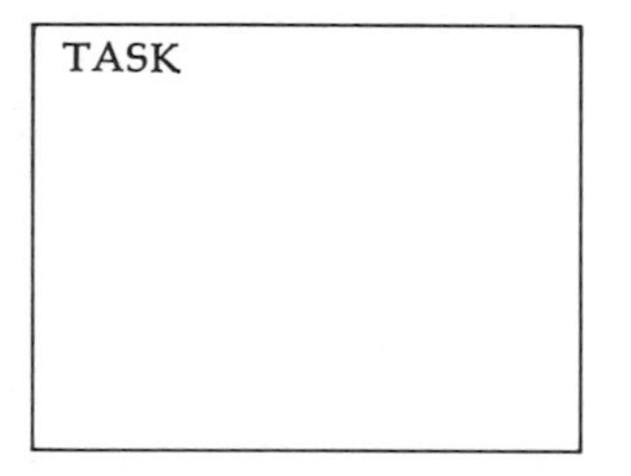

Stop for a moment and recall two teachers whom you have had in the past, one whom you considered to be excellent at evaluating students and one whom you considered very poor at this. Jot down a description *of the evaluation procedures used by each teacher.*

Now look at your estimates of the two teachers' evaluation procedures. Probably you responded best to the teacher you perceived as being very fair and as considering a student's overall performance rather than test results alone. The teacher whose evaluation procedures you rejected was probably extremely inflexible in his grading method and used test results alone to determine the final grade. Your view of these teachers may also have been affected by some other considerations: (1) whether you liked or disliked them, (2) whether you considered them to be good or poor teachers, and (3) whether you yourself were considered by them to be a good or a poor student. Students' perceptions of the teacher may vary tremendously within a single class; still, the teacher who puts test data before concern for his students' individual progress is likely to be viewed apprehensively by all.

We shall not go into the actual construction of test items, since there are many fine books available that deal specifically with such matters. Instead, we shall investigate another aspect of testing that is more relevant here. In lieu of the previous list of questions, we would propose the following:

1. How do I evaluate the performance of a student who understands content but scores poorly on examinations?
2. How do I evaluate the performance of a student who obviously is making good progress but does too poorly on tests to earn a passing grade?
3. Should I judge student performance on the basis of test results alone?
4. What aspects of student performance should I consider in determining the earned grade?
5. Do my evaluation procedures attempt to measure a student's progress in the area of rational-power development?
6. Do my evaluation procedures consider the developmental level of the learner?
7. Can I construct a test that will give me an indication of a student's overall progress and performance rather than just his ability to memorize facts?

Student Evaluation: I

It seems all too likely that "the examination is king" in most classrooms across the country and that the kind of examination that is king is not normally concerned with measuring effective learning. The following quotation sums up the truth about most examinations:

About the only wholesome grounds on which mass testing can be justified is that it provides the condition for about the only creative intellectual activity available to students—cheating. It is quite probable that the most original "problem solving" activity students engage in in school is related to the invention of systems for beating the system.[1]

[1] Neil Postman and Charles Weingartner, *Teaching as a Subversive Activity* (New York: Delacorte Press, 1969), p. 152.

Because examinations do not usually measure the amount of intellectual growth that goes on in students, they do not measure the amount of learning that goes on. But if examinations do not measure learning, what do they measure? Usually, they measure a student's ability to memorize material and repeat it upon prompting, and they measure the student's background. Quite obviously, then, they contribute to the development of only one of the rational powers—recall. If this judgment seems unduly harsh, try doing a small bit of research on your own. Stop the first ten people you meet on campus and ask them what they do when they are getting ready for an examination. If they use words like "review" and "cram," ask them to be more specific, and if necessary ask them if they really mean "memorize." Then go to a secondary school or junior high school and repeat this procedure. The examinations being used right now by our schools simply do not measure learning, unless you define learning as the memorization of information.

Where do learners get this information to memorize? From several sources, but principally from textbooks and the teacher. The teachers of the classes, which students at any level just sit through, usually assume that each learner has developed intellectually to the point where he can master the material if he wants to. They assume that the intellectual development of all learners follows a common pattern. Our contention is that all learners in a class are not likely to be at the same level of intellectual development, and teachers should not assume that they are. Teachers are so concerned with getting the learners ready for course examinations that they ignore intellectual-development levels. Postman and Weingartner explain the present situation in this way:

A "course" generally consists of a series of briefings for the great Trivia Contest. It's a kind of rigged quiz show. And it seems to work only if the participants value the "prize." The "prize," of course, is a "grade." An appropriate grade permits the participants to continue playing the Trivia game. All the while, let's not forget very little, if any, substantial intellectual activity is going on.[2]

"The great Trivia Contest" is, of course, the examination. If this quotation is true, and there is little reason to believe it is not, a rather depressing picture begins to emerge. Apparently, most people in education today believe that learning is represented by how much a student knows about sociology, arithmetic, chemistry, and the other

[2] *Ibid.*

disciplines taught in the elementary or secondary schools, and not by how much he has developed intellectually, which constitutes real learning. As long as the belief persists that the possession of information represents learning, attempts will be made to measure it with pencil-and-paper tests, and class time will be spent getting children ready for those tests. The teacher assumes that in order to do well on tests, there are certain "things" that all students should know, and uses all sorts of tricks, seductive procedures, and fancy hardware to ensure that those things are known.

The current overemphasis on testing is the principal ailment of education in the United States, and possibly in the world. Most modern testing procedures have nothing to do with intellectual growth, which *must* be the primary concern of the schools if for no other reason than that there is no other institution in our culture as equipped to foster that growth. From the time of the Puritans schools have demonstrated a remarkable talent for ignoring the development of the learner's intellect and for making use of only a few of the least attractive of his characteristics—his willingness to conform, memorize, and be a passive recipient of what is done *to* him.

In addition to the other drawbacks of current testing procedures, measuring an entire semester's work on the basis of an hour's test is patently unrealistic. Some teachers try to get around this criticism by giving a number of tests throughout the semester and using the average scores as a basis for the earned grade. However, we may again be doing in the classroom just the opposite of that which we profess to believe. We talk about individual differences among students, we suggest that students learn in different ways and at different rates, we say that we want students to learn to think rather than to memorize facts, we realize that the students come to us from different educational backgrounds, and we know that there is a wide range of proficiency in learning skills; yet, we give the same examinations to all students, apparently assuming that individual differences among students can be identified by test scores.

Content examinations do have some uses. Asking students to recall bits of factual information is useless if the teacher desires information about a student's degree of learning achievement. On the other hand, a testing device that determines how well the student understands the content of the course, as well as his ability to use that understanding, may be quite helpful to the teacher. Using tests which measure only recall is a highly questionable approach, *unless* the purpose is to determine which students are highly motivated or ambitious, to identify those students who have cultivated good memories, to pinpoint the good readers in the class, or simply to find out which students have learned to play (and win) in the "game system" of American education. What do we really have after we have charted student scores? Do we know which students have developed the ability to think rationally? On the other hand, how can we evaluate a student's performance and achievement if we do not methodically test his retention of content? And how do we deal with the problem of student grades?

Student Grades

If the tasks detested most by teachers were ranked in order, the assignment of grades to students would probably be near the top of the list. Perhaps education would have fared far better than it has if grading systems had never been invented. However, grades *were* invented, and like it or not, we are expected to be concerned with them. Although a great many teachers would prefer to abolish grades and grading systems, grades have become so widely accepted by students and parents that attempts even to alter the present system have been met with open resistance.

Almost universally, the grades A, B, C, D, and F have become accepted in American school districts. Once given, letter grades are fairly easy to interpret. An A generally means that a student is doing very well, a B that he is doing pretty well, a C that he is doing fairly well, a D that he has almost learned the course material, and an F that he has failed completely to do so. The difficulty for the teacher lies in accurately measuring how much a student has learned. As long as the teacher is willing to accept the idea that learning can be measured by the recall of factual material, then perhaps he is justified in defending such a grading model. If, however, he does *not* equate learning with factual recall, then he must question the grading system in which he participates. Logically, we would assume that an individual either has learned or has not learned something. Just how a teacher can justify saying that a student has *almost* learned the course material is somewhat beyond comprehension.

Over the past several years, many school districts have witnessed attempts to alter the grading system and to correct some of the problems and inconsistencies contained in the A-through-F pattern. One of these efforts, which has received wide attention, measures student progress by a three-point scale: Instead of using letter grades, the teacher rates the student's work as excellent, satisfactory, or unsatisfactory. A variation of this is to use only two categories: satisfactory and unsatisfactory progress. Another two-point scale rates a student's progress as consistent with his ability, or as unsatisfactory owing to insufficient application. Each of these student-evaluation methods has met opposition, or at least resistance, from several sources. Students have been conditioned through the years to expect the A-through-F grading system. Parents, as well as their children, apparently find it difficult to adjust to a system that does not allow comparisons among students. School personnel also have trouble accepting a system under which special recognition cannot be given both to outstanding achievers and inadequate students. Institutions of higher education have become geared to assessing transcripts of beginning freshmen in terms of the A-through-F system; this, too, is a hindrance to improving grading procedures.

All these factors have contributed to a hesitation on the part of school personnel to refocus attention on testing and evaluation techniques in the secondary schools. Even in school districts in which some newer grading approaches have been tried, students and their parents have had a tendency to continue to compare the progress of different students. Letter grading has left a lasting impression on those who have been exposed to it. The concept of competitiveness among class members for the recognition contained in high grades has been too strong to allow a switch to an effective and more legitimate noncompetitive evaluation system.

Student Evaluation: II

Regardless of the emphasis in the schools on grades and tests, teachers are constantly involved in evaluating students in other ways. If we are to be completely honest and realistic, we must recognize the great subjectivity involved in any testing procedure. Even the most objective teacher-made test reflects subjective judgments in the selection of test items. No two American history teachers would construct identical tests for their classes, even though both may have covered the same material. Thus, the teacher variable cannot be discounted. There is also the student variable. Two different students, after studying the same material, may respond to the same question in completely different ways. Each of them may have learned the material but interpreted it differently (because of variations in preparation and experiential background). To carry our argument just a little further, quite different interpretations of factual content may be made even by two historians; hence, the interpretations found in different textbooks may vary. Thus, content itself must be considered a variable that affects subjectivity.

Most teachers realize that testing contains, at best, many problems for both the teacher and the student that limit the meaning of the results. Even outstanding students will do less than their best work on occasion. There are probably few, if any, teachers who do not make a number of assessments of their students daily. These subjective evaluations may have to do with (1) student attitudes, (2) student preparedness, (3) student behavior, (4) physical appearance, and (5) student responsiveness to the teacher. The overall picture the teacher forms of an individual student consists of the impressions, good and bad, he has received over a period of time. He knows which students usually need individual help, which can work independently, which are potential classroom problems, which need teacher approval, which can grasp a concept quickly, and which cannot. All these things contribute to a teacher's overall evaluation of a student. Some teachers claim they can predict quite accurately the achievement level (or grade) a student will attain in a course by observing him closely during the first two weeks of the semester. What those teachers are doing during those weeks is making an overall assessment of a student's alertness, his attention to classroom activities, his daily preparedness, his general attitude, and his interest in the subject. Whether the teacher realizes it or not, his relationship with class members involves constant, continuous judgments, assessments, and evaluations.

Evaluation apart from testing is thus not new to the teacher. He has participated in such evaluations from the first moment he stepped into his first classroom. Inexperienced teachers are prone to make initial judgments concerning their students on rather superficial bases. It is quite easy for a new teacher to stereotype students and prejudge them on the bases of early impressions. A middle-class teacher is likely, at least at first, to look favorably on a student who is clean and has neatly combed hair and polished shoes, and less favorably on a child who is unwashed, wears soiled clothing, and has a pronounced body odor. To him, the first child "looks" like a student, while the other does not. We have certain preconceived notions about how a student should look and how he should behave; on these bases, we may be guilty of evaluating (prejudging) students before the learning process ever begins. Often, first impressions are proved wrong, but teachers cannot avoid making some kind of evaluation of all their students.

Often, however, teacher evaluations affect the grade earned by the student. Sometimes these influences on grades may be inappropriate —for example, when a teacher lowers a student's grade because he "talks too much" in class. In other instances, teachers consider a student's good attitude, his homework, and the effort he makes in class as justification for raising a grade lowered by poor performance on a particular test. Thus, student grades are often the result of many things besides test results.

Evaluation can serve a much more useful function than simply helping a teacher compute or adjust a grade. One of the important responsibilities of the teacher is to determine a student's preparation for participation, his learning disabilities, and his stage of intellectual development. By simply evaluating student attitudes, effort, and commitment to classroom preparation and participation, teachers may be judging symptoms rather than the real problems and assets of the student. The latter evaluations might not loom very important were teachers to realign their thinking on matters relating to the learning process.

If teachers could forget for a few minutes their concern with grades —and if we could eliminate completely from the classroom the competition for high and low marks—what would the objective for both teachers and students be? It would have to be *learning*. If the need to rank and grade students were removed, the teacher could concentrate on seeing that each student *learned*. If a student did not learn, the teacher too would have failed. Under these circumstances, the teacher would be forced to look for opportunities to identify a student's learning problems or disabilities and manipulate content in such a way that the student, despite his handicap, could come to grips with the content of the course. The teacher would have to focus on problems that interfered with a student's participation in the learning process and use this evaluation to further manipulate the ingredients of the classroom environment.

Throughout this text we have been concerned with the development of rational powers, the intellectual-developmental level of the learner, and attention to individual needs. Each of these criteria is tremendously important, but the last is perhaps the most difficult to meet. Evaluation is a very difficult aspect of the teaching-learning process for the teacher to understand, especially as it applies to individualization of the learning process. But if it is to have a useful function, it must be individualized. If it is not, then it cannot contribute to the learning process.

Evaluation, in its richest sense, has a very real place in teaching methodology. It means much more than merely grading. Assessment of an individual student's growth—where he was before interacting with content, and where he is after that involvement—is an important element of real evaluation. The teacher's assessment of such growth is an indication of his judgment of the student's progress in the learning process. Real evaluation is inevitably a subjective process. J. B. Stroud, at the University of Iowa, once said that he believed that if he worked with a student who read 250 words a minute and did not understand what he read, and increased that student's reading speed to 500 words per minute (and he still did not understand what he read), he had helped him, because now the student would waste only half as much time reading what he did not understand. We include this brief example to show that teachers must be careful in using subjective evaluation of students to determine progress in the learning process.

Many teachers believe that evaluation ends with their assessment of a student's progress; again, this would be a shallow interpretation of evaluation. If evaluation is to contribute to the learning process, the teacher's assessment of student progress or lack of progress must guide his further selection of content for the classroom curriculum. Used in this way, evaluation becomes a constructive part of the classroom curriculum. When the teacher's estimate of student performance indicates unsatisfactory progress, his next step should be to (1) identify the obstacles to the learning process, and (2) choose further student activities designed to either remove or circumvent those obstacles. Approached in this way, evaluation procedures become positive instead of negative aspects of the learning process for all students. Unlike testing programs, true evaluation is a constant and continuous part of the total classroom curriculum.

Now let us take a look at some additional problems the teacher faces in the general area of evaluation. We know that the classroom environment will reflect a range of student abilities simply because of individual differences. How should the teacher respond to a student who profits greatly from his participation in the learning process, who makes great progress in a single year in a particular subject, but who still is clearly the least competent student in the course at the close of the semester? On the other hand, how should he judge another student who is highly conversant with the content at the beginning of the course, is widely read, and understands the subject area extremely well, but who will not participate in the learning activities and makes little progress during the course? In neither case will grades give a fair picture of the learner. The first student may fail a content-oriented examination, but he has progressed considerably in the learning process; the second student may score 100 percent on the same test, but he has progressed little in the learning process.

This does not mean that the student who has made such tremendous progress should receive an A, while the other "good" student, who has not progressed, should fail. In a way, it is the teacher who has failed in his responsibility, by not devising content-based activities that would have prompted the good student to participate and, hence, to progress. The teacher also fails if he does not recognize the slower student's progress in the learning process, despite his poor scores when tested on factual material.

It is important for teachers to take a close look at their reasons for testing students, for reporting grades, and for evaluating progress (if they do). What is the value of evaluation? What is the comparative value of testing students on factual material? What useful functions do testing and evaluation serve? What are the purposes behind the evaluative procedures adopted and applied by the teacher in the classroom?

Let us pause for a moment and consider the rational power of recall. Although much has been written in these pages condemning the practice of evaluating students on their recall of factual information, we do not mean to denigrate this ability. We have taken this position because recall tests are directly associated with the traditional, unproductive, teacher-centered approach to learning. Without a doubt, there is a place for the evaluation of recall ability, but this should not constitute the entire evaluation program. Since recall is one of the rational powers, it is important to determine the extent of its development. But what about the other rational powers? Is it not as important to evaluate a student's ability to compare, to synthesize, and to analyze as it is to measure his ability to recall? Teachers who measure only recall are basing their entire evaluation of a student's performance and progress in the total learning process on a single aspect of it.

In studying evaluation, as opposed to factual testing, the teacher must first recognize three important points: (1) teaching is not synonymous with telling, (2) memorization is not synonymous with learning, and (3) recalling facts is not evidence of understanding. Probably no one reading this book would disagree with these three basic concepts. Yet, the schools are full of teachers who disregard them in constructing their entire testing and grading programs.

If the teacher becomes committed to evaluating his students rather than just testing them, he must establish bases for his evaluation. Several of these bases are indicated in the following questions:

FIGURE 10–1
In assessing student progress, the teacher must determine whether the student can explore a topic on his own.

1. Is the student able to adequately identify the problem he is attempting to solve? Can he outline clearly his investigative approach?
2. Does the student properly organize and describe the information he has found pertaining to his problem?
3. When the student studies the information he has gathered pertaining to his problem, can he accurately determine what theses that information will substantiate?
4. Is the student able to draw conclusions pertaining to his problem from the information he has gained in his investigation?
5. Is the student capable of approaching another problem, using the conclusions drawn from the investigation of a previous problem?

These are all points that might be used in evaluating student performance in the learning process, without benefit of paper-and-pencil testing. Since these criteria are concerned with student behavior, progress, and growth—not just recall ability—using them to evaluate performance is more meaningful.

A phase of student evaluation that normally receives little attention is student *self-evaluation*. A teacher should not simply ask a student what grade he feels he has earned. However, if we are concerned about whether a student has learned or about what he has learned, perhaps it would be more realistic to have the student tell us what he believes he has learned from a unit, a project, or an activity. Perhaps the teacher would get a more accurate estimate of student progress in this way than by subjective measures. Using such a procedure to substantiate his own estimate of a student's progress might be extremely revealing for the teacher.

Student self-evaluation may be used in yet another way. Perhaps our whole approach to testing and grading is inappropriate. Apparently we test students to get some idea of what they have learned from a course. Could it be that we should test, instead, what students *have not learned?* Possibly the stigma attached to low grades could be erased if such a direction were taken and followed. Testing then would serve, together with the results of student self-evaluation, to indicate to the teacher the areas in which the learning process has been unproductive for students, and which elements of his methodology should be revised or discarded.

Such a procedure, however, draws attention again to the dilemma faced by the teacher who is asked to convert student performance into grades indicating achievement. Evaluation by the student of his own progress is an integral part of the inquiry procedure. Aligning this self-evaluation with the assigned grade may be difficult. We do not deny that teacher evaluation of the student's performance is important, but there is an immediate inconsistency when we consider that inquiry requires the student to evaluate his own performance.

Many teachers have sought to get around this inconsistency (which can be destructive to the inquiry process) by using the following approach. They explore the teaching-learning experience with their students; inquiry thus becomes a joint activity, engaged in by both the teacher and the learner. When the student evaluates his own performance, he is giving his estimate of the end product. The teacher, on the other hand, as a fellow investigator, must treat the student's evaluation as only part of the data to be analyzed in reaching his own conclusions about the student's progress. The student must understand that his self-evaluation is only one part of the total set of data that the teacher must consider. However, it is also important that the teacher explain any inconsistency between his view of the student's performance and the student's own view.

Let us see how this joint approach to student evaluation works in a specific instance. In Chapter 3 we saw how the inquiry process might be used to study the Constitution. The teacher placed the materials to be investigated in the hands of his students and asked them to examine, analyze, and interpret them. In this example, there are many things the teacher can look for:

1. Did the student examine all the materials available, or did he refer to only one source of information?
2. Was he able to proceed on his own using these materials?
3. Did he exhaust the sources available when he encountered a problem?
4. How did he behave when confronted with an inconsistency or when he found that his assumptions were faulty?

FIGURE 10–2
Students need the experience of pooling and exchanging information, and of creating inventions.

5. When the teacher gave him a clue as to the direction his investigation might take, was he then capable of proceeding on his own?
6. When the teacher drew attention to the dates of the Thirteenth and Nineteenth Amendments, was the student capable of using this bit of information to distinguish between the two amendments' emphases, meanings, and applications?
7. When the student became stalled in his procedure, did he retrace his steps to check his data, and did he seek new sources to substantiate it?
8. When students shared or exchanged information, was he able to communicate his findings to others and to use the findings of other students in his work?
9. Was the student able to interpret the first ten amendments in terms of his own rights and responsibilities?
10. Could he draw logical conclusions about the Constitution on the basis of his findings?
11. Was he able to apply his interpretation of his individual rights to contemporary social problems? When confronted with such questions as, Why are separate but equal school systems for the races unconstitutional? What authority exists in the Constitution to make taxing a tax unconstitutional? What evidence exists in the Constitution that supports or denies support to the Electoral College? Was the student able to use his findings to examine other areas related to the Constitution?

12. Was there any indication that the student was becoming more capable of translating the concepts invented by the class to explain contemporary problems?

There are always many pieces of data a teacher can use in evaluating a student's progress in learning to interact adequately with content and with other class members. The student's own self-evaluation should serve to substantiate the teacher's estimate of his progress. If the teacher has been alert in observing his students, his evaluation of their progress is likely to be rather consistent with theirs.

One word of caution: The teacher should not forget that some of his students will be concrete-operational, while others may be formal-operational. Thus, some will be more able than others to apply generalizations to other problems. It is easy for the teacher to fall into the trap of assigning top grades to the formal-operational students, without considering the limitations under which concrete-operational students are functioning.

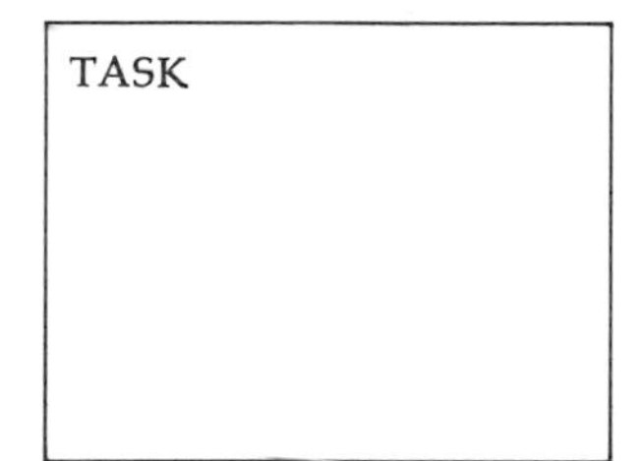

Reread the passage in Chapter 3 on teaching the Constitution. In what other ways might students' handling of this inquiry enable you to evaluate their general progress in the learning process?

Grading is an unnatural addition to the inquiry process—in fact, it is an unnatural addition to the learning process. However, the teacher who must face the reality of assigning grades may find that his dilemma is lessened if the students understand that it is his duty to assess their performance, and to make judgments based on that performance. Obviously, the closer the teacher's estimate of the student's performance is to the student's own estimate, the more likely it is that the student will view the teacher's judgment as legitimate. A hopeful note for the teacher is that many who use this procedure claim that their students do an incredibly fair and honest job of assessing their own performance.

Finally, evaluation procedures should meet the three criteria essential in judging any aspect of the teaching-learning process. If teacher-evaluation procedures are used to select activities that will help the student to come to grips with the course content and develop his ability to think rationally, they have a legitimate base and justification.

If evaluation procedures adopted by the teacher recognize the problems encountered by the concrete-operational student and help him

FIGURE 10–3
Teachers need to assess whether students have utilized all available sources before inventing a concept for them.

to move toward the formal-operational stage by identifying the most productive media, activities, and content, they have a legitimate base and justification.

If evaluation procedures developed and applied by the teacher consider the individuality of the learner and his abilities and disabilities, and allow room for adjusting the classroom curriculum to meet his needs, they have a legitimate base and justification.

Should the teacher approach evaluation bearing these points in mind, he will have made the greatest contribution to his students a teacher is capable of making. *He will have helped them to learn, and to learn how to learn.*

This viewpoint, of course, opens the door to another problem. School administrators and parents also need to develop a broader stance toward evaluation. Administrators, parents, many teachers, and students have certain expectations concerning tests. However, the fact that many expect tests does not mean that we should continue our traditional attitude toward testing, if it is wrong. If our present form of evaluation is a barrier to learning, then it should be abolished or changed.

It is the business of the school to see that all those who are connected with the learning process, directly or indirectly, understand the difference between testing factual knowledge and realistic student evaluation. Our society has become so indoctrinated with the idea of the test as an essential part of the learning experience that it will require much effort to correct this attitude.

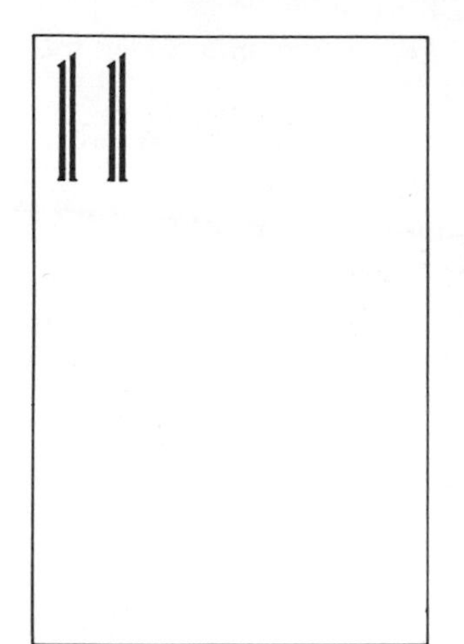

11 New and Persistent Problems

The problems of our educational system can be grouped into three general categories—professional, financial, and parental. Financial problems we shall ignore here, not because they are unimportant but because they are outside the scope of the book. To deal with the financial problems of the school, we would have to investigate such topics as tax bases and rates; teachers' salaries; materials, equipment, and maintenance costs; and local, state, and federal support to education. There is, however, one thought you might ponder.

When schools were first started in this country, each small community took the responsibility for educating its own children. Since the probability was very high that those so educated would live out their lives in the general vicinity, the community was rewarded and reimbursed for its investment. Financial support of the schools became not only an obligation but an investment the community would directly profit from. In today's mobile society, however, predictions cannot be made with respect to where an individual will spend his life. Nebraskans become New Yorkers, Texans become Alaskans, and everyone becomes a Californian. South Dakota's educational investment in an individual may benefit Oklahoma, and New Jersey's may profit Oregon. You may be tempted to think, "What's the problem? Each state educates its own, and each benefits from the other." Theoretically, that is true; but you need only consult the records of what each state spends per pupil to know that the states are not providing the children of this country with *equal* educational opportunities (even when an adjustment is made for the location).

How can this inequality be stopped? Some years ago the states asked themselves this question and decided that each state would have to provide financial support to the various districts within its boundaries, in order to equalize educational opportunity for the children of that state. Could it be that the time has arrived for the citizens of this entire country to take the financial responsibility for providing equal educational opportunities through federal support of education? The federal government has provided aid to schools almost since the nation was founded, but it has always been in the form of grants for a specific purpose, such as setting up a vocational education program or providing library facilities. The federal government has never paid for the general expenses of running the schools, such as teachers' salaries and building maintenance costs. Perhaps the time has come for the federal government to help *support* the schools, and not just aid them in specific areas.

TASK	*What are your feelings on the subject of federal financial support? Jot down your ideas, and be prepared to discuss them in class.*

Professional Problems

Using time

During the last few years there has been much discussion about the distribution of time in the school day. At the secondary school level the assumption has usually been made that each class should meet for a set amount of time each day. Furthermore, accrediting agencies have given their seal of approval to schools that have followed their recommendations concerning the amount of time that should be devoted to each subject each day. Generally, each subject is allowed the same amount of time daily to market its wares. This division was introduced because of a theory that learning occurs most efficiently if a little time each day is devoted to each content area, and because of the administrative convenience of such an arrangement. Perhaps there is some validity in the latter argument, but it ignores the factor of intrinsic motivation. When a teacher succeeds in "turning on" a class with an activity and time runs out as the investigation reaches its zenith, both the class and the teacher are frustrated. The next day, the same motivation will not be present at the beginning of the period, and a portion of the time will have to be spent getting the students back to where they were at the end of the preceding period. For the teacher who uses the inquiry method, the single-period-each-day schedule is probably, at best, 50 percent efficient. For the teacher who sees his job as telling the learners what he believes they should know, little time is lost from day to day; he simply picks up each day where he left off the day before. For him, a single period each day is probably best because his students are doubtless tired of listening to him at the end of 55 minutes anyway. But the single-period-a-day schedule puts the inquiry-centered teacher in an unnecessary bind.

There are two ideas here that should be examined. First, should each class meet every day? And second, should all subjects be given the same amount of time? What is the alternative to having each class meet every day? Perhaps classes should meet twice a week for a time longer than the conventional 55-minute period. Perhaps meeting for 90 minutes, three times a week, is better for a class than meeting for 55 minutes, five times a week. (The total difference is five minutes per week—not even time for two good jokes.) The emergence of *modular scheduling* in some of the nation's leading secondary schools is an effort to provide longer periods for inquiry-centered activities. The modular schedule also provides some short periods, when brief lectures covering information that everyone should have can be given to several hundred students at one time.

There are, no doubt, other ways of arranging the students' time that might be considered. Why must a student study each subject for a semester or an entire year? Because they always have? Suppose, for example, that eleventh-grade students took only two subjects, English and chemistry, for half a day each for nine weeks, and then were finished with those subjects for the year. Under such a system the learners would have the opportunity to really steep themselves in the discipline. When this plan is proposed to teachers and administrators, they usually say that time would be wasted and the students would get bored. If the conventional show 'em-tell 'em-ask 'em style is used, this rejoinder is valid. Being told about the giants in American literature for 55 minutes each day is bad enough, but imagine how you would feel if you had to endure this from 9 A.M. to noon every day! On the other hand, suppose that each student in the class had his own research project, such as "The Impact of Slavery on the Literature of the 1860s," "The Effect of the Depression of the 1930s on Short Stories," or "How Closely Do Newspapers Adhere to the Rules of Latin Grammar?" Do these topics sound like thesis title for a master's degree? Perhaps you are right, but remember the purposes for which American literature and grammar are taught in an inquiry-oriented school system. Although we are interested in acquainting the students with these disciplines, they are basically vehicles to lead the learner to develop his ability to think. If a student has the opportunity to pursue his own project, participate in discussions led by the teacher on currently interesting topics, and engage in a dialogue about his own project and the projects of others, three hours may pass quickly. Perhaps this plan, a concentrated study of each subject for a shorter time, is the only one that will turn a class into a community whose members are interested in each other's work and, more importantly, in each other. Most people do their best work when they are in the company of those with whom they feel comfortable. Another advantage of this plan is that the teacher and students will have the time to utilize outside resources. Field trips can be made to the school library, the public library, local industries, laboratories, and governmental establishments without taking time away from other classes. Such a system would require allowing each teacher about nine weeks a year to plan; prepare materials; seek out suitable areas for student research (some students may not be able to come up with a topic themselves, but will become very involved in a project suggested to them); evaluate the resources of the community; and preview films, filmstrips, and other media. Teachers, of course, would be required to be conscientious in using this time, and not look upon it as a vacation. But we have spent enough time investigating our first point. It should be clear by now that there are many alternatives to the present system that ought to be considered.

The second point that must be examined is whether all subjects should be allotted the same amount of time each day, each week, or each year. As you might imagine, this is a very explosive issue because it requires evaluating each discipline as a vehicle for achieving the central purpose of education. We have examined the structure of the several disciplines in Chapter 5, and nothing more need be said by us on that topic. We would only add that often art, music, and other creative activities, such as short-story writing, are allowed time in the curriculum only after the "solid" subjects (English grammar, mathematics, social studies, and science) have been accounted for. There is reason to believe that achievement in the latter subjects would increase if more creative activities were provided. Could it be that the creative activities are more concerned with developing the learner's ability to think than are the so-called solids, which stress mainly the coverage of specific content or the mastery of specific skills? Reading, for example, has always been considered an absolutely essential solid in the first grade. At the risk of being redundant, we would like to repeat here a quotation from Hans Furth given in Chapter 4.

While the written word is the means par excellence for expanding a mature intelligence, the early pressure on reading must be exposed not merely as contributing little or nothing to intellectual development but, in many cases, as seriously interfering with it.[1]

Furth goes on to say,

Neither the process of reading itself nor the comprehension of its easy content can be considered an activity well suited to developing the mind of the young child. . . . a school that in the earliest grades focuses primarily on reading cannot also focus on thinking.[2]

Perhaps, all content is not of equal value in developing the learner's ability to think; and teachers, administrators, and others connected with our schools must begin to make curriculum judgments on the basis of the usefulness of each discipline in developing the rational powers.

Using educational materials

A persistent problem in the schools is the way teachers view the materials and particularly the textbooks the school provides. There is no doubt that the easiest way for a teacher to behave (notice we did not say teach) is to begin the first day on page one of the textbook and finish the last page the final day of school. If the transmission of information is the goal of the school, this procedure is acceptable. However, that school does not really need teachers; reading supervisors and proctors are all the personnel needed.

A textbook should be used as *one* resource from which information can be pulled to help solve problems that arise in an investigation. If the textbook or other materials provided lay out specific answers to the problems, they are of little value. If, on the other hand, they explore the nature and structure of a discipline and furnish information that can be used in problem solving, you will find them very useful. Fortunately, there are many excellent resource materials available today that are not written in a style that gives answers but rather are real narratives of inquiry. We urge you to discard a textbook that lays out answers for students; you should select materials that lead him to understand something of the structure of a discipline. This is not an easy task, but it is an essential one if inquiry-centered

[1] Hans G. Furth, *Piaget for Teachers* (Englewood Cliffs, N.J.: Prentice-Hall, 1970), p. ix.
[2] *Ibid.*, p. 4.

teaching is to be used to lead a learner to develop his rational powers and pass through the stages of the Piagetian model of intellectual development. Within the last few years teaching materials that are organized on the inquiry principle have become available in science, mathematics, English, and, to some degree, social science.

A closer look at equality of educational opportunity

Because of the limitations imposed on the educational process by the element of time as it is used (and misused) in the schools, many educators have devoted themselves to investigating more flexible patterns and, thus, to finding a more legitimate framework for the learning process. In addition to time, the limitations of materials, equipment, and teaching talent have considerable influence on education in a particular school. Another factor (closely related to the time element) that may impede the learning process is the limited curriculum in some local school units. This has been one of the stronger arguments for consolidation of rural school districts. The American philosophy of education requires that the system meet the needs of all students, yet many who would profit intellectually from various courses cannot get this exposure in their school.

Course limitations are a problem not only in rural schools. In many large city school districts identical circumstances are present in individual school units. The curriculum is not the same in all schools in an urban district. Thus, a student who should be allowed to pursue advanced courses in a particular area often cannot. On the other hand, a student who needs remedial work in basic skills also cannot get the help he needs because of the limitations imposed by the absence of special programs, inadequate materials, and the lack of qualified teachers in the local school.

One approach to urban education that may alleviate these problems is based on several long-standing concepts in American education: equality of educational opportunity, the neighborhood school, specialized schools, maximum utilization of school equipment and educational facilities, educational programs designed to meet the needs of students and the community, efficient utilization of teaching talent and ability, and flexible scheduling. This plan, developed by Robert F. Bibens, is known as the *Cluster Plan for Urban Education.*

The Cluster Plan suggests that the educational leaders of an urban district should identify the areas of the school curriculum that are inadequate and provide inequitable opportunities for secondary students. Such curricular areas could be academic or nonacademic, or a combination of the two. After identifying the areas in which the curriculum was deficient, the districts would then create special centers located within existing neighborhood schools where these subjects would be taught. Each neighborhood school would continue to offer its regular selection of coursework, excluding those courses taught in the centers. One major urban school district, in exploring the idea, suggested the following form of organization as appropriate for its particular needs:

1. Special centers would be designated within existing neighborhood secondary schools to handle all courses in social studies, mathematics, science, and foreign languages.
2. Each secondary school in the district would maintain classes for its resident student body in all subject areas except those handled by the center, thus preserving the neighborhood-school concept.
3. Each neighborhood school would fulfill two functions: (1) that of a regular high school and (2) that of a special center for a particular subject area.
4. Specialized equipment and facilities would be provided for each center. Teaching talent would also be concentrated in the centers, increasing the depth and scope of courses within the content area. In addition, each center would have a special subject-area consultant responsible for maintaining the integrity of and providing leadership in the teaching-learning process.
5. A modified version of modular scheduling would be applied in the centers. Participating students would be brought to the center twice a week, for sessions of approximately two-and-one-half hours' duration. During this time block they would be exposed to a variety of classroom activities and experiences. Periods of this length would force members of the teaching staff to take another look at their classroom methodology. Obviously, teachers would be unable to hold the attention of their students for two-and-one-half hours of presentation or lecture; thus they would be pushed toward developing classroom activities designed to involve students and to encourage student participation in the learning process.

The potential advantages of the Cluster Plan are tremendous:

1. No student would be prevented from taking a subject because of its unavailability in his home school.
2. Expensive and specialized equipment would not have to be purchased for all the secondary schools in a district.

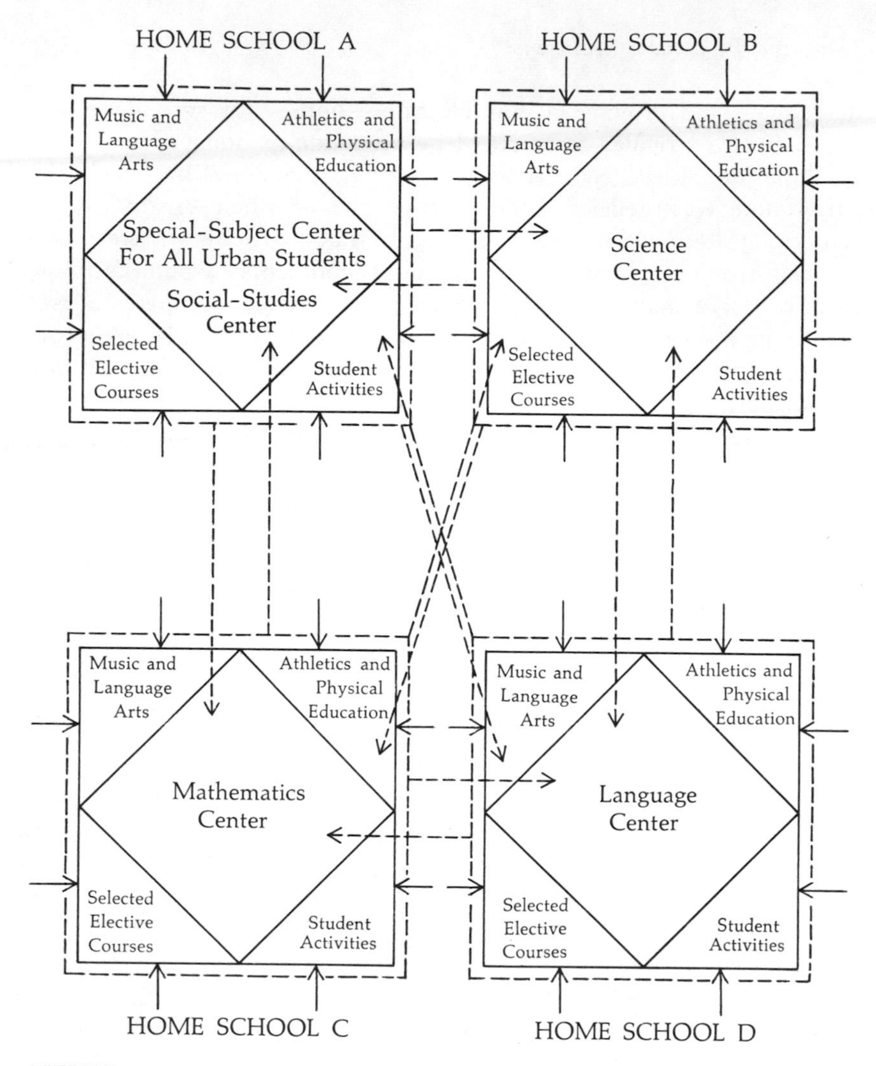

FIGURE 11–1
Students move from their home-base schools to special-subject centers.

3. Teachers trained in a certain academic area would have a better chance of receiving teaching assignments in that area.
4. Subjects that normally are not part of the regular secondary school curriculum could be offered to all students.
5. The concentration of teaching talent in a special content area would make it possible to give individual attention to students needing this kind of help.

6. The responsibility for instructional leadership within the center would be assumed by an individual trained for such a role.
7. The framework of the plan would permit teachers to encourage students to pursue their interest in a content area as far as their capabilities would allow.
8. A closer watch could be kept on the quality of teaching in a specific area. This situation would encourage the more capable and productive teachers and discourage unsuccessful teachers from remaining in the profession.
9. Individualized programs could be developed within each time block, thus enabling both students and teachers to get away from the "lock-step" concept of education.

These are only a few of the potential advantages of the Cluster Plan for Urban Education. Certainly, we are not suggesting that it is the whole answer to the inequities and limitations of the present system. Other administrative and organizational innovations to improve secondary education have been tried (see Chapter 6) and will continue to be tried. The Cluster Plan cannot solve all the problems of the schools; regardless of the organizational pattern superimposed on the instructional environment, the learning process will not be improved from its present status until individual teachers improve the quality of student experiences within their classrooms.

Instead of considering the Cluster Plan as just another of the countless administrative innovations designed to alter present curricula, we would prefer to consider it as an attempt to remove some of the rigidity and restrictiveness from existing organizational patterns. Hopefully, it would support a more responsive and flexible approach to the learning process, reestablishing with educators the responsibility for providing opportunity for the fullest possible kind of educational experience for all students in a school district. Educators have long recognized the inflexibility of the subject-centered curriculum and the lack of practical attention to individualization of the classroom curriculum. The Cluster Plan will not correct these deficiencies in our approach to secondary education, but it may assist teachers in their attempts to legitimize classroom procedures. No design or plan by itself can guarantee inquiry and student involvement. On the other hand, inquiry can be achieved within *any* organizational plan, if it is the teacher's philosophy. The Cluster Plan simply removes some of the barriers that discourage administrators, teachers, and students from moving toward a more legitimate approach to the teaching-learning process.

Evaluation

One of the most persistent problems in education is evaluation. To solve that problem teachers must first understand what it is they wish to evaluate. We believe that the true focus of evaluation must be the progress made in achieving the objectives of education. If an educational activity has been chosen based on the criteria for curriculum selection described in this book, you can, at the same time you evaluate learners' performance, evaluate what progress has been made toward achieving the central purpose of education and what progress the learners have made in intellectual development. Factually oriented examinations and the majority of standardized tests will not help you to make this kind of evaluation. You can, however, use the techniques and procedures described as relevant in Chapter 10.

Occasionally you will encounter a school system that rates its students *and* teachers by some external evaluation criterion, such as a standardized test. You should not concern yourself too much with these examinations because the probability is high that they cannot measure progress toward the real objectives of education. If you teach in a school where such tests are the rule, you may have only two choices: You can ignore the outcome of the tests, or you can prepare your students for them. If your school puts great stock in these tests, and if your success as a teacher is rated by your students' performance on them, your choice (if you wish to stay at the school) is clear—you must prepare your students to take the tests. One way to do this is to use past copies of the examination as a guide. While using past copies of a test in this way is not really professional behavior, a school which uses evaluation techniques that do not measure progress toward the central goal of education is not acting in a professional way either. If the external evaluation criterion measures progress toward the real goals of education and your teaching is inquiry-centered, preparing your students will not be necessary.

The school as an instrument of social change

Earlier in this book we mentioned that schools are often asked to be agents of social change. That function is not necessarily one the schools have sought, but it is one they have. No doubt there are other institutions in our culture that could, if they chose, be equally effective in promoting social change. The school, after all, has access only to children. Anything that is done, therefore, to bring about social change through the schools tends to be somewhat one-sided and is often challenged by parents. Institutions such as churches are better suited to bring about social change because they have access to both parents and children. Churches, unfortunately, seem to view their responsibilities from a frame of reference that does not include fostering this sometimes painful process. The fact that churches in some parts of the country have maintained separate facilities for blacks and whites suggests that they have not only not accepted responsibility for social change but have acted to retard it.

What is the role of the school in effecting social change? We can give no final answer to that question, but we can isolate some factors that give us a rather dim frame of reference. The first of these is that all children, regardless of race, creed, or national origin must be treated with respect and dignity. That is, of course, one of the foundation stones of an inquiry-centered program. Every child in the schools must be given the opportunity to find his own level of achievement and encouraged to pursue it. If all students are treated with dignity and respect, they will in time learn to treat others with that same dignity and respect. No social change would have a greater impact, and the schools can foster this attitude through their own attitude toward students.

Our culture would also be changed profoundly if each citizen were taught to see himself as having a unique creative potential. There is only one way that an individual can discover the extent of his own creativity, and that is to be allowed to create something on his own. Inquiry-centered teaching not only allows but encourages each learner to develop his own explanations of problems. It also trains a learner to inspect other explanations carefully and compare them with his own. Just as nothing succeeds like success, nothing encourages an individual to be creative like creating something. Writing a story, solving a mathematical problem, designing an experiment, or interpreting a phrase from the United States Constitution in his own way, and having that story, solution, design, or interpretation accepted by the teacher and his peers, encourages creativity. If a child learns in school that he can be creative, he is likely to continue that creativity as an adult. Creativity brings about social change. It is responsible for all our technological breakthroughs, improvements in law, and great works of art, music, and literature. Not all your students will be George Washington Carvers, Martin Luther Kings, or John Kennedys, but they will use their creativity to change our social order.

Perhaps the most important contribution the schools can make to social change is to create a learning environment that will demonstrate how human beings must interact with one another in order to bring out the best in each individual. Guided inquiry gives each learner the opportunity to interact with others and to learn what he must do to secure their cooperation. In other words, perhaps the schools could make their greatest contribution to social change simply by encouraging learners to discover how to get along with each other.

Many of the institutions that provide the public with entertainment and information could not survive if a creative public viewed their products in a logical, rational way. Newspapers, movies, magazines, television, radio, religions, veterans organizations, theaters, and many other public institutions influence the manner in which the citizens of this country think. If our schools were to concentrate on producing a citizenry whose rational powers were fully developed and who operated at a formal level, many of those institutions would not survive or would have to change or cease to exist, to the profit of our social order.

TASK

There are, no doubt, other professional problems that you feel should be discussed to make this section complete. Make a list of such problems, and get the reaction of your classmates to them.

Parental Problems

The title of this section is really a bit unfair because the vast majority of parents are not problems. Perhaps a better title would have been "Teacher-Parent Interactions." There are some aspects of teacher-parent interactions that are so important that every teacher should be sensitive to them.

Parents usually want the best education possible for their children. That means that they will cooperate with the school in providing that education. But to secure their cooperation, the teacher must be able to show parents how the program of which they are in charge is beneficial to the children. Teachers must, in other words, be able to articulate their educational objectives and explain to parents how the home can help children to achieve these objectives. Parents must be kept informed regarding new programs, particularly the purpose of those programs.

Disciplinary problems sometimes are so severe that parents must be informed and asked to do what they can to help the situation.

This can be a traumatic experience for both the parent and the teacher. The teacher has a professional responsibility to fully explain to parents how he views the problems and to give parents every opportunity to explain their view of the situation. It may be necessary for him to explain his disciplinary procedures and those of the school. Often, a difference in disciplinary attitudes at home and at school may be the root of the trouble. After such a parent-teacher conference, the teacher is obligated to keep the parents informed about the progress being made. Disciplinary problems severe enough to bring the adults responsible for the child to school can usually be solved only through the combined efforts of the family and the school.

The school's assessment of the academic progress of a learner (his grade, in other words) can sometimes bring a parent to school. When this happens, the teacher should be honest and open about the criteria he is using to evaluate the child and how the child is progressing in terms of those criteria. It is unwise in such situations to compare the progress of the child with that of other class members; such comparisons are usually unfair to all the children concerned. Instead, the teacher should base his explanation of his evaluation of the child on the objectives he wants the class to achieve, and he should be prepared to let the parent know what he (the parent) can do to help the child raise his standing in the class. This potentially hostile situation would not arise if schools would abandon the present grading system. Perhaps some day schools, parents, and colleges will be mature enough to let that happen.

In this chapter we have treated only a few of the new and persistent problems facing the schools. We have not attempted to provide an exhaustive treatment because that treatment would require a book in itself. Most problems can be solved by selecting curricula that will lead a learner to develop his ability to think, raise his intellectual level so that he is at home with formal operations, and realize his potential as an individual. If schools and teachers can accomplish these goals, our culture will have made a unique contribution to mankind.

Index

71 72 73 7 6 5 4 3 2 1